Live Your Road Trip Dream

Travel for a year for the cost of staying home

Phil and Carol White

RLI Press | Wilsonville, Oregon

RLI Press
P.O. Box 1115
Wilsonville, Oregon 97070-1115
888-522-TRIP
www.roadtripdream.com

Editing and proofreading: Marvin Moore
Design: Martha Gannett
Composition: William H. Brunson Typography Services
Cover photograph: Getty Images
Author photograph: Tim Holmes

Printed in the United States of America

Library of Congress Control Number 2004092485
ISBN 0-9752928-0-3

To travelers everywhere who have road trip dreams.
Go live your dream!

Contents

Acknowledgments

We couldn't have had this great adventure without the support of our families. Like most families, they were incredulous and disbelieving at first, but ultimately they provided the best possible support: their blessing that we go do this crazy trip, and for that we are so thankful. Mom, Tom, Lois, Andie, Christopher, Amy, Jack, Eric, Kristen, Phil Jr., and the grandkids—you're the best!

Throughout the trip our friends both at home and in locations all over the country gave us great support, opened their homes to these road-weary travelers, and kept us up-to-date on everything going on back in Oregon. Thanks to all of you.

This book has been a long time coming as we worked with potential publishers and learned about this business. We have been privileged to have the encouragement and participation of many friends who provided advice, focus-group feedback, and much-needed suggestions. Our thanks to the following friends and family whose coaching and energy helped shape this book: Meredith Bruinier, Haley Dahlquist, Stacey Hyatt, Marianne Klekacz, Lois Legerski, Sue Llewellyn, Wendy Lucia, Cathy Lunsford-Bowles, Paul and Tara Maull, Anne McAlpin, LeAnne Mantero, Joy Moran, Marty Ritter, Patty Solberg, and K. C. Weary. Special thanks to Valerie Marsh, who so carefully read and edited the draft of the manuscript, and to my daughter, Andrea Edmonds, for editing the book proposal.

And finally our thanks to Martha Gannett and Marvin Moore, whose humor, patience, and ideas brought everything together into this wonderful book that we are so proud of. You provided every bit the same professionalism that a corporate publisher would have supplied. Thank you both so much—you are amazing inspirations and great coaches.

Introduction

Traveling for a year? It is either one of your fondest dreams—or your worst nightmare! It's something many baby boomers have long thought of doing after we are through with the family-raising stage of life and before we succumb to old age!

My husband, Phil, and I are two early boomers who, like many of our contemporaries, have had the good fortune and opportunity to leave the full-time work world early—with all the possibilities and decisions that this life change brings. Early in our lives, we did all "the right things," like many children raised in the '50s and '60s. We went to college (no running off to Europe for six months for us!), graduated, got jobs that we stayed with throughout our careers, married, and raised our families. Never did we have the luxury of taking off on an adventure for more than a few weeks at a time.

When we left the workforce, we found that we became just as involved and immersed as we had been when we were working. Of course, the time is now filled with things of our choosing—playing with the grandchildren, serving on boards and committees, traveling, golfing, exercising more regularly, and so on. But nonetheless, a new routine develops that makes it just as difficult to break away. Since a long trip around the United States is something that had been on our wish list for some time, we decided that now was the time—while "untangling" the web of our new life was still relatively easy.

Another consideration was the fact that right now we are both healthy and our families are healthy. This is something none of us can take for granted, and it can change at any time. Wouldn't it be sad if we put off the trip—as it is so easy to do with something like this—and then found we *couldn't* do it due to our health or family obligations?

If you are looking for a book about "the ten best places to eat and sleep in Cute Town, USA," this isn't for you! Yes, we will tell you about some interesting places along the way, but the focus is on our experiences planning a trip of this type. We include our travelogue, not because we think what we did is important, but to give you a glimpse of what it is really like to be on the road for an extended period of time.

We visited and wrote about all the national parks in the "lower" forty-eight states, plus many of the national monuments, seashores, and other types of parks. We visited Phil's favorite football stadiums from a lifetime of watching sports. We experienced all kinds of activities from golf (our favorite), to whitewater rafting, to sailboating on the Great Lakes, to snorkeling in the Keys. We talked to ordinary people with experiences that enriched our own. They stretched our intellect and imagination and provided perspectives that we will cherish forever.

We decided to write this book due to the lack of a comprehensive resource about how to plan an adventure of this type. People we met all over the country were fascinated with the idea of actually doing this. They peppered us with all kinds of questions. Soon it became apparent that we should gather some thoughts and maybe put together a notebook for friends who are interested. We got a little carried away!

This is written totally from a tourist perspective. We neither asked for, nor received, any favors or freebies along the way. We just tell it as we experienced it with no commercial obligations to fulfill.

So come along, envision your trip of a lifetime, enjoy the scenery, and see the USA from your armchair and who knows, you may find yourself making the decision to "hit the road" too!

Part 1 | The Plan

The essence of this book is encapsulated in "The Plan." What we have heard time and again from people both at home and on the road is that they would love to do a yearlong trip like we did, but they don't have a clue how to begin getting themselves organized to actually make it happen.

When you finish reading this section, you should have all the information you need to begin to plan your own trip of a lifetime—whatever that is for you. It could be a trip around the United States like we did, or it could be a long trek through Asia, or a motorhome trip through Europe, or a sailboat trip around the world. We have included worksheets, budgets, common sense, a little psychology, and some humor to help you on your way to wherever your dream takes you.

The rest is up to you.

You Too Can Make This Happen

It's early January. It's raining out—what else in Oregon?—and I am sitting down with a cup of coffee to pay the bills. I come upon a renewal notice for *Golf for Women* and mechanically begin to write out the check. "*Wait!*" my subconscious says to me, "Why are you doing that? You won't be here to read it! You're going on a yearlong trip, remember?" And so the serious decision-making of preparing for "The Trip" begins. At first the tasks seemed almost overwhelming. So many things to think about—it's enough to make you cancel the whole idea before you get started! With that first small step of not renewing subscriptions came a torrent of activities over the next six months.

Make it your trip

Everyone has dreams. What we hope to do in the next few chapters is to help you turn your dream into reality. Not *our* dream—*your* dream. What we did on our trip is not really important. *How* we went about it can help you turn your vision of the perfect trip into your reality. Everyone has issues and concerns that make them drag their feet. The difference between whether you can make it happen or whether you can't is not how many obstacles you have, it is how badly to you want to do something totally life-changing—totally for yourself. We will give you the tools to change your dream into reality, but the implementation is yours to enjoy. Our hope is to get you off the couch and believing that you too can do this.

Small trips versus one big trip

One thing you may be asking yourself is, "Do we really need to commit a year to this? Couldn't we just do a bunch of smaller trips?" And of course, the answer is yes. But there are several really good reasons to consider one larger trip—and whether it is a full year or not depends on what you want to accomplish (more about that in Chapter 4).

First, as you will read in Chapter 2, there are real financial advantages to doing one long trip. Freeing up your income stream to spend on the trip is a necessary part of the planning for most people. Some of the strategies we employed wouldn't be available if you were taking a series of shorter excursions.

Second, there is the whole idea of planning and actually getting out of the house. After you've read this book, we think you will agree that you don't really want to go through this amount of detail more than once!

If you do decide that a series of trips is the way to go for you, then we would strongly encourage you to plan them all at once—and then stick to your schedule.

Can this be done in a series of trips? Absolutely. Will you gain the same benefits we found from taking one long trip? Probably not.

Be a kid again

Finally, the factor that we feel speaks the loudest to doing it in one long sweep is the "kid" factor. How long has it been since you could basically leave your responsibilities behind and focus on just doing what *you* want to do? Only a trip of extended length can allow you to be that kid inside again. Before we left, we had no concept of how freeing this would be. We had done enough planning that we really could let most things happen on "autopilot," and we could explore, experiment, and try new things every day. Once we got the rhythm of being on the road, we could feel our curiosity begin to creep out of someplace deep inside us. We were less inhibited— we'd strike up conversations with **The techniques that we will discuss can be applied equally well to a trip across the USA, in a foreign country, or on an around-the-world sailboat trip.** people almost anywhere and stop to look at something "just because." We also found new perspectives about the way things are in this country. There is no doubt that in some way you will come back from this experience a different person from the one who left.

Related to the whole idea of freeing yourself to experience the trip fully is the notion of focus. If this is just an extended vacation of sorts, you will not truly "leave it all behind." You will make compromises with yourself—"Oh, I can handle that, I don't need to make arrangements for this to be taken care of"—and pretty soon, you will be focusing on home obligations and not fully on experiencing your trip of a lifetime. You will inevitably have to take some of your life with you, but we will show you how to minimize that in order to focus on your trip.

Although our vision for our great adventure focused on the United States, the techniques that we will discuss could be applied equally well to a trip in a foreign country or an around-the-world sailboat trip. The choice is yours, and the planning is basically the same—just some of the details will vary.

By now you are most likely beginning to formulate your own ideas of how this could work for you—what your trip could include. But the nagging voices are already talking to you—the roadblocks are beginning. Acknowledge them as items that you will have to address and work through. Do not let them become reasons to close this book and forget the whole idea. You can make it happen. We'll show you how.

Chapter

Financing Your Dream

Once you get past the "dream" stage, the first serious issue that faces all of us is how do we afford to do this? In the next few pages, we will try to give you some tools and thought processes that we used to conquer the challenges. These ideas are, of course, not the only road to success, but they are certainly ones that worked for a couple of compulsive list-makers with bad memories.

Where will the money come from?

This trip may most likely be done by someone who has already retired, but that is not the only way to make it a reality. We started contemplating the idea well before retirement. What you *do* need, of course, is a source of funds for the year. We will show you how to virtually eliminate your current expenses so that you aren't paying double to make this adventure a certainty. If you are retired, you can utilize the same money you are spending today at home to finance your trip. If you want to do this before retirement, then you are probably going to have to come up with a combination of funding sources as well as the time to make it happen.

The sources can be retirement income, savings/investments— or how about a paid sabbatical? There is an excellent book on the market called *Six Months Off,* by Dlugozima, Scott, and Sharp, that explores ways to finance extended trips without going broke.

A seminar by one of the authors is what got us going on making our dream a reality. Another braver idea, if you are really intent on doing this *now*, is to take out a loan and consider it an investment in your future. We guarantee that you will come back vastly enriched from the experience and with an understanding of this country that can't be gleaned any other way.

If you are retired, you will naturally still need to review your own monthly financial situation and your vision for a trip of this type. Our goal is to show you how you can eliminate your current expenses and re-deploy the money to your trip.

What to do with the house?

The first big decision we had to make was what to do with the house. Since we still have a mortgage to pay, that decision was a major factor in the budgeting process. It appeared to us that there were basically four choices:

- Leave it empty for the year
- Lease it unfurnished
- Lease it furnished
- Sell it

If you are renting, the process may be somewhat easier if you decide to just move out, but the same decisions still apply.

To decide which alternative is best for you, add up all the ongoing expenses if you left it empty. The "Household Expenses" chart on page 8 will get you started.

Once you know what it would cost to leave it empty, then you can decide if you can afford to—or want to—do that. If you make the decision to leave it empty, you need to realize that it limits your goal of freeing up your cash flow to use on the trip, as those costs will continue. Otherwise, you can decide which of the other alternatives makes more sense.

Household Expenses

Mortgage (or rent) $ _____

Second mortgage $ _____

Homeowner's fees (if applicable) $ _____

Property taxes (if not in monthly payment) $ _____

Homeowner's insurance (if not in payment) $ _____

Utilities that would have to continue (heat, cooling, water— $ _____
    what would be needed depends on where you live)

Yard work, pest control, or other work to keep the $ _____
    property safe and kept up

Security service (if applicable) $ _____

    Total $ _____

Considering the alternatives

Some simple checking with realtors, looking at the newspaper, calling property managers, and so on, can establish what the lease market may be for your area. Our community has a lot of major employers that bring people in on temporary assignments who would be potential lessees. And we have other rentals, so we are comfortable with that whole process. If you do not have experience in that area, it would probably be wise to have a professional help you with the lease process and the ongoing management while you are gone. While you are considering leasing options, you need to consider whether to rent it furnished or unfurnished. Do you have a place to store your goods? If not, what would it cost to store them? How about getting them to and from storage? What about insurance while in storage?

The final choice would be to sell your property and invest the proceeds for the year. This is not a bad alternative if you are considering a change. When a trip like this becomes viable, you are probably in the midst of a life change anyway! Either your kids are on their own now and you may want a change of housing, or you have retired and may be considering a change, or you are having your own personal rebellion and taking off in mid-career. If any of these fit your situation, give this course of action serious consideration. Investing the equity for a year can add a sizable amount of additional capital upon your return or can provide funds to help finance the trip. One additional consideration is the potential emotional trauma of not having a place to live upon your return. Some people find this to be a bigger deal than others.

Deciding on an option

After considering the pros and cons of each alternative, we decided that trying to lease the house furnished was our choice. Once our research showed that we could probably lease to a visiting executive or professor, we had a major portion of the ongoing expenses covered. We calculated that renting it unfurnished was not a preferred option for us. The cost to store our possessions, including getting them to and from storage, would be about $8,000—about half the cost of leaving the house empty for a year— plus all the hassle and risk of renting it on top of that. We considered selling the house (and this became our backup plan if leasing failed), which would of course eliminate the mortgage and allow our equity dollars to grow for a year. However, since we both love our community and wanted a place to come home to upon our return, we decided to lease it as our first choice.

Pricing your home to lease

There are a variety of approaches you can take to this, but the most obvious is that you want to cover your expenses if at all possible. The lessees will pick up the utilities, but you need to make sure that your mortgage(s), homeowner's dues (if any), taxes, and insurance are covered. If you are hiring a property manager, that cost should

For leasing our home, a website was a key marketing tool. People could look at the property from the comfort of their home anywhere in the world.

also be included. Once you know the total cost, relocation firms or property managers can help you decide if this is a realistic price for your area. Obviously, furnished is going to lease for more than unfurnished, so if you can bear the thought of someone using your possessions, this will give you more dollars toward covering your expenses—or maybe even creating some positive cash flow toward the trip.

Since we were leasing our home furnished, we also included the cost of our housekeeper every other week. This accomplishes more than making sure the property is kept up. Since you most likely don't know the people you are leasing to, it is a good idea if someone on your "team" is keeping an eye on things and has access to your cell-phone number if anything is amiss. Good screening and deposits help in this area, but the housekeeper gave us a lot more peace of mind about leaving our home.

Marketing your home

Starting about three months before our departure, we put together a marketing plan that included all the major businesses, colleges, relocation firms, realtors, and other businesses here in our community. We built a website with pictures of the house and put together a nice color flyer about it—with the floor plan on the back—which we distributed to anyone who would take one! You never know where that "perfect" person will come from. Our target market was people moving here from out of town, many of whom were coming to work for either high-tech firms or colleges, both categories of whom are computer-savvy. Because of this fact, we felt that a website was a key marketing tool so people could look at the property from the comfort of their current home. Our Internet provider includes a simple-to-use web-page builder and storage space for no additional monthly fee. This kept us from having to hire someone or to go out and buy—and learn—a web-building software program. We found their web builder quite adequate for this simple purpose of providing a brief description and showing pictures of the house.

We made calls to everyone who could potentially help us, had an open house, and followed up every possibility. We were rewarded with just the right couple six weeks before our departure date. A realtor who had taken our flyer had an "over the backyard fence" conversation with his neighbor, and this neighbor was looking for a house for a business associate to lease, preferably furnished. The realtor gave him the flyer, and a day later, the deal was done. You never know where the success will come from, so don't be afraid to let everyone know about your property. This couple rented it just from the flyer and the website information. They never even saw it before sending the deposit!

We spent about $200 total marketing the property. We never advertised it in the newspaper, although we would have done so during the last month if our more targeted plan hadn't yielded results.

If you choose to market your house yourself, you will find in the appendix a selection of flyer ideas and letters that we put together to aid you in getting started. Again, if this is not your forte, you should seek the assistance of a professional to help market the property to avoid frustration and disappointment before you ever leave on the trip.

A backup plan

Even the best-laid plans do not always work, so it is important to consider what you will do if plan A doesn't work out as you envisioned. Your house might still not be sold for your price by departure day, the right renter might not appear, or you can't put the necessary plans in place to leave it empty. Have a plan B!

What about the cars?

The second big consideration was the cars. Do we keep them and store them, and if so, where, or do we just eliminate the expense (payments, insurance, a year's worth of depreciation, and so forth) and buy a couple of cars when we return? We decided "good-bye cars!"

We purchased a 19-foot self-contained van that was fully out-fitted for all the necessities of life. We considered it a large car, not an undersized motorhome! Neither of us was comfortable with the idea of driving one of those "big rigs"—and there are a lot of places you can't go with them. We wanted the freedom to be able to go pretty much anywhere we wanted (more on this decision in the next chapter).

Again, you need to have a plan B. One of our cars did not sell for the price we wanted and what *Kelley Blue Book* said it was worth. Our daughter continued to market it for a few more weeks after we left, but still no sale. So rather than sell it for cheap, we decided to hold on to it, wrap the payment in with the van payment, and store it with a friend while we were gone. We kept the insurance active on it so that our friend could drive it as needed. In fact, she decided this would be her "Friday Car." Wherever she went on Friday, our car went with her. This avoided the problems of long-term storage of a vehicle, and she had fun having a different look on Fridays!

With the major financial responsibilities planned, you can turn your attention to the other details of your life that must be considered and other arrangements to be made.

Handling family responsibilities

Although our children are all grown, on their own, and doing well, my mom is still living and we check in on her regularly. Phil has a brother whose affairs we handle as well. We needed someone to manage those responsibilities. Our daughters graciously decided they could take care of those things for us. We always knew those girls would come in handy one day!

Each family circumstance is different and requires sitting down with the parties involved and deciding how to best accommodate their needs. This can be difficult, as the people who depend on you might not want you to go on the trip—not because they want to deny you the opportunity, but more likely because the idea of change makes them uncomfortable. Or the fear of what might happen if you were gone—the fear of the unknown—causes them to resist. You need to recognize that this is what's going on, not that they are really trying to keep you from going.

Before you approach the family members involved, you should have your action plan together. A sound way for their financial and emotional needs to be met is critical. You may have to give them some time to think about your ideas for their care and happiness. With a well-thought-out plan and your conviction that you are going on this adventure, there is a much better chance of the conversation going well. The outcome you want is their agreement that your plan will work for them. This conversation, however, should not be the first time your loved ones have heard about the trip.

This brings up a good point. It is best to begin "socializing" the idea of going on an extended trip well before it happens. We started talking about it seriously in the family six to eight months ahead of time. This way it isn't a big surprise when you get down to talking about the specifics of taking care of your loved ones while you are gone. Properly done, you can even build excitement in the family so that they are actually helping you plan how everything will be handled.

Depending on your situation, there could be financial impacts for you. Any costs that you will incur while you are gone need to be added to the budget. For instance, you may need to hire someone to pay bills for a loved one or to order medications on a regular basis. We were lucky to have family members who could and would take on these kinds of responsibilities. The kids all stepped up to more regular contact with Grandma and made sure that Uncle Tom was included in family gatherings too. There was actually a nice benefit of our leaving these new responsibilities to the kids, as they all became closer to their grandmother. And their uncle developed a new relationship with them and their children that he didn't have before. It turned out to be a bonus we never would have expected. They felt more included and competent, and they knew we were always just a phone call away on our cell phone if anything came up that they didn't know how to handle.

Keeping your investments on track

Most Americans these days have some form of investments, whether a 401(k), IRA, rental properties, or stocks and mutual funds. These, of course, must be considered while you are gone.

In today's environment of online access to accounts and 800 services to brokers, most types of investments can be managed as easily on the road as at home. In Chapter 6, we discuss the electronic aspect of the trip more thoroughly. But suffice it to say, this is no longer a major obstacle to traveling.

If you have rental properties, you will need someone to oversee those while you are gone. Again, we were lucky to have a child skilled enough in this area to receive the rents (including our now-leased-out primary residence), handle any maintenance issues, and even re-rent the homes with a little long-distance assistance from us. Wouldn't you know that both of our longtime renters bought homes while we were gone, and both houses had to be re-rented. It never fails! If this family arrangement isn't an option for you, perhaps a like-minded rental-investor friend would take it on for a small fee—or a couple bottles of their favorite beverage! Another option is to hire a professional property-management firm. Don't forget this item in your budget. We did pay our daughter who took on this task, as it was quite a bit of work on a pretty regular basis. It is also tax-deductible as a rental expense.

Other things to consider

Before we begin building the budget for your trip, let's discuss a couple more items you may want to consider. A year is a long time to be away from home, assuming that this is indeed a trip, not a new "full-timer" lifestyle. Depending on when you embark on your journey, you will probably want to build in a trip home during the year.

Since we left in June, the holidays were an ideal time for us to go home for a visit. We simply left the van in Raleigh, North Carolina, and flew home for four weeks. We had included these expenses in our original budget. We watched the fares on the Internet until we saw something that was very reasonable. Since we hadn't sold both of our cars, we even had a car when we arrived—an unexpected bonus. Because our home was leased, we didn't have a home to come home to, but we arranged to house-sit for some friends who were out of town for the holidays. It worked out great for both of us. We fed their dog so they didn't have to board her, and we had a lovely home to stay in. We did have a couple nights "overlap" in a hotel to account for in our budget, as we opted not to stay with the kids during that already hectic time of year.

As hard as you try to eliminate all your expenses during your absence, there will be a few things you need to continue to pay, such as health-club memberships, country-club dues, and any ongoing consumer loans you may have. On your memberships, be sure to check for lower dues rates for "nonresident" members. If you are going to be gone a year or more, most clubs will change your status to a lower-rated classification, which will save you some money.

There are many additional things that you will need to address before you leave which can possibly have a small impact on your budget. We will discuss them in Chapter 3, "Deciding to Go," and Chapter 5, "Getting Ready to Go."

Building your budget

Now is the moment of truth. Can you *really* do this for the cost of staying home?

We propose two budgets for your consideration. The first, a more "deluxe" version, is the one that we actually used, and the second is a more "frugal," yet reasonable, plan for those who want to be more conservative. Of course, it is always easy to spend more money—a bigger and more deluxe rig, fancier motels, more extravagant souvenirs, more expensive entertainment and attractions, and the list goes on. If your income allows, then by all means go for it! But we think we represent a pretty average experience.

Budget 1

The table "Our Actual Budget" shows you our original budget, how we computed it, and then what we actually spent. You will see that on some items we were close; on others we were significantly over or under. We were just using educated guesses—but you have the benefit of our actual experience. As you read the travelogue portion of the book, you will get a sense of how closely our lifestyle on the road might match your own, and you can then gain a much better idea of how to adjust your budget for your own habits.

Two things happened on the road that negatively impacted our budget: a traffic accident involving an uninsured motorist (triggering our deductible and additional expenses to get that straightened out) and a broken ankle during the summer. This caused our expenses for hotel nights and restaurants to go up and for camping nights and groceries to go down during several months while

Our Actual Budget

Item	Computation	Monthly (× 4.3 weeks)	Annual	Actual	% of budget
Gasoline	750 miles per week divided by 13 mpg × $1.75/gallon	$436	$5,232	$4,338	83%
Gas—rental car	—	—	—	$98	—
Motel lodging	$80 per night × 4 nights per week	$1,376	$16,512	$22,160	134%
RV lodging	$25 per night × 3 nights per week	$323	$3,876	$978	25%
Food—restaurant and groceries	$60 per day × 7 days per week	$1,806	$21,672	$22,206	102%
Attractions and entertainment	$35 per day × 7 days per week	$1,054	$12,648	$7,385	58%
Dry cleaning, laundry, personal grooming	$20 per week	$86	$1,032	$804	78%
Cards, postage, birthday/wedding gifts sent home	$125 per month	$125	$1,500	$970	65%
Souvenirs and photo developing	$2,000 for the year		$2,000	$942	47%
Clothing (some as souvenirs)	$100 per month	$100	$1,200	$1,089	91%
Cell phone, long distance, Internet access	$125 per month	$125	$1,500	$2,164	144%
Transportation cost (van payment)	$503 per month × 14 months	$503	$7,042	$7,042	100%
Van maintenance, repairs, and insurance	$300 per month	$300	$3,600	$2,070	58%
Accident—unreimbursed		—	—	$627	—
Tolls, subway, and additional transportation en route	$600 for the year		$600	$571	95%
Miscellaneous (prescriptions, newspapers, etc.)	$100 per month	$100	$1,200	$1,126	94%
Equipping van and supplies en route	$2,000 for the year		$2,000	$1,768	88%
Deduct for holiday trip home (less lodging, meals, and gasoline)	$1,160 per week × 4 weeks (you don't incur the first five items while you are home)		($4,640)		
Total			$76,974	$76,338	101%

it healed. More about both of those incidents can be found in Chapter 8, "Handling Emergencies."

We also didn't contemplate the fact that we wouldn't camp while traveling the cold winter locales, as most campgrounds are closed. Also, our rig was too confining to be closed up in for extended periods of camping. More about this subject can be found in Chapter 3, "Deciding to Go."

Now, we're sure you are thinking, "Yeah, right, how could anyone come that close on a yearlong budget?"—but we swear that although we kept track on a monthly spreadsheet, there was really no budget-watching that went on during the year to try to manipulate the numbers. We just enjoyed the moment and let the chips fall where they may. We wanted to make this experience as real as we possibly could. When you read Part 2 of the book, you will see that we enjoyed a number of extravagances during the year just because we felt like it. This is really how it happened.

Because of variations in costs in different parts of the country, we fluctuated between 80 percent of budget in low months to 142 percent the month we were in Boston, New York City, and Washington D.C. Don't let this scare you; just know that you need to plan for it.

Budget 2

We realize that $76,000, plus some expenses at home, which we will discuss in a moment, is not a budget that everyone can work with. But we did learn some things along the way that we believe could result in a lower budget amount, which is shown in the table "A More Frugal Budget."

You might even be able to reduce these numbers further. Maybe you already own a suitable vehicle free and clear. Maybe your tastes in things to see involve just the natural beauty of our land, and not museums, golf, and sailboat charters. Maybe you want to stay full time in your rig and cook all your own meals. These things will change your numbers. Just make sure to allow enough money so

A More Frugal Budget

Item	Reason for lower expense	Monthly	Annual
Gasoline	Less driving, a higher-mileage vehicle, and lower gas prices would reduce the cost.	$300	$3,600
Motel lodging	Our $80 budget (an average) was more than adequate, and fewer motel nights per month would lower the cost.	$600	$7,200
RV lodging	$25 per night is a deluxe campground, but money could be saved by camping more and utilizing less expensive locations.	$350	$4,200
Food—restaurant and groceries	Although we oinked our way through the budget, we could have eaten "in" more and been more conservative in restaurant choices.	$1,000	$12,000
Attractions and entertainment	We actually spent about $20 per day and had many fabulous experiences—and this number is highly dependent on your interest areas.	$450	$5,400
Dry cleaning, laundry, personal grooming	$40 per month should be more than adequate.	$40	$480
Cards, postage, birthday/wedding gifts sent home	$100 per month should be adequate, but it depends on your family's habits in this area.	$100	$1,200
Souvenirs and photo developing	The more limited your space, the fewer things you will buy—although it is easy to go overboard in this area, and what will you do with it all when you get home?		$1,000
Clothing (some as souvenirs)	$75 per month is about right; you will need and want a few new things along the way.	$75	$900
Cell phone, long distance, Internet access	Although we had excellent plans in this area, we underestimated usage, but we stayed in touch with family and friends more than we thought we would.	$150	$1,800
Transportation cost (van payment)	Our payment included our car at home that we didn't sell and our road vehicle—and two months of extra payments before we left.	$350	$4,200
Van maintenance, repairs, and insurance	This number depends greatly on the age of the vehicle, type, etc.	$200	$2,400
Tolls, subway, and additional transportation en route	$600 was about right, as we took several train trips, a plane trip to Nantucket, etc.—but you must judge your own use.		$600
Miscellaneous (prescriptions, newspapers, etc.)	$100 per month	$100	$1,200
Equipping van and supplies en route	$1,000 for the year		$1,000
Deduct for holiday trip home (less lodging, meals, and gasoline)	The first five items are eliminated when you are home, if you decide to take such a detour.		($2,700)
Total			$44,480

that you don't have to cut your trip short or not do things you want to. Remember, this is a once-in-a-lifetime adventure. You want to enjoy it!

Even though we came out with a $79.14 average on 280 motel nights including taxes, we had a wide variation. The larger cities cost more, as do resort areas during high season. We had lots of nights in the $50 to $60 class and under. Most were very nice. We always utilized AAA, AARP, corporate, or some other local discount; the same was true with most attractions.

Other costs

We have talked about some of the other costs that you will have to consider, as well as the cost of a trip home if you decide to do that. The "Additional Expenses" checklist details some of those items for you to consider in your own budget.

Not everything will apply to your situation, but we want to give you as many "memory joggers" as possible to help you on your way.

Putting it all together

Now that you have considered most every expense you might encounter and have added up your sources of money to pay for this, turn to the appendix and make copies of the "Master Budget Worksheet" we've prepared for your use. Use pencil and keep erasing until you have a workable solution for your road trip dream. If you use MS-Excel, you will find a template on our website that you can download and modify to your heart's content.

We know that finances are a very important part of the decision-making process for a trip like this, and we hope that we have given you enough information so you can come up with a budget which suits your situation and desired type of trip. As you read through the rest of this book, you will see things that will cause you to go back and change some of these figures. That's good! This is your trip, not ours!

The old saying "Where there is a will, there is a way" certainly applies to this endeavor. It is very easy to say, "Oh, I can't do this; it costs too much, it takes too much planning, I have insurmountable obstacles"—and the excuses go on. The truth is that if you really want to have this incredible experience, you can make it happen. We'll share all the information we've discovered that can help to make this a reality. The rest is up to you.

Additional Expenses

Ongoing expenses

Club memberships	$ _____
Consumer loans	$ _____
Insurance (health, life, etc.)	$ _____
Other _____	$ _____
Total	$ _____

Other costs of being gone

Property management	$ _____
Care for others	$ _____
Repairs to property(s)	$ _____
Other _____	$ _____
Total	$ _____

Expenses for trip home during year

Airfare or transportation cost	$ _____
Rental car or local transportation	$ _____
Hotels and lodging	$ _____
Parking for travel vehicle—distant end	$ _____
Meals and groceries	$ _____
Holiday gifts, decorations, etc.	$ _____
Miscellaneous (personal services, doctor appointments, etc.)	$ _____
Total	$ _____

Chapter 3

Deciding to Go

Now that you've thought through the pesky area of financing the trip and realize that it really can be done, it's time to address all the other issues involved in making the decision. While money is an important topic, it is far from the only criterion in deciding to live your dream. This chapter addresses such practical aspects as what to tell the family, what to do with the family pets, missing your support system and home, deciding how to travel, and the most often asked question: how to be with your traveling companion on a 24/7 basis without going crazy!

Breaking the news

Saying it makes it real. The sooner you start telling people you are planning to go on this adventure, the sooner you will start believing it and orienting your thought processes around the idea. Even if you are not 100 percent committed to the idea yet, it solidifies your own commitment to start "socializing" the idea with friends, family, and organizations with which you are involved.

Even a year ahead is not too soon to start. You will find that you need about six months of intensive planning time to get everything done without making yourself crazy or a complete slave to your schedule. So the sooner you pick a date to leave and begin telling people that you are going, the easier it will be when you begin doing your planning in earnest.

People's initial reaction may be to resist or dismiss the idea, and this is especially true for people who depend on you for support of some type (financial, emotional, social, and so on). As we mentioned in Chapter 2, the earlier you begin talking about the idea with them, the more time they will have to incorporate the plan into their thinking. A series of discussions that cover the "what, when, why, and how" of the trip will help your friends and loved ones understand the importance of the decision to you and how they can support your decision.

> **Build a good plan, communicate it early and lovingly, keep a problem-solving can-do attitude, and never lose sight of your goal.**

Those who depend on you most will need particular attention. You need to be considerate of what they are feeling. Most likely they are thinking, "What will happen to me while you are gone?" Have a plan ready to address those needs. Once they understand that they will be taken care of, they will usually be in full support of your trip. The table "Some Potential Scenarios" on page 24 addresses some of the questions that could come up and offers some ideas on how you might find a solution for each concern. Certainly this list is not exhaustive, but hopefully it will get your own ideas flowing for how to handle your family's issues.

The bottom line is to do everything you can to provide for your obligations, but be firm that you are going on this adventure. Your firm resolve will motivate people to rally around you and become part of the solution, not part of the problem.

Building support

Here is where your skills as a cheerleader and motivator will become handy. Your own enthusiasm for the project can be contagious, and most people will ultimately be excited for you and can help you build consensus in your circle of friends and family.

Some Potential Scenarios

Area to be addressed	Potential solution
You pay the bills for your elderly father	Put most of them on a bill-payment plan from his bank, the utility companies, etc. Have a friend or family member pay miscellaneous ones each month when visiting.
Your disabled sister depends on you to mow her yard and grocery shop for her	If there isn't a family member who can take over these duties while you are gone, hire someone to do the work and include the cost in your budget.
You visit shut-ins at a local nursing home who have come to look forward to your visits	Find a friend or recruit someone from your church to start going with you and integrate them into the facility before you leave on your trip. Get the folks excited about your trip and offer to send e-mail or postcards of what you are doing. They will love that idea.
You have a three-year commitment to your community's planning commission, home-owner's board, etc.	Turn in your resignation early so that they have time to replace you and you can help orient the newcomer. This happens all the time. Don't let your guilt become a deterrent to your trip!
Your mother depends on you to manage her medications, get her to the doctor, etc.	Again, this is one of the areas where you can ask someone in the family, her circle of friends, her church, and so on, to fill this void while you are gone.
You baby-sit your granddaughter two days a week	If your son/daughter can't make other arrangements on their own for new childcare (the best option), then you may have to offer to find and pay for the care while you are gone. This is another item to include in your budget.
Your brother worries that you won't keep providing that extra income he counts on each month	Assure him (if it is true!) that you will continue to take care of that, and then set it up on an automatic payment directly to him or to his checking account.
Your business partner is concerned about what will happen to your clients while you are gone	It will take some negotiation to plan for not only the workload but also the split of profits, payment of expenses, and so on. A weekly conference call could help keep an even keel, or completely turning the business over to her for a year may work. Don't overcommit to your involvement or neither of you will end up happy with the arrangement.

When we first told people we were thinking about doing this, no one believed us, especially the kids. "Parents don't just run away for a year!" they exclaimed. I'm sure they thought we would "get over" this crazy idea and life would go back to normal. But as time grew closer and we began involving them in the planning by asking their opinions and assigning them duties while we were gone, they soon realized that we were actually going to do this. They became very supportive, even though they initially felt that their support system would be diminished. Other than not being available to take the kids off their hands for an afternoon or evening with Grandma and Grandpa, they actually saw new benefits to the time away. The postcards arrived pretty regularly, their phone was always handy to give our cell phone a call, our website showed them fun pictures of what we were up to, and the learning opportunity on geography was undeniable.

We were fortunate to have not only family but also friends who could and would help us to make this a reality. We made them all part of the process of getting ready to go and part of the trip while we were gone. Finding ways to include them, get them excited, and bring new experiences into their lives all ended up being positive developments that couldn't have been predicted ahead of time.

Here are some ideas for ways to include people in your planning and your trip:

- Make an adult child responsible for your mail. Forward everything to them, have them review it all, throw away the junk, pay any miscellaneous bills, and occasionally forward anything important to you. Remember that they can call you on your cell phone with any questions.
- Add one person to your checking account to take care of unexpected issues and to do any banking business. This could also be important if something were to happen to you on the trip.

- Enlist a "techie" friend to help you build a website, learn e-mail, or consider the options for GPS systems.
- Secure e-mail addresses from everyone you talk to and build a list so that you can send out mass e-mails to keep them up with what's going on while you are on the road.
- Ask someone with some spare space to be your "warehouse" while you travel so that you can ship treasures and out-of-season clothes to them along the way.
- Have someone be responsible for getting the local news and gossip to you each month—via e-mail, of course!
- If you do something involving children (i.e., volunteer at school, teach Sunday school, serve as a camp counselor, etc.) or have a teacher friend, set up part of your website for them to follow your adventure. Post geography questions, pictures, and other information that is appropriate to their age and to the area you are currently traveling through.
- Ask a marketing friend and/or a realtor to help you learn how to market and care for your home while you are gone.

The more committed you become to your trip, the more enthusiasm will build around you. We guarantee that your positive attitude will go a long way toward encouraging others to support you. Build a good plan, communicate it early and lovingly, keep a problem-solving can-do attitude, and never lose sight of your goal. You too will soon be on your way to your trip of a lifetime.

What about the pets?

We had pets in our lives when the kids were growing up. We have now chosen to consider each other our only pets! But for many folks this is a major consideration. We can tell you what we observed along the way.

Many people travel successfully with their pets, and there is no reason that you can't take most dogs or cats with you. They seem to enjoy it as much as the adults do. Most RV parks and even many motels have "walking areas" for your friends. We also saw many kenneling opportunities at large attractions, so you don't have to leave those companions in the car.

If you believe that taking your pets is not a good idea, for whatever reason, there are other solutions. The obvious one is to loan them to a loving family that either has pets or would like a "trial run" with yours. If your pet is a snake or some other exotic, this may be more difficult.

Another thought is to include the pet as part of the lease on your residence. This could either limit your potential caretakers or be seen as a bonus. We worked this strategy in reverse when we came home during the holidays. Since we had no home to come "home" to, we circulated an e-mail among our friends a month or so ahead of our arrival and offered to pet-sit for someone going on a trip during the holidays in exchange for a bed. Sure enough, friends of friends thought this was a terrific idea—no need to board the dog and someone reliable to watch over the house!

Children, grandchildren, and other support systems

This is just a short plea for sanity. The most common refrain we heard—and still hear—was, "I could never leave my grandchildren that long! How did you do it?" We also heard it in relation to children, dogs, neighbors, and parents, but most often it was about those darling little humans that grow way too fast.

We too love our grandchildren to death. We now have eight, and we see some portion of them almost every week. We wouldn't miss their growing up for anything and continue to arrange our lives to live close to them. But we also know that life is short, and we never know when our time here will be over. We were good parents. We prepared our children well for life. We did our jobs and more. We willingly and gleefully gave of our time and our talents and continue to do so. We never took long vacations away from them, and we now take the grandchildren with us from time to time and will do more as they get older and easier.

But at some point in life, don't you just want to scream, *"But what about me?"*

We decided *our* time had come. If we didn't grab it now, we might never get the chance. It was our turn to do something special for ourselves.

If you still don't believe you can do it, think about some of the things your grandchildren would miss:

- That phone call at the top of Bear Tooth Pass, 10,000-plus feet, and that little voice saying, "Hi Grandma, what'cha doing today? I love you," and you telling them about looking down on mountain lakes and glaciers and about the bears in Yellowstone Park—maybe we'll go there together one year.
- Those pictures of Grandpa in silly positions with his hands in Colorado and Utah and his feet in Arizona and New Mexico at Four Corners. "Where is that, Mom?" "Let's look on the map, honey, can it be true?" Another lesson learned.
- That meeting at the airport after six months away and the look on their little faces to finally see you again. Priceless!
- Arranging a little detour in your trip so you can join them on their vacation and they can see how you have been living. A day at the Smithsonian, a day at the park, or even dinner together can be memories they will never forget.
- If you really can't stand the thought of separation and if space allows, how about having them join you, one by one, for part of your trip? What a special time for both of you!

We know how important this factor is for many people, but we really plead with you to consider yourself first for a change. If extensive traveling is indeed of interest to you—or we assume you wouldn't be reading this book!—then take a deep breath, kiss the grandchildren, and plunge ahead with this crazy idea!

Missing important events

There is *never* the perfect time to take this trip. We missed class reunions, weddings, birthday parties, retirements, births, funerals, and many family get-togethers. These will all happen while you are gone. Life does go on around you. We finally decided that we have been very lucky to live around family and great friends all our lives and that this little "blip" of time wouldn't change that. We thought about all the people who spend their lives moving around or who live far from family, and again we counted our blessings that we would miss only a few events in the scope of things.

We made a conscious decision to do what we could to support those events we were missing and to include those people in our trip and thoughts to the fullest extent possible. We always sent e-cards or postcards to mark events. We sent presents when we would have bought presents at home. E-commerce certainly makes this easy these days. We made phone calls when appropriate. We encouraged people to visit our website, and we often posted greetings or special messages there. We received digital pictures in e-mail so that we could see what we had missed. In other words, we acted just like people who live far away from home.

If there is an event that you just can't miss, consider it as part of the trip experience and include a trip to the location as part of your budget. We knew that we wanted to "take a break" and come home for the holidays, so we included that in our plans. We left the van for a "checkup," hopped an airplane, and spent a wonderful four weeks with our families. Your break might be a class or family reunion along the way or a trip home for the arrival of that new grandchild.

You can simply make the extra effort to stay in touch and to be a part of lives and events. Your trip will be over in the blink of an eye, and although you will undoubtedly miss some significant events, the enrichment that you experience on your trip can never be replaced.

Choosing your traveling home

There are scads of books that discuss this topic in excruciating detail, so we won't take up space explaining it all again. They cover every type of vehicle, the pros and cons, how to maintain them, how to buy them, where to store them, and everything else you can imagine. Once you've decided to go, we suggest that you buy one of these books to help you make your personal decision on what is right for you. What we will tell you here is how we decided that our Pleasure-Way, 19-foot, Class B van was the perfect vehicle for us.

Envision your adventure
The absolute first thing you have to consider is what your trip will be like.

- Do you want to go fewer places and stay for a while in each?
- Do you want to be on the move most every day?
- Will you explore the back roads of our country or stick mainly to the interstates?
- How much gear do you need for your adventures?
- How many personal items are essential for your comfort?
- What kinds of weather will your route cover? What does that mean for clothing requirements and vehicle comfort?
- Do you want to be able to sleep in your vehicle? How elaborate does it need to be?

Each of these items has an impact on what type of vehicle you decide on. Your "home on the road" decision will impact your flexibility, your comfort, your driving, your ease of setup/teardown, and your finances. You can do a yearlong trip in everything from a large car or SUV to the fanciest motorhome available. Your choice of vehicle all depends on what you want to do and what you are comfortable living in.

If you will be staying in motels every night, have little or no desire to make sandwiches along the way, and can travel with minimal "gear" and a couple of suitcases full of clothes, then a car makes great sense. Your gas mileage will be better and you will have complete flexibility in where you take your vehicle and when you move to your next destination/adventure.

If, on the other hand, your needs for a yearlong trip are more extensive, then the fun begins—because the choices are so broad.

How we decided

The choice of vehicle was one of the first items we tackled on our long list in order to get ready for the trip. Once we had a general outline of what we wanted our trip to look like (see Chapter 4), we knew that there were a lot of things we wanted to see. We knew that we wanted to spend time in each state, we wanted to do some "camping," we wanted to have a comfortable amount of our "things" around us, and we wanted to stay off the interstates as much as possible. We also knew that neither of us had ever driven anything larger than a station wagon and didn't particularly want to add "big rig" training to our list!

We did Internet research, bought a couple of books, and started going to RV shows—something we'd *never* thought we would see ourselves doing! Because of our parameters, the more we looked, the more we became intrigued with the idea of either a Class C motorhome—generally defined as a "cab-over" design built on a regular truck chassis—or a conversion-van type of rig.

Conversion vans are each custom-built inside using a "delivery" van or an automobile van as the starting point. We saw a wide variance in quality and found that the used market was pretty undefined, which would be a concern once we returned and wanted to sell the vehicle. But we were intrigued with the ease of handling, the gas mileage, and the cozy interiors.

We ultimately thought that most of the Class C's were either underpowered for their size (too small of a truck body), top-heavy (high center of gravity)—think of a windstorm in Kansas!—or lacked design appeal (admittedly a personal preference). They do provide decent gas mileage and are generally roomy for their size.

We had eliminated the larger motorhomes early in our search strictly because we didn't want to learn to drive one. And we really didn't want to tow a car behind one, which is almost a requirement. Also, they are not easily maneuverable for exploring back roads, and they offer poor gas mileage. But they can't be beat for overall creature comfort: lots of room, lots of storage, and lots of gadgets—which we just saw as more things to go wrong that we wouldn't know how to fix! If you are doing a trip where you are planning to stay in your traveling home all or most of the time and you are not moving every day, you might want to seriously consider this type of vehicle.

The other choices include a trailer, a camper on the back of a pickup, or a fifth wheel—which is really a motorhome pulled by a truck or pickup. We didn't think we wanted to ride in a pickup for a year, so we nixed those choices early on. We also didn't like not being able to move back and forth between the cab and living area while moving down the road. And the choice of a fifth-wheel or trailer would also have entailed learning to maneuver a towed vehicle.

While we were at one of the RV shows, we spied a cute little unit way in the back. You could hardly see it for all the big rigs on the floor. We found out it was a Class B motorhome. We had not seen the Class B on the Internet, nor were they talked about in the

RV books. They were fairly new, and we were told that they had a limited market appeal. But we knew it was for us. They are built on a van chassis, are beautifully finished inside with every-

Class B RVs are so cleverly built and so convenient to drive, they are really in a category by themselves.

thing you could need, have a standard resale market (dealers, etc.), and get decent gas mileage. They are cozy but very well laid out.

We found there are several large manufacturers of these products. Winnebago makes the Rialta, and Pleasure-Way and RoadTrek (both from Canada) make the ones you will most often see on the road. There are a few smaller players—and maybe new ones we don't know about—but these are the ones we considered seriously. We felt that the Rialta, with its Volkswagen engine, wouldn't provide the horsepower we wanted going over mountain ranges. It has a neat layout and seems more spacious than the others. It is also lower to the ground, which is nice for getting in and out, but we thought that could be a problem for road clearance.

Let us spend a little time telling you about our decision-making to buy a Class B, because there is not a lot of information out there on these units, and we think they are a pretty neat choice. We did our serious comparisons between the RoadTrek and Pleasure-Way. Both have substantial dealer networks, both hold their value about equally well, both have well-laid-out interiors and adequate headroom for a six-foot-two-inch husband, and both sell for about the same price. By the way, if you consider one of these, the pricing may initially take your breath away for their size. You can certainly buy any other size RV for less money per square foot than a Class B. But they are so cleverly built and so convenient to drive, they are really in a category by themselves. Also, they hold their value much better than a standard RV. That is at least partly because you can drive them like a regular automobile when not using them for traveling. They have seatbelts for four or more, get good gas mileage (we got about 14 mpg on average over 35,000 miles), and can be parked with relative ease in a standard parking space. They are about the same length as a Suburban—just taller.

So how did we decide between the two? Part serendipity, part research, and part customer referral. We asked everyone we saw with one or the other brand (we often saw them at the grocery, downtown, at Wal-Mart, at sporting events, and so forth) and we found that the Pleasure-Way owners overall seemed more satisfied with their vehicle than RoadTrek owners. The Internet also proved to be fertile ground for reading about people's experiences with one or the other. Just type the brand name in any search engine (such as Google) and you can read for days! The major complaint from the RoadTrek owners seems to be that they lack power. They are built on a smaller engine than the Pleasure-Way. I understand there have been some changes in both brands since we bought ours, so it is worth checking out again. Ours always had plenty of power. As long as we didn't get behind a slow truck, we could whiz over the Rocky Mountains—which we did several times—at highway speed and were always comfortable passing on the highway. We also felt that the Pleasure-Way was laid out better inside—more usable storage, lighter and brighter (we had a white interior), a larger bed area, and a better-laid-out kitchen. Again, a lot of that is personal preference. We went to both dealers and talked to sales and service people. We felt, in our area, that the dealer representing Pleasure-Way was more informed and more interested in the product. We also found the Pleasure-Way dealers around the country to be very helpful and knowledgeable.

The serendipitous part of the decision involved finding an absolutely immaculate, "gently" used Pleasure-Way sitting in the driveway next door to a friend's house—for sale! We were already leaning in that direction, but this "find" sealed the deal for us.

Because Class B's are built on a standard chassis (ours on a powerful Dodge 3500), you can get them serviced at any regular car dealership. We didn't realize the importance of this until we were on the trip and found that RV dealerships are always booked out well in advance, whereas you can call an auto dealership, tell them you are traveling, and get in the same or the next day—

without fail! Since we didn't plan anything ahead (we never knew where we would be in two weeks in order to call and make an appointment!), that turned out to be a big advantage, because those 3,000-mile oil changes come around pretty often. Call the dealer, go have lunch, and you'll be back on the road! When you travel over 30,000 miles in a year, all the servicing that you would do at home in several years is condensed into one year.

Even our most nerve-wracking experience was resolved without a hitch by a Dodge dealer. We broke a shock—that big heavy-duty kind—in Yellowstone Park. We came back to the "Rolling White House"—our van's name—one day and saw something hanging down. "This does not look good," I told Phil. A service station was nearby, and they confirmed it was indeed a broken shock, but they had nothing of that size to replace it with. After determining it was not critical, just serious, we simply drove carefully and enjoyed the rest of our park experience and limped into Billings, Montana, a couple of days later. We called the dealership late on the afternoon we arrived and explained the problem. The dealer did not have a replacement on hand, but he said, "Let me see what I can do and call you back." He truly embodied the spirit of customer service. Near closing time, he called our cell phone and said he had found one and would have it there first thing in the morning: "See you then!"

Just a note about service: *Don't skimp!* This is not *just* your vehicle; this is your home and your special once-in-a-lifetime trip. You do not want to break down. We followed the "heavy-duty" maintenance schedule and never had a problem the entire year. Remember, our vehicle was not new—which was an even bigger incentive to keep it in tiptop shape. We always found the dealerships to be great. Everyone was interested in what we were doing and treated us royally at every stop. They made helpful suggestions, checked our records for what had been done previously, and generally made sure we went safely on our way each time. Congratulations are in order to the Dodge dealerships, large and small, around the country.

Our decision—post mortem

So would we pick that vehicle again? The answer is absolutely yes, but with one caveat. We loved the small size for handling, parking, gas, adequate storage, and driving. For 95 percent of the time, it was everything we could have needed or wanted. We did, however, find it a little confining in the evenings. Even though the seats both swivel around and there is a table between them, the interior is rather small for two good-sized people to move around in. When we camped and it was nice outside, we could hang out at the picnic table, take a walk, go swimming, have a barbeque, and so on, and it was perfect. But when the conditions were less than ideal, Phil, particularly, got a little claustrophobic inside the unit. This led us to camp less than we had anticipated. Sleeping was not the issue—in fact, he loved having the TV/VCR right at the foot of the bed; it was just the moving around inside during the evening hours. That was our only disappointment, and it may not be a factor for you. Rent one for a week before you buy if you have any concerns in this area.

We did find we used it in some ways that we hadn't originally anticipated and that were really handy. Having a bathroom on board can be a *real* lifesaver. Think of being stuck in the middle of nowhere while the road crew is working. Another fun option is firing up the stove by a beautiful waterfall and having a hot gourmet lunch with last night's leftovers. Easy as pie! Having cold water in the refrigerator at all times is wonderful. How about getting to your motel late, being tired, and cooking your dinner right in the parking lot in front of your room and eating in your room in your 'jamas? It was a lifesaver more than once.

You may be thinking, "Tired? What's with that? They're on vacation!" Trust us, you will have many tired days; in fact, you will have to take "vacations" from your trip! We know that sounds ridiculous, but as much fun as all of this is, you do have to have some downtime—just like at home.

The novice view of RVs

Having never driven—or even ridden in—an RV, and neither of us being very mechanical, we were nervous about any decision involving this type of vehicle. We're here to tell you that if we can do it, anyone can do it. Once we got the hang of it, we could set it up in less than fifteen minutes and be having our cocktails!

We read all the material, which was pretty confusing, but then we enlisted a friend with an RV to take us out in ours to practice. We went to a nearby RV park and told them that we wanted to practice. They laughed and let us play around to our heart's content. We hooked everything up, ran some water, turned everything on and off, flushed the toilet, unhooked everything, went to the dump station, saw how that worked, and then went back and did it all again by ourselves while our friend watched. We had it down—kind of. Before we left on our "real trip," we tried a weeklong trip—just to be sure. On that trip we learned a lot more. But there were no horrible disasters, only silly things that made us laugh. Read more about that in Chapter 11.

You just have to think of it like a house. It has a plumbing system, a heating system (actually two), a water system (also two), an electrical system (well, actually three), an air-conditioning system (two), and a septic system. Just like a house! Once you learn the basics, it all makes sense. We had a laminated card with setup and breakdown checklists (see appendix). We needed this for about three weeks, and then it was all automatic. Also in the appendix is a chart of the systems. This chart would have made our learning a lot easier! Each manufacturer varies a bit, but this is the general idea. Don't let this fear stop you from buying a "rig" if that is the most appropriate choice for your trip. Just keep your sense of humor and patience handy.

The great 24/7 "getting along" issue

Speaking of "humor" and "patience," if you don't take those along with you in large doses, you will be heading home in the first month. Guaranteed.

Nothing seems to strike fear into the hearts of couples faster than the idea of being together on a 24/7 basis for even a week, much less a year! This is unequivocally the *most* important issue to face before you decide to go.

Actually liking your spouse (or traveling companion) is probably a prerequisite for attempting to do this. If you can look that other person in the eye and say, "You know, I really do like spending time with you," then keep reading. If not, find a new companion for the trip, or read the rest of this book just for its entertainment value!

We never even gave this a thought as we made up our mind, as we genuinely enjoy each other's company and like to do many of the same things. We just naturally spend a lot of time together, so we really thought nothing of it. However, 24/7 does have its challenges, even for the most "together" of couples.

Support, support, support. If you don't do this and be sensitive to each other's needs, moods, and quirks, you could be really miserable on the road. Think about your current day-to-day relationship. Do you like spending time together even if life doesn't let you do it often? Do you enjoy the same activities? Do you have fun together on vacation? Do you find it relatively easy to help each other out and plan for things together? If you can answer yes to most of these, then you already have the foundation for a successful year together on the road.

> Make exercise a part of your routine. We took a walk almost every day at the end of the day to reflect and to recharge our batteries.

That's not to naively say you will always get along. You will both have bad days and good days, but it is really your frame of mind that says, "We are going to support each other through those times, and this too shall pass! We have a lot of fun and interesting times still ahead of us, and we'll have great memories to take home." And if you don't keep a positive outlook, you are surely headed home.

Arranging some space within the space is also helpful. If each person has even just a drawer or shelf that is all theirs, or a time of day when the other one just leaves them alone, then togetherness becomes more inviting.

We'd also put in a plug for exercise. We all know that it is good for us, both mentally and physically, and now you have the time to do it. We found that an hour of yoga—by a beautiful river, near a stream, viewing the mountains—was very calming. We also took a walk almost every day at the end of the day to reflect and to recharge our batteries. Whatever works for you, just make sure it becomes part of your routine. Having that daily bit of structure will go a long ways toward mitigating the "too much togetherness" that we've been discussing. Each of you can do it alone if that works better for you.

So what do you do when those bad days come, when you've just had it "up to here" with the other one and you want to run screaming from the campground? Just separate for a while and go do something individually. It may mean that one of you reads while the other golfs. One of you goes to a museum while the other one goes to a sporting event. You lie out in the sun and send him to get groceries (yeah, right!). Just do something to put distance between the two of you for a day. When we went home at the holidays—six months into our adventure—we figured out that we had been apart only nine hours in those six months and we still liked each other!

If you are not currently a "cozy couple," talking about it and setting some boundaries and routines ahead of time could help ease the transition to more togetherness. Taking time to discuss it and practice it could definitely make the difference between success and failure. This trip should not be another chore to live through but rather a life-changing, exhilarating experience to cherish forever.

When you return to your home, you will be a changed couple. We found we were closer than when we left, and our experiences continue to enrich our lives and conversations in a way that no other event could possibly have done. It could be the spark that keeps you together for the next fifty years of your life!

Chapter

Planning the Route

When we first began fantasizing about our trip, we mused, "Gee, we can stop anywhere we want, anytime we want—we've got a *whole year!*" Well, that is true, but you can't stop everywhere you want, every time you want. This is another case in life where choices have to be made. We've often said that we could do a whole additional year and never visit any of the places we went the first time. This country is really amazing!

You can't do it all

As much as you might think you will be able to see everything you want in the time frame that you choose, *you won't be able to*. We suggest that you pick a theme or areas of interest to help focus your trip. Even then, you probably won't make it to everything. Things will happen to make you change your itinerary, or you'll add other things that necessitate reprioritizing your list. But that is OK! It shows that you have allowed the flexibility in your schedule which is so important to a successful trip.

We chose national parks, historic architecture, small towns, and college football stadiums—guess who chose that one!—as our areas of focus. During the trip, we added state capitals, mostly because the capitol buildings across the country are such historic buildings, filled with interesting stories and beautiful architecture.

Don't get so locked into your plans that you don't allow room for spontaneity. You want to explore the unexpected opportunities along the way.

Our focus on seeing all forty-three of the national parks in the continental United States—plus we threw in about fifty of the monuments, seashores, historic parks, and so on—gave us a reason to go places where we wouldn't have otherwise gone. That total commitment to seeing all of them provided us with some of the most spectacular scenery and serendipitous moments of the trip.

It seemed we would never get to Big Bend National Park—way down in southwest Texas. Through sandstorms, heat, and miles of nothing, we forged on, and it turned out to be one of our favorites. Four parks can only be reached by water, which added another challenge to seeing them. They were all well worth the trip, and getting there was half the fun. Glimpses of some of these adventures are in the second part of this book, and for those who are interested, a complete travelogue can be found on our website.

Your trip may not have you on the move as much as we were, but again, make this *your* dream, not ours. Find those experiences that you will treasure and share over and over again both with each other and with other people.

Picking a theme

Some of you may have a firm idea of what your adventure will include. You have thought about it and planned it in your head for a long time. Others will have only a vague idea of what they would like to do. If you need inspiration to get started, there are a couple of techniques you may want to try.

Brainstorming with your travel partner or friends is always a good technique to get ideas flowing. The thing to remember with brainstorming is that there are no bad ideas. Often one of the most off-the-wall thoughts will trigger the perfect idea. So let the ideas flow, make a list as you go, and weed out the crazy thoughts later.

The second technique is to buy some travel magazines—or to surf travel websites—to get ideas of what is possible. Once you have decided to take this road trip, you will just naturally have your antenna up and begin to see everything as a possibility. The trick will be to narrow down what you really want to do.

We began visualizing our trip on a weekend getaway. Because you are relaxed and away from the hubbub of everyday life, this is an ideal time to bounce those ideas off each other and begin focusing on your dreams. One last piece of advice: Don't get so locked into your plans that you don't allow room for spontaneity. This is the trip of a lifetime, and you do want the opportunity to "be a kid again" and explore unexpected twists and turns along the way.

Here are some additional ideas to get you thinking about your own aspirations:

- Play at least one famous golf course in every state.
- Trace the development of our country through the railroad expansion.
- Follow the Lewis and Clark Trail (or some other historic theme).
- Visit the headquarters of every company in which you own stock and see their operations up close.
- Ride all the famous roller-coasters in the country.
- Visit historic inns.
- "Antique" your way around the country.
- Visit all the famous baseball/football stadiums.
- Hike on all the famous trails (i.e., Appalachian, Pacific Crest).
- Visit museums in every state.
- Paint or photograph sites in every state.

The ideas are endless. It is just up to you to fulfill your dreams.

Don't over-plan

This brings us to a *major* piece of advice. Do not, we repeat, *do not* try to plan each day of your trip before you leave. Don't even try to plan each week in any detail. Now, we know that this will make some of you very nervous. Where will we stay? How will our friends know when to expect us? What if we can't get into our favorite museum? And on and on.

By the time you finish this book, hopefully you will be convinced that you can do your trip without a detailed schedule. We'll show you how to plan "on the fly" and make it fun and not intimidating. You do have to keep that sense of humor we talked about earlier and be willing to accept that things won't always go according to plan, but isn't that true of life in general?

If you try to plan your every move, you will begin to feel like you are on a forced march to that next commitment, not on a trip of joy and exploration. In fact, we will go so far as to say that you will end up hating yourself and not enjoying the experience. Frustration will set in when you can't keep up with your schedule, reservations, and false deadlines. You just can't predict that far ahead.

Breadth versus depth

When we left on our trip, we didn't realize that playing every day and living your dream could be so tiring! One of our motivations for taking our trip when we did was health and fitness. We were both in our fifties, pretty fit, and in good health. But you never know how long that will last, so do it while you can.

Depending on the kind of trip you have envisioned and your personal lifestyle, you will need to discuss how to best execute your trip. If your goals lend themselves to seeing fewer places but with more exploration in each area, then consider a vehicle and itinerary that allows you to stay in one place longer and to explore in a "hub and spoke" pattern rather than continuously moving forward like we did. Because you will be setting up and breaking down as well as packing and unpacking less frequently, the wear and tear on your minds and bodies will be less!

If, on the other hand, you want to cover as much ground as possible and see a wide variety of things in this vast country, make sure your physical and mental condition can keep up the pace. We mentioned earlier about taking "vacations" from your trip. We know that sounds ridiculous, but it's true! No matter how wonderful every day is, you will still need some downtime. We simply acknowledged that we were "road-weary" and looked ahead to a spot where we wanted to stop and spend a few days, and then we planned our "vacation."

One such stop was along the shore of Lake Superior in a wonderful little Wisconsin town. Bayfield was one of those finds along the way. People we had spoken with at a restaurant one night said it was not to be missed. They were right. We golfed, we sailed, we lazed around in the sunshine, we did laundry, we shopped, we cooked, we attended a wonderful concert at Big Top Chautauqua, and we generally recharged our batteries for the next leg of our trip. Little did we know that our first big challenge of the trip lay but a week away when I suffered a broken ankle. But more about that later. During the course of the trip, we took one of these little mini-vacations about every two months. They made all the difference in our mental, if not our physical, outlook!

Laying it all out

Once you have your theme or goals set, then you should begin to lay the trip out, not in a detailed way, but at least in a general way. Believe it or not, it is easy to let a year slip through your fingers and not see everything you have envisioned. A general schedule, perhaps month by month, will ensure that at the end of the time you will have covered the ground you wanted and will have seen most things you planned, along with many things you didn't plan. Your memory will be overflowing with the knowledge and perspective you have gained, and the stories, both funny and uplifting, will be etched in your mind forever. This is the beauty of a long trip, and it absolutely cannot happen in a couple of weeks or even a month or two.

Naturally, your goals will somewhat dictate your route, but weather, specific events you want to attend, and other personal factors will also help mold your route. For us, weather was a big factor, as we wanted to avoid ice and snow at most any cost. We didn't want to sightsee in the cold, and we certainly didn't want to drive in it. We know, we're wimps! For the most part, our plan worked. Naturally, November and December along the eastern seaboard weren't like summer, but we had appropriate clothes and really enjoyed some great days, even with some pretty low temperatures. We had only one day of any snow, and that was at Virginia Beach, of all places. We outran it all the way from Williamsburg and got tucked into a lovely condominium overlooking the ocean and just watched it snow on the beach!

By the time we got to the Southwest, it was starting to heat up, but again, you plan for it, dress for it, and think of the people who live in that heat! One of our favorite hot spots was the Furnace Creek Inn in Death Valley. Temperatures ranged from the high 80s at night to over 110 degrees during the day—but what a true oasis in the desert this was. Because it was off-season, the rates were more reasonable, and it was a real treat. We felt like we were in the Casbah!

Our itinerary is included in the appendix to help give you ideas. This itinerary was the sum total of our route planning before we left. We didn't stick to it completely—which was a good thing!—but it did give enough structure to keep us on track yet the flexibility to change as opportunities presented themselves.

Maps, books, and the Internet

Maps and books will become your friends. They are integral to both the planning and execution of your trip. If you start your planning six months to a year ahead, you will have time to savor the possibilities and read about different places that you may want to include in your itinerary. Use them as a tool, but don't become a slave to them or use them to plan an exact route.

As you can see from our itinerary (see the appendix), we grouped things we wanted to do by state. That worked pretty well, even though we visited some states more than once. For instance, our route took us through eastern Kentucky in the fall and southern and western Kentucky in the spring. Ultimately, we got to see most of the items on the list, just at different times.

Plan on taking a few books with you to reference along the way. Our personal favorite was *Road Trip USA: Cross-Country Adventures on America's Two-Lane Highways*, published by Moon Travel Handbooks. We enjoyed their zany presentation and casual, fun-loving outlook on things. It closely matched our own approach to traveling. Our route crisscrossed their routes several times, so we found ourselves going back to it many times to find hidden treasures. The "Rolling White House" had some great compartments right above the seats that were perfect for storing maps, books, CDs, audiotapes, and other necessities of the road!

Here's one tip we learned the hard way: Pick a brand of map and don't change. They all have different ways of marking things, and when you get used to looking at one type, picking up another is very confusing. We had AAA maps for every state prior to leaving, but we lost one several months into the trip. The AAA office wasn't handy, so we stopped at a gas station and picked up another map. Big mistake! Our eyes were so oriented toward the "AAA style" that it was almost impossible to read the new one quickly and accurately. We soon found the local office of AAA to replace our lost map.

Speaking of the American Automobile Association, a travel club of some type can be a valuable resource both in preparation and along the way. Most of the memberships include towing insurance—make sure it includes RVs, if you are driving one—which you hope you will never need, but you should have it available anyway. But it's their travel assistance that can be invaluable on this type of trip. We had AAA prepare what they call a "trip tik." Basically, it's a suggested route that includes the items on your itinerary. We found the trip tik to be useful at times, especially the detailed maps when approaching large cities, but we found that we didn't follow it most of the time.

What we did find to be invaluable were the AAA guidebooks. We secured one for every state before we left, stored them in the van, and discarded them as we completed a state, thus freeing up valuable cargo space. In retrospect, we probably should have secured them a few months at a time, because the ones for the second half of our trip were mostly outdated by the time we reached those states. There are both lodging and camping varieties, although the camping ones are not as complete as the Woodell's or Trailer Life guides. We found the best aspect of the AAA guidebooks to be the information on attractions. Hours, days, prices, telephone numbers, and directions made seeking out special places easy. The discounts on attractions and motels that we were able to use during the year paid for the price of the membership many times over.

Every state has AAA offices, which we found to be convenient, friendly, helpful, and a great resource for information, either locally or along the way ahead. OK, enough advertising for AAA. Pick a travel club that you like, but pick one for sure!

In Chapter 6, we talk about all things electronic, but the Internet is such a fabulous tool for planning a trip like this that we have to mention it here. Every state and most cities have websites with more details than you can possibly digest. The National Park Service site has up-to-date information about the park system, and any kind of hobby or event of interest can be found by doing a search. Like much of the Internet, it can be overwhelming and you can find yourself spending way too much unproductive time "surfing" around in la-la land! Use it as a planning tool before you go and as needed on the trip, but don't forget that the goal is to see things for real—not on web pages!

> **The stark reality of this trip is that weeks and sometimes months will go by where you will see not one other person you know.**

Friends along the way

You will come to crave visiting friends along your route. No matter how well you get along with your companion, you two will soon be sick to death of talking to each other! The stark reality of this trip is that weeks and sometimes months will go by where you will see not one other person you know. Read that sentence again and let it sink in: *not one other person you know*. You will come to crave these visits with friends, family, and even other people you haven't seen for a long time.

Make these visits part of the excitement of your trip. Contact your friends and relatives as you make your plan, share with them what you are doing, and let them know *approximately* when you will be in their area. At this point, don't commit to anything more specific than "in the spring." You don't want to have to sprint to be at their house on a certain day unless it's for a wedding or an important event you have agreed to put in your itinerary. Be sure to add them to your e-mail list and take their phone number with you so they can track your progress and you can keep in touch with them as you get close to their area. Most people will understand your need for flexibility and make accommodations for your crazy road trip.

Don't overlook the possibility of seeing someone you haven't seen in a long time. You will most likely really enjoy these visits and may even renew some old friendships. Phil had lost track of a junior high school friend but had continued to hear about his life over the years through a mutual friend. We were able to get in touch with him and his wife and had a grand visit with them. It was such fun for both of them sharing experiences, reminiscing, and teasing each other as if they had never been apart. We ended up building a special part of our website just for her first graders, and that twenty-first-century "pen pal" arrangement became one of the highlights of our trip (see Chapter 6). Near the end of our trip, we were able to meet up with them again for a second visit. The gifts and picture book from "my" first graders—who by now knew more about the geography of our country than most sixth graders!—are among the most treasured of our mementos.

When to schedule ahead

Never schedule ahead. Well, that's not totally true, but it is close. If there is something so high on your priority list that if you didn't get to do it (and if it can only be done on one date during the year), it would be a great disappointment, then by all means, book a room ahead and make sure that your plan will accommodate being in that location at that time—even if it means you have to backtrack, speed up, or slow down.

During the trip, we agreed to meet a friend from home in New Hampshire and travel to Boston with her while she was on vacation. She is originally from Boston and wanted to show us "her city." While she, thankfully, kept her plans pretty loose until we got into that part of the country—we knew it would be "in the fall for the turning of the leaves"—we still ended up missing a lot of upstate New York and most of Vermont in our dash to meet our agreed timeline in New Hampshire. That was kind of a bummer, but we had a great time with her as our tour guide. Not only did we get to see Boston, but we also got to catch up on what was going on at home and have someone to talk to that we knew! It just means we'll have to take another trip back to that beautiful area to see the things we missed.

Another time, one of our children had a business meeting in Washington D.C. He brought the family along and we had a really fun weekend in our nation's capital. Another chance to talk to someone we knew! In fact, it was so bad that even though we were not yet near Washington D.C., we made special arrangements to leave the van in Connecticut and take the train down to D.C.—just so we could see them and enjoy the time together.

So even though these rendezvous were not pre-planned before we left, we still took advantage of the opportunities to work them into our adventure.

The other time to schedule ahead is if you want to plan a trip home during your adventure. If you decide to go for a whole year, you may want to come home for a special event such as a wedding, birth, or holiday.

Since we went from June to June, Christmas was a perfect mid-trip break. About two months before the holidays, we began projecting where we might be and which airports could be handy. We then began watching the airfares on the Internet from various choices until we nabbed a really good fare. Again, flexibility played a key role since we could choose to be in one of several places and our exact travel dates were immaterial.

Speaking of holidays, this trip could be a great chance to spend some of the holidays during the year with family or friends who don't live near your home. It can make a nice memory to do something different for Memorial Day, Fourth of July, or Thanksgiving. Experiencing the lives and cultures of people in other parts of the country was one of our favorite parts of our trip.

Chapter

Getting Ready to Go

As the time grows closer and closer to your "D-Day" (departure day, of course), the tasks will become overwhelming. But don't let the details derail your plan! Now is the time to let your best organizational skills kick in. This chapter will help you through most of the issues.

The lists: nailing down the details

Unless you have a completely photographic memory, you will need lists. We started six months before we left with big topics broken down by month, and we ended with very specific activities, day by day, for the last two weeks before we left. If you are at all like us, you will go to bed many nights thinking you will never get everything done—but you will. If you are really "organizationally challenged," find your most organized friend and enlist his or her help.

Here are several of our favorite techniques:

- **Do/Call/Get.** Break your lists down by things you need to *do* at home (pay bills, water plants, clean out the refrigerator), people you need to *call* (make doctor appointments, call realtors about leasing the house, change utilities to renter), and things you need to *get* (new rain jacket, tires for the car, take clothes to storage, clean out locker at athletic club). This technique allows you to focus on a subset of the tasks depending on whether you are at home, making calls, or running errands.

- **Break down the "chunks."** On big tasks that have several steps, break them down into more manageable "chunks" and put each of the smaller activities on your lists. You will find that the big tasks get done in a timely fashion and without a huge effort because you've done a little at a time.
- **Calendar the tasks.** Set deadlines to have certain items completed by—especially those large tasks that take several steps. Block out time on the calendar to work on projects and treat that time as already committed just like any other appointment that you schedule.
- **Prioritize.** Each week prioritize the activities for the week—the "must do now" group, the "want to complete this week" set, and the "if I have time" activities. Cross things off as you complete them—that feels so good!—and make sure the "must do's" are getting crossed off first. Reprioritize the lists each week.

Learning to navigate

How are your map-reading skills? Have you ever driven a vehicle of the type you have decided on? Do you have a good sense of direction?

These are all questions that need affirmative answers before you leave! At least one of you needs good map-reading skills. In the previous chapter we suggested using the same brand of maps throughout the trip. It really does make the navigating job easier. If you haven't done much traveling that requires maps, start reading them now with every trip you take—even if you know where you're going.

If all else fails, buy a GPS system with all the maps for the areas you will travel. Even if you have a good sense of direction, can follow signs well, and read maps like an expert, a GPS is not a bad idea anyway, as you will undoubtedly get temporarily lost at some point on the trip.

Discounts/clubs/passes

Depending on what you have planned for your adventure, you will want to take advantage of all the discounts possible.

National parks

If the national parks are part of your itinerary, be sure to buy one of the annual passes. You can buy them at any national park. Wait until you get to the first one so you will have a full year from that date. They give you free admission to all the parks, monuments, and so forth. This pays for itself many times over.

National chains

Many grocery-store and drugstore chains now have discount cards. Make sure you have a couple from your favorite major national chains.

Most hotel chains have discount programs. If you are planning motel/hotel stays as part of your trip, be sure to take advantage of these. We particularly liked the Days Inn September Days Club. It is not well advertised but always offers good rates.

AARP/AAA/corporate

Most motels offer some combination of these discounts. Always ask about those for which you may qualify. If you have your own small business, you probably will qualify for a "corporate" rate.

Motor clubs and AARP have negotiated discounts with many major attractions around the country. Always be sure to ask when purchasing your tickets, because the discounts are often not shown on the ticket-price reader board.

Camping clubs and timeshares

If you are taking an RV of any type on your trip, you should be sure to join Camping World, KOA, and the Good Sam Club. Some are free, and some have a nominal fee, but all provide good discounts to their members. Others are worth investigating, but these are at least the basics.

Early in the trip, we came across a private campground. We wondered what that was all about, so we pulled in to find out. We ended up joining Resort Parks International, one of the large campground-membership clubs. It cost $500 and covered hundreds of nice campgrounds for a $5 per night fee, some condominiums at low rates, and another large group of campgrounds for free. We figured that since most nice campgrounds charge around $25 per night, the membership would pay for itself in no more than twenty-five nights ($500 divided by the $20-per-night savings). Well, this was true, but we found that the nice campgrounds and condos were seldom located where we were and that the free ones were pretty basic. We didn't break even. A lesson learned for us, but your experience might be different.

If you own a time-share of any type, be sure to check out whether they offer discounted "last-minute" bookings. Many of them allow you to book inside a couple of weeks on a space-available basis for practically nothing. If you are doing a trip where you will be in one place for an extended period of time, this may be a good opportunity to use your time-share for that year.

Other discounts

The "Entertainment" books, no matter which city you buy, have discounts for lodging all over the country, mostly at 50 percent off. If you are planning to utilize motels for some of your stays, this could be a very good resource. If you are staying in an area for any length of time, you may want to investigate buying the local "Entertainment" book for lodging and attractions in that area. It could quickly pay for itself.

As the World Wide Web continues to expand, there are more and more discount coupons available for all types of products and services. You may want to scout some of those sites for current discount offers a few times during the year.

Insurance

Insurance was one of the most difficult areas for us to negotiate. We spent countless hours trying to figure it all out. Conflicting information, stalemates, and unsolvable problems seemed to be the name of the game. In the end, we left home totally insured, but it wasn't easy. We hope these tips help you with easier navigation of the insurance industry.

Homeowner's versus landlord policies

Homeowner's insurance was the most troublesome area for us. If you sell your house, you no longer have homeowner's insurance. That seems reasonable, but the contents of your automobile/RV are covered by your homeowner's policy, not your auto policy, so what about your golf clubs, laptop, cameras, or wedding ring?

Similarly, if you rent/lease your home while you are gone, you no longer have a homeowner's policy; you now have a landlord policy, which doesn't cover either the contents of your home—which is a problem if you rent your home furnished or store some items there while you are gone—*or* the contents of your vehicle. *Yikes!*

A couple of really good insurance agents finally sorted it all out for us. We were able to add a rider to our landlord policy that covered the contents of our leased home since the furnishings were part of the rental price. Then, because we were storing things at our daughter's house and it was our "residence address" (because our mail was being forwarded there), we were able to add a schedule to *her* homeowner's policy that covered the major personal items in our van. We had to identify what we wanted covered, item by item. It cost less than $100 for the year.

The lesson is this: Keep digging. If you get one "no," keep asking questions of both your own agent and others. This took us literally several weeks of work to make it all happen.

If you don't belong to an auto club, you may want to join one for this trip. They offer many services that can more than pay for the membership cost.

We also had jewelry scheduled on our former homeowner's policy. That problem was more easily solved by putting the jewelry in our safe-deposit box, such that no coverage was needed. And while we are on the subject, as many experts will also tell you, don't take expensive jewelry along while you are traveling.

Automobile or RV policies

If you are taking a standard automobile as your conveyance on your trip, check with your agent just to make sure that your coverage is proper for this extended vacation.

If you have chosen an RV of some type, you have a couple of additional issues to handle. Most RV policies are written for either limited travel or full-time use. Be sure to get a full-time policy, or upgrade your existing policy if you are taking a vehicle you already own.

If you don't belong to an auto club, you may want to think about joining one for this trip. As we covered in Chapter 4, they offer a lot of services that can assist you on your trip. And now, more than at home, you may want to have towing coverage also. This is your trip of a lifetime. For the small amount that towing coverage costs, isn't it worth it to avoid the risk of inconvenience when you are in a strange location with no family or friends available to come help you? Both automobile and RV packages are available from most auto clubs or through Camping World.

Another coverage that's available is called "bumper to bumper" RV insurance, which covers all the systems on board your RV. No, these aren't covered by your regular RV insurance. This policy covers things like your stove, refrigerator, roof air conditioner, and many other amenities. The cost is fairly steep and has a time *and mileage* stipulation, which we didn't realize. We found that our mileage had run out in about four months. If you have a fairly new unit and you do the recommended maintenance on the systems, you may want to think carefully about investing in this expense. If you are traveling a lot of miles on your adventure, it would take a major system failure for you to break even. If, on the other hand, your unit is older or you have a more limited travel range, it might be a worthwhile investment.

Medical insurance

Most health plans cover you anywhere in the United States, but you should check with your plan provider for any caveats or special circumstances.

We had our provider note our records as to what we were doing, and it made for very smooth sailing when I broke my ankle. After the initial emergency trip to the nearest clinic and a subsequent trip to a "real" hospital with an orthopedic doctor, they helped us find "in-plan" doctors along the way and even smoothed the unusual claim process by assigning a customer-service agent to help us. This avoided the silliness of having to check with our primary-care physician (who never saw the broken ankle) each time we saw a new doctor along the way. There's more about this in Chapter 8, "Handling Emergencies."

Legal things

This is a great time to make sure that all your affairs are up to date. It's unlikely that anything will happen, but taking an extended trip provides a perfect time to review that everything is just as you want it.

Take a look at your will, organ-donor cards, life insurance, and advance directives to make sure they reflect your current thoughts.

If you haven't taken care of these items, now is the time. It would be complicated enough for your loved ones to get you back home without the added frustration of improper documentation for them to manage.

Have all the necessary legal and identification documents with you. Put a note in the glove box as to where in the vehicle the documents are stored.

This brings up the issue of power of attorney. If something disabling happened to you, it would make it much easier if someone in your family had power of attorney to be able to sign legal documents in your stead. Some people are comfortable with this notion; others are not.

Also, we added our daughters to various checking accounts. One daughter was added to our personal account (see the next section too) and the investment-properties/rentals account, and another daughter was responsible for Phil's brother, whose affairs we manage. This way they could both handle day-to-day transactions on our behalf. We also left safe-deposit box keys with them. We made no changes on our brokerage accounts, as we had professional managers there and we could access the accounts as needed.

Voting turned out to be problematic. We live in a state where all elections, even the big national elections, are vote-by-mail. We have no polling place. So we assumed that our ballots would be forwarded with all our mail to our daughter. Wrong—ballots are never automatically forwarded. So for the first time in many years, in 2000 we did not get to vote in that crazy "no president" election. If you want to vote while you are gone, check with your local elections office as to what you can do. We probably could have re-registered at our daughter's address or applied for an absentee ballot and had her manually forward the ballots to us, had we only known.

One last item is to be sure to have all the necessary legal and identification documents with you. Carry a complete set of anything you might need—car title, passport, immigration papers, advance directives, emergency-contact information, insurance information, medical information, etc.—in the vehicle in a secure spot. Also put a note in the glove box—the first place police will check—as to where the documents are stored. Always carry your emergency-contact information with you. Make sure those persons listed know your vehicle description and license number in case you are injured away from your "home."

We debated about keeping the title to the vehicle with us but decided that the risk outweighed the hassle of getting it to us if we totaled it or got a crazy notion to exchange vehicles part way through the trip.

Enough of the depressing stuff. We always believe that being prepared helps ensure that the bad things won't happen.

Banking, bills, money, and mail

Your options for this part of your planning have become so much more robust in the last few years that this is almost a non-issue if done properly. If you have resisted all the new electronic tools, now is the time to get on board. It will make your life on the road so much easier. We have found that errors are easier to detect and happen less frequently with electronic media, but you do have to get them set up correctly.

Banking

Check with your financial institution(s) and see what they offer. Sign up for bank by phone and/or Internet access, if you haven't already done so. If these services are new to you, sign up a few months ahead so you can practice and be familiar with them before you leave on your trip; there's no need to have the frustrations of training while you are enjoying your adventure.

Once you have signed up for these services, you will see that you can transfer money from account to account, check your balances, see what transactions have cleared, find out how your investments are doing, buy/sell/change investments, and a myriad of other options. There is very little you can't do online or with telephone-automated systems. The Internet services are easier to use because you can visually see everything just like on a statement, whereas you have to listen and write down the information given on an interactive voice system.

You can check each account every day on the road if you are so inclined. But let's hope you don't.

Bills

Sign up for auto-pay on everything you possibly can:

- Mortgage(s)
- Vehicle payment
- Insurance
- Dues
- Credit cards
- Cell phone and Internet

Sign up for auto-deposit on all of the incoming resources possible:

- Pensions
- Distributions from IRAs
- Rental income
- Social Security

You can check every day if you want to make sure that everything is being done correctly. The nice thing about electronic systems is that once they are set up and working properly, there is no human intervention to mess them up, so they normally just click along perfectly. Just get them all set up a few months before leaving so that you'll have time to fix anything that didn't get set up correctly the first time!

For the occasional unscheduled bill that comes in,

- The person on your checking account can check with you by phone and then pay it.
- You can call the company and put it on your credit card; most companies are glad to accept this form of payment these days.
- As a last resort, you can have it forwarded to you on the road.

We had less than a dozen items that our daughter had to actually act on during the year. Makes you wonder why you get so much mail at home, doesn't it?

Money

With everything at home now under control, you can think about how to conduct transactions on the road. We feel that debit cards are the easiest and best for everything—except hotels, which we'll explain in a minute. You can keep track of exactly where your finances are with a debit card, because they post to your account immediately. It virtually eliminates the need to carry cash. We never carried more than ten or twenty dollars with us at any time. Using your debit card for everything also gives you an accurate record of what you spend on your trip, if you care. The only things we used cash for were incidentals such as a newspaper, a coin-operated vending machine, or a rare "cash only" attraction.

We normally got our pocket cash by adding the amount to a grocery-store debit transaction. Occasionally we'd get stuck and have to use an ATM and have to pay their fee. Most credit unions don't charge for ATM or debit transactions, but check your bank's policy.

Now for motels/hotels—a little-known secret that we found out the painful way: When you check into a room, the front desk runs your card for a predetermined amount—often over $200 for even a one-night stay in an inexpensive place. The average desk clerk has no idea how to override this and will have no idea what you are even talking about. So what is the problem?

The way debit cards work, this $200 is debited against your checking account immediately, and it is no longer available. It sits in this "suspense" state waiting for the "real" charge to come through that matches the $200 *exactly*. When you check out the next day and the charge is only $50, it doesn't match, so now you are debited for the $50, *and* the $200 is still waiting for a matching charge. After a few *business* days (three, at our bank), the "unmatched" charge drops off, returning the $200 to your account. So you can see that if you check into a different hotel every night for several nights running, you could have upwards of $1,000 in the "suspense" account waiting for matching charges that never appear, plus the actual amount of your stay—$50, in the example above—each night! We couldn't figure out why our checking account was overdrawing.

The answer is to put hotel/motel charges on your credit card and just pay the credit-card charges from your checking account once a week or so. This is ever so easy if your credit card is issued by the same institution where you have your checking account; you just transfer the funds from checking to the credit-card payment.

Another way to manage your money on the trip would to be to use a credit card for everything. You get the same convenience and the same recordkeeping, and you avoid the motel problem, and then you just pay the whole bill once a month when your funds are deposited into your account. You could also accumulate credit-card "reward points" this way, which would be an added benefit. Why didn't we think of that?

We did carry five $100 traveler's checks in the van. We came home with $400 of them. But that one time we needed it, we really needed it—no credit/debit cards accepted, not enough cash on hand, no ATM available, no out-of-state checks accepted, but we did have our trusty traveler's checks. Saved by American Express!

Mail

As efficient as all the electronic services are, you still will get mail while you are on the road. Almost all of it is inconsequential. Our daughter maintains that we are personally responsible for the deforestation of America! Just think how many trees we could save if we eliminated junk mail.

She dutifully received and sorted through everything, saving receipts in a file, writing the occasional bill payment, answering invitations from people who didn't know about the trip, looking at a few catalogs herself, and throwing out the vast majority of what the mailman brought.

If you aren't lucky enough to have children or a friend who will bear the burden of sorting not only their own mail but yours too, then you will probably have to use a mail-forwarding service.

For a fee, they receive all your mail and forward it to you when you call with a forwarding location. If you are moving along each day, this is a little tricky, as you have to project where you will be in five days. Always pick a small town with only one post office. It is much easier to find your General Delivery mail in a one-post-office town. They even get kind of excited to see who is going to pick up this unfamiliar parcel. The reason we know this is that we had a camera break which had to be mailed to us when it was repaired.

Also, don't forget about fax. If you have a document that requires a signature while you are gone, most motels and some campgrounds have fax machines where it can be sent. You could also receive it on your PC if you have fax software and a printer. If a fax signature is acceptable, then just fax it back, or at the very least you only have to deal with the mail from you back to them. This is much easier than trying to catch up with a mailed document.

Traveling with pets

We saw many people on the road happily traveling with their pets. There are quite a few books that deal exclusively with this subject, so if you plan to take man's best friend along, you may want to invest in one of those helpful guides.

During the planning stage, make sure to schedule a checkup and get the pet's shots up to date. As you think through the adventures of your trip, make sure you have considered your pet's arrangements: motels, campgrounds, kenneling while you are at attractions, and so on. This is where one of the books on the subject can be very helpful.

Packing the vehicle

When you get to this stage, it will really sink in that you are going. This should be an exciting—albeit frustrating—time. As soon as you have your vehicle, start thinking about where everything will go. In the appendix we have listed every single item that was in our van. This should give you a good starting point for your own list.

Start early "staging" your gear. Then put half of it away.

- **Think multi-use on everything.** If it doesn't have more than one use, chances are it doesn't need to go.
- **Start making two stacks**—"must go" and "candidates"—and keep eliminating from your "candidates" stack. This goes for both clothes and household items.

Make every inch count.

- **Zip-lock bags are your best friend.** Dump things out of boxes and into zip-locks—they take up much less room. Remember to cut any important information from the box or write it down and put in the zip-lock—things like how much water to add to rice, that great pancake recipe, and how to make biscuits.
- **Velcro strips with adhesive backs** are very handy for everything from attaching your cell phone to the dashboard—no more digging for it!—to closing that annoying gap in the curtains.
- **Plastic bags with one-way valves** allow you to store off-season clothing and occasional-use items. It is amazing how small a winter coat becomes in one of those bags.
- **"The Organizer"** was a real time and space saver. All those little items we could never keep track of went in a full-length, over-the-door organizer that we found in a catalog. It had over fifty pockets of varying sizes, and we stored everything from envelopes and stamps to nail polish to batteries to

staplers to aspirin packs in it. We could always find the little things in our van!

- **A shower caddy** of some type is really helpful if you will be utilizing showers at campgrounds or will be moving back and forth from your vehicle to motels. You will always have those toiletry items ready to go and all in one place.

When you go on your "trial run" (see Chapter 11), you will learn a lot and be able to adjust your supplies before you leave. Another good idea is to "live" in your rig in the driveway for a couple of days, especially if you aren't "old hands" at this RV thing. It's much easier to run into the house for things that you've forgotten than run to the store. The danger here, of course, is that you run in to get things that you really don't need; think of what you have already packed that can do double-duty for what you think you need.

Luxuries

This may seem like an unusual category, but it is really very important. A year is a long time, and you will want to have some of your favorite things from home along on your adventure. Think of small things that you can easily carry which will comfort you along the way. Here are some ideas:

- Favorite down pillow and comforter
- Small flower vase—maybe crystal
- Massage oil
- Relaxing CDs
- Heating pad
- Favorite wine glasses
- Family pictures
- Favorite coffee cup

Clothing

Depending on your everyday routine, you may need to adjust your attitude toward your wardrobe. If jeans, T-shirts, shorts, sweats, and other casual wear are your normal mode, you'll be ready to go. If, on the other hand, you are used to dressing up more, you do need to reassess. Phil was in the clothing business his entire career, so this was a big transition for him. It took him about a month on the road before he settled into his daily dress of drawstring cotton shorts, a T-shirt, and Tevas. Most of the "nice outfits" he so carefully packed went home in the first shipment. I tried to tell him . . .

> **Pick a color scheme that you like (black/khaki, navy/brown) and build everything around it. Don't take anything that can't be mixed and matched.**

Leave most of your "dry-clean-only" items at home. You probably want to have one nice outfit (dress and sweater or jacket; sports jacket, slacks, and mock turtle or shirt/tie) if you plan to include some nice resorts or restaurants in your itinerary. While there are only a few establishments left that require them, you will probably feel more comfortable and look less like a tourist if you have such an outfit. Besides, getting out of your regular travel clothes even becomes an event!

There are quite a few catalogs now that cater to the traveler's clothing needs. If you wish to buy a few things, those are a good place to find easy-care items that still look nice. Such retailers as TravelSmith, Norm Thompson, and Chico's (women only) all offer an array of travel-friendly pieces that coordinate well.

Be sure to maximize your clothing choices. Pick a color scheme that you like (black/khaki, navy/brown, black/red) and build everything around it. Don't take anything that can't be mixed and matched. In the appendix, we list everything we took and the colors. A few contrasting tops will help break up the monotony, but you'll save a ton of space if you think through what you take carefully.

You will undoubtedly buy a few things along the way, so have the basics in neutral, darker colors, and you'll have fun buying some interesting pieces to change the look.

Oh, and when you get home, you'll want to burn everything you took—you'll be so sick of it!

Personal things

A big deal for women is haircuts. My hairdresser went through all kinds of gyrations trying to help me figure out what to do: long hair pulled back, short hair with a perm or without, don't get it cut until I get home—what foolishness! When I needed a haircut, I started looking around the town we happened to be in for locals whose hair looked good and was styled similarly, and I asked them where they got it cut and off I went. One lady even called her hairdresser for me! People were great everywhere, and I got good haircuts every time.

Another thing I had to come to terms with was my nails. Although I don't get regular manicures or have artificial nails, I do like them to be polished and looking nice. Resign yourself to the fact that they won't look good all the time. This adventure holds too many fun, active, nail-breaking times to worry about it. But having a mani/pedi is a great way to treat yourself, get away from your spouse for a while, and hear the local gossip!

On a less "fluffy" note, don't forget to schedule a physical and have your teeth checked and cleaned before you go. At least start out in good health. If you are a fanatic about your teeth, make an appointment for when you come home during the trip also.

If you take any prescription drugs, check with your insurance company (if you have such insurance) to see how much you can purchase ahead. Some companies will only allow a ninety-day supply. Most of the national pharmacy chains now have interconnected computers, so you can get refills anywhere along the way where they have locations.

Have your doctor write a prescription for a year's supply, and keep that on file with your pharmacy chain. This should prevent having to make emergency calls to your doctor for refill approval as you are moving along. Just having the written copy with you won't help, as you can't get a prescription filled from a doctor who is not licensed in the state where you are currently travel-

The day that you actually pull out of your driveway will be so exhilarating! You will be *ready* to get going and get away from all the pre-leaving craziness.

ing. Again, a little pre-planning can save lots of headaches along the way and wasted time resolving issues when you could be experiencing your next great event.

If you wear glasses or contacts, be sure to take an extra pair (or extra sets of contacts) with you along with your prescription, just in case you lose or break both pairs.

Saying good-bye

The time is almost here. Your lists are dwindling, the rig is packed, and you are close to "D-Day." But wait—there are just a few more things!

Be sure to make a special effort with any relatives who are nervous about your departure. Make sure their needs are covered and that they have your cell-phone number. Include them in as many of the pre-leaving festivities as possible.

If people want to plan parties for you before you leave, let them. This will take the burden off of you to get around and say good-bye to everyone individually, and it will be a fun way to start your trip.

Have a send-off party the day you leave—just coffee and treats served in the rig for those who want to actually wave good-bye. You'll be *so* organized by then.

Oh, one last thing: When you have your cell-phone number, e-mail address, website address (if you decide to do that) all nailed down, get some personal/business cards made. Include both of your names, your usual home address and telephone number, and your traveling information (e-mail, cell, etc.). These are great to give to your friends before you leave so they can keep in touch, and they are wonderful to give to all the people you'll meet along the way. You can do them on your computer or on the Internet, or they are inexpensive to have your local print shop do for you. We are still using ours even now.

You will be feeling nervous, excited, and afraid you'll forget something important. *Relax!* All your pre-planning will pay off and your great adventure of a lifetime will begin. The day that you actually pull out of your driveway will be so exhilarating! And believe us when we say this: You will be *ready* to get going and get away from all the pre-leaving craziness. What you don't have by now, you either don't need or can buy along the way. The quiet of the open road awaits.

Have a great trip!

Staying in Touch

One of the best parts of your great American adventure will be sharing it with others as you go. With today's technology, staying in touch is so easy and getting more efficient all the time. Ten years ago, a trip of this type would have been much more difficult to enjoy with family and friends. But high-tech solutions aren't the only answer, and you may still use old-fashioned ideas like postcards and journals, at least part of the time.

Electronic gizmos

Even though we just said that electronic devices aren't imperative, they certainly enhance the enjoyment of the experience. There are so many different items to choose from, and the choices broaden every week. We can only share our experiences; researching current options is up to you.

Cell phones

I can't imagine taking a trip without a cell phone. Not only are they important for emergencies, but they allow quick communication with family, attractions, and campgrounds, and they have myriad other uses along the way.

With today's ever-falling prices, having a cell phone is not expensive. The real key for this trip is choosing a carrier that offers coverage in all the areas where you plan to travel and that has a plan which fits your needs.

Get your film developed along the way and mark on the back of the pictures where and what they are. You will *never* remember it all when you get home.

We chose the AT&T Wireless Nationwide Plan with no roaming charges and no long-distance charges. We were able to check our approximate usage online and varied our included minutes (and therefore our monthly cost) depending on the activity that month. Since we signed up in our home location, we had a local cell-phone number, and our friends and relatives at home could call us toll-free because they were simply dialing our local number, just as if we were in town. Very slick! We experienced very few times that we did not have cellular service. Even at the top of 11,000-foot passes we could hear those precious words, "Hi Grammie!"

We also had voice mail included in our service, and that was really handy since we didn't keep our phone with us all the time and there were occasions when we were actually out of range. Again, it freed us up to enjoy what we wanted and not worry about missing important messages.

Don't forget the car-charger too!

Laptop computers

A laptop computer is another device we can't imagine not having along. But maybe we're more compulsive than most! If you decide to have a personal website, a laptop is a must for creating the information as you go along, and if you want full-featured e-mail (attachments, video, etc.) it is almost a must. This is starting to change now with the advent of additional services on cell phones. Right now, I would take both a computer and a cell phone due to speed and convenience. But in a few years, who knows?

One thing you should now consider is a cellular modem. When we took our trip, the speed was very limiting for surfing the Internet, but things are changing. Wouldn't it be convenient to be moving down the road and checking out campsites for that night or bidding on motel reservations at Priceline.com? Wow!

We also had a small printer on board. We decided against the battery-powered type due to cost and need. We had electricity virtually every night and found that plugging it in the few times during the year when we needed it was workable.

Digital cameras

Digital cameras were yet another learning opportunity for us, but one that turned out to be important. If you want to e-mail pictures or to put pictures on a website, this is a must. They come with a piece of software to load onto your computer for downloading and editing. Some require a cable for downloading, and with some you use the memory cartridge in a special port on your computer. This is another area that is evolving rapidly. If you don't have a digital camera, spend a little time checking out the latest models and features that fit your needs. They really aren't hard to learn how to use.

One thing to remember is that once you have downloaded the pictures onto your PC, you can erase the memory card, so you don't have to keep a year's worth of storage on the camera. A digital camera is one item that it is easy to overbuy for your needs. Think carefully about how you want to use it and buy accordingly.

Other cameras

We used our digital primarily for the website and used our trusty 35mm for everything else. We even had a little pocket point-and-shoot for when we didn't want to carry the larger cameras with us. This also gave us built-in "backup" protection in case a roll of film didn't turn out or got lost. Our digital camera lost its main program and had to be sent off to be fixed, so we weren't totally without a camera during the three weeks it was gone.

Pictures are such an important part of a trip that redundancy isn't a bad idea. We took over two hundred digital pictures and thirty-eight rolls of film during the year. But think about it: that is less than a roll a week, or just a few pictures a day. As they say, the memories are priceless.

Tip: Get your film developed along the way and mark on the back of the pictures where and what they are. You will *never* remember it all when you get home a year later. We found one-hour or overnight services almost everywhere—even in some campgrounds. If you take a lot of pictures, ship them home with other things during the year, but don't just keep the film with you undeveloped or it will be a nightmare to figure out. If you are really compulsive, number the envelopes to keep them in the order of the trip.

GPS (global positioning systems)

We debated over GPS and finally decided not to buy it before we left. It was one of those things we figured we could always purchase along the way if we needed it.

Our experience was that there were a few times it would have been handy, but overall, we really didn't need it. However, if you are "directionally challenged" or don't read maps well, you probably should seriously consider one of these systems. They are very slick, portable, and relatively easy to use.

Two-way radios

These are also called "family channel" radios—the modern-day walkie-talkies. We received these as a gift and found them to be pretty handy. We had a way of losing each other in museums, parks, and towns. So having these—when we remembered to take them—saved us a lot of time searching for each other. We won't tell which one of us kept wandering off!

E-mail and Internet

Choosing your provider for Internet service is very important to its success and cost-effectiveness.

On the road, dial-up service is still the prevalent way of connecting to the Internet. We saw a few motels that had DSL connections, but we found none at campgrounds. We did not use Internet cafes, but some of them are now installing high-speed connections. The other "big new thing" is WiFi—wireless Internet access—but it is currently limited mostly to large cities.

That being said, be sure to choose a vendor that has a wide variety of local numbers across the country for access and an 800 number for when you aren't in one of their "local" cities. This will keep your cost down since connecting to any local number is usually included in your monthly cost, while connecting via an 800 number normally incurs a cost. We paid ten cents a minute on our AT&T Worldnet 800 service.

Having a mail program on your computer (such as Microsoft Outlook or Outlook Express) will save you money if you connect via 800 service because you can download your messages, disconnect, read them, reply, and then reconnect to send them. This is also an advantage if you are in a shared environment like a campground or cafe where others are waiting to use the service. If you don't have an e-mail program on your computer, you will be using your vendor's Internet-based service and will need to be connected the entire time that you read, compose, reply, send, and delete messages.

Keep checking the status of new technologies, but remember that you probably won't be in large cities much of the time. Think about what is available in rural America, unless you are going on a big-city-only adventure.

If you are planning to have your own website, you have more decisions to make. One reason we chose AT&T Worldnet was that their monthly charge ($16.95) included sixty megabytes (60 MB) of web hosting and templates to help you design your space. We ended up using Adobe PageMill to design our website, but the AT&T service helped us get going on the learning process.

An added benefit of setting up your own website is that it becomes a "backup" device for all your pictures and documentation.

A website does take some skill to develop, but you don't have to be a "geek" to do it. Like with any computer application, you can spend a few hours with the tutorial and then you are off and running. It is a great way to stay in touch, as your friends can surf your website anytime they want to see what you are up to, and you only have to post the information one time in one place—no more big e-mail lists or multiple e-mails to send and respond to. But there is definitely a time factor in maintaining your website. We spent a few hours two to three times a week in the evening loading pictures, updating charts, and writing about the trip. This also became our journal of the trip and the basis for much of this book, so it served more than one purpose.

An added benefit of a website is that it becomes your "backup" device for all your pictures and documentation. The web-hosting company (AT&T, in our case) maintains (or should maintain—which is something to check out) a daily backup of all their websites, so you can be assured of always having information on file that is no more than one day old. If your PC crashes, all you have to do is download from the web host and you are back in business—once you get the PC reloaded from the crash.

One of the fun things we did to amuse ourselves was to have contests on the website—things like guessing how many miles we will drive before Christmas, name the rig, and guess the date and time we will roll back into our driveway. We had prizes and a lot of fun with our friends and family.

If you decide not to do a website, weekly e-mails to your list with picture attachments are another potential way to stay in touch. If you decide not to take a PC at all, a popular service with RVers is PocketMail. This is a small device that lets you receive and send basic e-mail to and from their service.

Also, if you don't have a PC along, be sure to keep some type of journal. Another service available is called MyTripJournal.com. It has maps, journal space, and picture space, and it's easy to use—sort of a website already pre-built for you.

You just can't remember everything, and it is so much fun to go back and relive and remember this great trip. We have resolved many disagreements via our online journal!

Phone cards and phone credit cards

It used to be that everyone traveled with a telephone credit card issued by his or her home telephone company. Those cards still exist, but they have been all but taken over by the new prepaid phone cards. Since you will no longer have a "home phone" to bill to, the prepaid cards become the best option. Yes, I know you have a cell phone with you with unlimited long distance, but what about those times when you have no cell coverage and need to make a call? We used our card only a few times during the year, but when we needed it, we really needed it. Buy one just in case.

Postcards, gifts, and other mail

All of us have friends and family who have not joined the electronic age. My sister, who lives away from the rest of the family, was in charge of printing e-mail and some of the website information and mailing it to Mom, who is still mystified by computers. She really enjoyed keeping up with the trip through those e-mails, converted to snail-mail communications.

We also sent Mom postcards periodically, which added another dimension to the trip for her. Because our grandchildren are still small, we frequently sent postcards to them. Although their moms showed them the website pictures, the postcards were much more tangible to them.

We devised a special section on our website just for kids. We posted pictures and geography questions just for them almost every week.

Just because you are on the road does not stop birthdays, holidays, anniversaries, and other special events from happening. Just like at home, you will probably want to send greetings—either via an Internet card or a real greeting card. This is another good way to stay in touch. We both received lots of "e-greetings" on our birthdays that year.

While we're on the subject, gifts can be handled the same way. Gifts or gift cards from your favorite web-store, flowers (via either FTD or the Internet), or things you have picked out in your travels and sent home can provide that personal touch to special events. Most stores are glad to ship for you. This isn't the year for heroic displays of your creative talents.

We also amused the grandchildren with little treasures from time to time. It would be easy to go broke doing that alone—and we really had to contain ourselves. Handmade bows and arrows from South Dakota (the mothers may not yet have forgiven us for that one!), T-shirts from New England, and live cactus plants from Arizona are but a few ideas.

Here's another fun idea: If you aren't a big picture-taker, postcards written to yourself with thoughts about the location depicted on the card and sent home (to whomever is getting your mail) make a great picture journal when you finally get home.

Community service

Many of us are continually looking for ways to "give back" or to provide a service to others. This trip of a lifetime is a great opportunity for community service. We came upon our chances quite serendipitously.

Before we left we were chatting with the editor of our community newspaper. We both thought it would be fun to do a monthly column. She called it "On the Road with the Whites." Not quite Charles Kuralt, but we e-mailed her 700 to 1,000 words each month and a couple of pictures about what we were doing. The column was a big hit. In fact, she said that some people told her it was the first thing they turned to in the paper! We still run into people who recognize us from the column.

Our other chance came after the trip had started. We were visiting old friends of Phil's in South Dakota who were both teachers. Marty thought it would be fun for her first graders to follow along on our website. She saw it as a way to teach geography, current events, reading, and computer skills. We decided to go one step further. We devised a special section on the website just for the kids. The pictures were captioned just for their level, and we posted age-appropriate geography questions almost every week for them. The word spread and pretty soon several classes were following our travels.

Marty said that Fridays were their favorite day because they got to go see what Phil and Carol were doing. Occasionally she would have them compose e-mails to us, and near the end of the school year they did a booklet of pictures and writings for us about the experience. It is one of our most treasured memories of the trip.

So think what you might do. We're sure there are other great ideas out there that didn't come our way. Maybe connect with a group of home-schoolers, a retirement home, or a scout troop. Discover a way to interact and use your talents. It was really an enhancement of the trip for us and was so rewarding. If you don't have a website, how about sending some e-mail correspondence or postcards and providing the recipients with a big map on which to follow along? Everyone can help kids learn or provide enjoyment for adults!

Chapter 8

Making Decisions along the Way

The second part of this book will give you a "travelogue" look at what it is like to be on the road every day for a year, but we want to pass along some of the specific things that we discovered as we moved along. Although you will undoubtedly have the opportunity to discover many interesting twists and turns on your own, this section will hopefully save you some time along the way and provide lots of usable tips.

Eating and sleeping

Although eating and sleeping are surely not the focus of your trip, they are necessary ingredients that will consume time each day. We did not call ahead for lodging or campgrounds unless we were going to be getting into an area after 7 p.m. There was only one night on the whole trip when we really had to scramble for either a motel or campground. One of the nice things about having the van was that we had the flexibility to either camp or stay in a motel when things were tight, and we could either cook in the van or eat out, regardless of whether we were in a motel or campground—total flexibility.

Motels
Utilizing a motel guidebook of some type is a good idea. This gives you an idea of what the rates are in various cities, what types

of accommodations are available, and where most of the motels are clustered.

There are also always motels not in the guidebooks. They are either too new to have made the book, or they don't qualify for some reason. That doesn't make them bad; in fact, some of the cutest places we stayed were "unlisted" properties that were quaint and clean. You just have to look around a bit if you like those types of accommodations. Always ask to see the room if you are unsure.

If you are driving an RV of any type and are planning to stay downtown, *always* ask about parking. Remember that you need to have level parking, and it must be over-height.

We used the prices in our AAA Tour Books as a baseline for comparison. We found that many times you could walk into a motel, especially if it was late in the day, ask for their "best rate," and beat the prices in the guidebooks. They want to fill their rooms and would rather take a little bit less than have you walk away. This is especially true with locally owned establishments.

Price is always negotiable. If you want to stay a few days and they are obviously not busy, ask for the "off-season" rate or another type of special. We were able to negotiate some really good deals at resorts, casinos, and condominiums in particular. If they won't negotiate the rate—or even if they do—you can often get a more desirable room than the standard. You no ask, you no get!

If you are not sure where to find a place, take the "business route" into town. Most of the older places and some new ones are often found along that stretch of highway. The chain motels are usually clustered together at interchanges or along the main highway. If you are trying to stick with one chain for their "perks," this is where you'll find them.

If you are driving an RV of any type and are planning to stay downtown, *always* ask about parking. Remember that you need to have level parking, and it must be over-height. Most places have a few over-height spots, but be sure to ask, and make sure they reserve one for you. Once we had to pay a night watchman in downtown Chicago to watch our vehicle in a loading zone all night—not a very restful night! It was all because we forgot to ask, and it was the season opener of the Bears a few blocks away, and there was no parking of any kind anywhere.

Campgrounds

Trailer Life or Woodell's produce the most complete books on campgrounds. We bought the CD-ROM version of Trailer Life's and really liked their rating system. They provide three different "scores": amenities, bathroom cleanliness, and scenic value. We found their descriptions to be accurate and informative.

If you belong to a camping club, you will have their directory. In addition, KOA produces a directory of their locations. We found KOAs to be the Best Western of the camping world—all a little different but with the same basic good quality and amenities.

If you are in a bind or are looking for cheap or free places to stay, you can find them. If you have a generator on board, you can "boondock" in a Wal-Mart parking lot (at least at this time), or oftentimes hospitals will let you park in their lots. Just be sure to ask. And there are many forest locations where there are few, if any, amenities other than beautiful scenery. If that type of rugged camping appeals to you, there are lots of books detailing those locations. We're just not into that much dirt anymore.

Just like at motels, don't be afraid to look around at the sites and ask for what you want. We found everyone to be very accommodating when possible. Another advantage of a smaller RV is that you can fit into just about anywhere, and we got some really nice locations because of that.

Food

One of the treats of a trip like this is trying the various cuisines around the country. We always asked at the office of the motel or campground for suggestions. Virtually every suggestion we took turned out to be a winner. We got to sample lots of regional specialties and take part in some local traditions. If you are at all adventurous, don't miss those opportunities.

Eating out can really become boring—which is another reason to consider taking an RV on your trip. It offers you the ability to home-cook whenever you want, as often as you want. We almost always had breakfast from the van and most days fixed lunch also. Finding a good lunch spot along the way was seldom difficult. A city park, a rest stop, a county or state park, or a scenic overlook all make great stops with wonderful vistas. And people will be so jealous when you fire up that gas stove and heat leftovers or make wonderful grilled sandwiches. This was all just part of the ambience of the trip!

On motel nights when we were tired, we would get takeout from a deli or restaurant and eat in the room. You have all the plates and utensils you need in the RV, and it is so much more relaxing after a hard day of sightseeing. You can even do soup and sandwiches or something else simple right out of the RV.

We kept a small cooler on board for picnics away from the van or for when we went to an outdoor event. It was also very handy poolside during the cocktail hour.

We barbecued a lot on the trip. Our favorite meal was meat on the grill, a green salad (the pre-washed bags are wonderfully handy), and either foil-wrapped potatoes on the barbecue or rice/pasta cooked in the van. Packaged sauces are a quick and tasty addition for variety. It's not gourmet, but with minimum fuss a complete meal can be prepared in no time.

We also became the masters of the one-dish meal when the weather wasn't good or no barbecue was available. We didn't carry a portable grill because it would have required too much room in our tight quarters. Here's how the one-dish meal goes: Brown a couple of chicken breasts/pork chops/ham slices/firm fish/hamburger patties—or whatever you like. Remove them from the pan and sauté a few vegetables of your choice (fresh or frozen). Add rice for two and the appropriate amount of water, or use packaged scalloped potatoes according to package directions, lay the meat back on top (yup, right in the water—trust me), cover, and go have a beverage while it cooks. Voilà—a completely balanced dinner! If you want leftovers for the next day, just increase the quantities appropriately. It's so easy—and only one pot to clean!

Tip: If you are at a loss for a spot to stop to eat, look for where the truckers or UPS drivers are congregated. They always know the good places with great values.

Visitor centers

We found most visitor centers to be of great help. They know all about "specials and deals" and have a great wealth of knowledge about the local scene. They can help with rooms when things are tight. They know where the best values are located. They can help with tickets to attractions and special events, good restaurants—and just about anything you would need.

If you are still deciding what you would like to do in an area, they have great recommendations, and they always have lots of brochures if you just want to browse for a while.

What to see and do

Naturally, the specifics of what you see and do will depend on what type of adventure you have planned for yourselves. But deciding what to see each day will be a major focus of the previous evening or morning coffee. Here's where you can get out your books, surf the Internet, ask around the campground, or look at the brochures you've picked up at the visitor center on the way into town. Most of the time you will have the next day or two generally planned, but you want to be flexible so that you don't miss something exciting. We found some of our best tips on places to see while standing in line somewhere, swimming in the pool, or just talking to the locals.

Take advantage of all the discounts. Even if it is just a dollar off each, when you are doing major sightseeing, those dollars add up.

Here is another place where your travel guides come in really handy. They will give you the rundown on days of operation, opening and closing times, credit-card status, price of admission, and other pertinent details.

We always bought a copy of the local paper everywhere we went. We wish we had saved the front page from each one—it would have made an interesting souvenir of the trip. Not only do you get the flavor of the locality—politics, sociology, culture, and customs—but you will sometimes find out about things you wouldn't otherwise know about—everything from highway closures to coupons for restaurants to local entertainment options.

Speaking of discounts—we worked every angle!—don't forget to use any reciprocal memberships you may have. If you belong to the art museum or zoo back home, they often have reciprocal membership agreements around the country that provide discounted or even free admission to the reciprocal location. And don't forget about other organizations' discount programs—everything from AAA to the "Entertainment" books. Even if it is just a dollar off each, when you are doing major sightseeing, those dollars add up. We more than paid for our AAA membership with those discounts alone.

And here's another tip for visiting the most popular destinations: go early or late, because there are many fewer people than in the middle of the day.

As interesting as all your adventures will be, remember that too much togetherness will eventually start wearing on you. Occasionally, pick two different things to do—and the dinner conversation will be fresher than rehashing what you saw together that day. When you find yourselves on "sightseeing overload," it is probably time for one of those "vacations" that we talked about earlier. Find someplace you enjoy and just hang out for a few days—no attractions or driving, just R&R: read, play cards, golf, hike, or whatever it is for you. You will find it is very rejuvenating, and soon you'll be ready to go again.

Filling the drive time

We loved driving—most of the time. The big cities are really nerve-wracking, but driving through the country on the back roads was really fun. No matter where you are in this great country, there is something interesting to see. We really tried to avoid the freeways as much as possible. Yes, you'll get somewhere faster, but you miss so much of what makes America great—small towns, scenery, little-known places, wonderful people, and serendipitous findings.

One lovely fall afternoon, we were driving through the backcountry of New Jersey, headed for Princeton. All of a sudden, we passed a small sign that said something about "USGA Headquarters." Being golfers, we had to find out what that was all about. So we turned around and headed down the road. It was definitely a treat to see the lovely museum and shop tucked in the rolling hills, but learning about how golf clubs and golf balls are tested for meeting required standards was extremely interesting to us. Hardly anyone was there, so we got the grand tour of just about anything we wanted to see or ask about, and we walked away with a few unmarked golf balls. These were plain golf balls from all the big manufacturers with identifying numbers handwritten on them in ink indicating that they had been anonymously tested for acceptability. And we gained a fun story to tell our friends back home when we used the balls.

Here is a list of things to do if you get bored of the scenery as you drive along:

- **Read to each other.** Read aloud from books, articles, or travel information about the destination where you're headed or the state you've just entered.
- **Listen to local talk radio.** The variety of thought patterns in different parts of the country is amazing.
- **Practice your navigation skills.** Try out a secondary route or a scenic loop.
- **Call the grandkids.** They always love to hear from you and will talk as long as you want to.
- **Listen to books on tape.** This became one of our favorite things. Sometimes we had to keep driving just to finish a book or chapter. Jon Krakauer's *Into Thin Air* had us spellbound through Nebraska.
- **Reminisce.** When was the last time you talked about your first date? The house you grew up in? Your favorite teacher? These are all wonderful discussion topics, and there are so many more.
- **Write in your journal.** Journal either on paper or electronically if your PC batteries are charged up.
- **Listen to music.** Music is always a good backup plan, and there are some wonderful stations around the country.
- **Make a list.** Itemize the groceries you need, things to ask the kids on the phone, and so on.
- **Correspond.** Write postcards, birthday cards, or ?
- **Listen to the sweet sound of silence.** Ahhhh!

Most days we didn't cover more than 50 to 150 miles, so we didn't have great expanses of time on the road, but depending on your plan, you might find yourself with fewer days of travel and longer distances each travel day. That is another issue for you to consider as you develop your goals for the trip.

Necessities on the road

Just because you now have the carefree lifestyle of the road doesn't mean that you don't still have a few responsibilities! Very few—but necessary evils.

Groceries

The big thing to remember here is to not buy more groceries than can fit in your refrigerator and cupboards! Unless you choose a really big vehicle, you probably want to limit your visits to Costco.

Here are couple of reminders from earlier chapters: Get the national "club cards" of your favorite chains to maximize your savings, and remember that zip-lock bags are your best friend. When you buy cereal or rice or anything else in a bulky container, empty it into a zip-lock right away for space economy and freshness.

When we are at home, we like to buy in bulk and stock up on sale items. Unfortunately, that philosophy had to go out the window for the year we were on the road. Even storing a few rolls of toilet paper or paper towels can become a challenge.

When you begin to pack your vehicle, just include the most essential items and expand from there. Spices, staples, and cleaning supplies are a good place to start. As you see how much room you really have, add things as you go. Our little van had a pullout pantry that could really store a lot of items, if you planned carefully. When you are looking at what vehicle to buy, really think about the storage space and try to visualize where everything will go. We found a lot of differences in the usefulness of various layouts. Even though some appeared to have more storage, the layout, sizes, and accessibility were vastly different.

Laundry

Unless you have a really high-end unit with a built-in washer and dryer, you'll be faced with going back to your college days and finding laundry facilities. Fortunately, most of the nice campgrounds have clean, bright laundries. If you are lucky and it isn't busy, you can actually make short work of the task by utilizing multiple machines—something most of us can't do at home! Many motels also have guest laundries, and these were quite adequate. Just remember to keep all those quarters and the detergent handy.

We started out with quite a few "dry-clean-only" items. Those quickly went to the back of the closet and were eventually shipped home. If your trip keeps you in one place for a while, it's not such a big deal, but if you are moving along most days, trying to get other than very occasional cleaning done is a major inconvenience. Save being a peacock for when you get home. It just doesn't work on the road. Wash-and-wear is the name of the game.

Shipping

As winter passes into spring, you'll wonder why you need all those heavy clothes taking up space, even if they are "deflated" in a one-way-valve plastic bag. Additionally, you have probably accumulated souvenirs that are stuck all over the vehicle. It's time to ship some stuff home. Hopefully, you've made an arrangement with someone who can receive a few parcels during the year to store for you.

Find a mailing service. They can help with boxes, packing materials, and getting the accumulation on its way. Yes, it is a little more expensive, but we found that the convenience and their helpfulness outweighs the small additional cost, and it gets you back on your way exploring your trip of a lifetime.

Taking care of your vehicle

Since your chosen vehicle is both your home and your transportation, you will want to give it extra special care. There are mountains of books on the selection and care of RVs, so we won't cover the detailed information that they do. We carried *The Complete Guide to*

Full-Time RVing, by Bill and Jan Moeller, and we found answers to almost every question we had relating to taking care of the rig.

Maintenance

You don't want to have to interrupt your fun with a breakdown when a little scheduled maintenance at *your* convenience will avoid those problems.

Even more than at home—where you have friends, AAA, or a service station handy to help with any problems—do plan time to either do or have done the routine maintenance. If you have a car/truck-based vehicle—or just a plain old car or truck!—you have a much wider selection of service points, such as quick-lube places, the car dealer's service shop, an independent, or even an old-fashioned service station still found in some parts of the country.

We chose to have Dodge dealers do all our service around the country. We religiously followed their "heavy-duty" schedule, and we found the dealers everywhere to be helpful and knowledgeable about what should be done and when. We always were able to pull into a medium-sized town, find the dealership, and get serviced the same day—or at least by the next morning. This is a big plus for a truck-chassis-based vehicle. Even procedures that took up to half a day were quickly accommodated. Usually we were a big attraction at the dealership and got to talk to everyone about what we were doing on our trip, hang out, go for lunch, or just walk around town. Just make sure they know you are an "oversize" vehicle when you call, because they need to have a heavy-duty lift available for you. We had no problems the entire year, partly because we were fanatical about maintenance.

The few times we called around for RV service (for the stove, refrigerator, and so forth), the wait was several days to several weeks. We found it impossible to get anything done on the spur of the moment. This has been confirmed many times by others who have big RVs. When you are traveling along like we were, you can't possibly predict an exact location, date, and time that far in advance. This is another thing to consider when planning your trip and choice of vehicle.

Fortunately, we had few real RV system issues. When we went home for the holidays, we left the van at an RV shop—which also kept it safe and out of long-term parking at the airport for four weeks—and they did some preventative maintenance and a few repairs at their leisure while we were gone. It was a win-win. We got our servicing done and avoided parking at the airport, and they could work on it when they had time.

Be sure to do visual inspections frequently. As we mentioned earlier, in Yellowstone Park, we noticed something hanging down under the van. Unfortunately, we had broken a heavy-duty shock on the terrible roads there. Even though we were close to a full-service gas station, they didn't have that type of part. We limped into Billings a few days later, and the dealer located one overnight and had us going the next morning.

Gasoline

Finding the good gas prices became another form of entertainment. Here are some of the things we learned:

- Generally, avoid freeway intersections. We found few exceptions to this rule.
- Avoid isolated towns. Low volume and high delivery costs do not make up for cheap rent! Don't get yourself caught where it is your only alternative.
- Small towns near larger cities are often good due to ease of delivery and lower operating costs (rent, pay, insurance, etc.), especially if there is some competition amongst several stations.
- For the same reasons, middle-class neighborhoods in large cities are good.

- The best bets are business routes (often industrial areas) and truck stops.
- Costco and grocery-chain gas stations, when they are available, are excellent choices.

Roads

No matter how well you plan your route, you'll encounter bad roads and detours. The northern states have only two seasons: winter and construction. Some detours take you miles and hours away from where you think you are headed. If you are really in a hurry to get somewhere, a check on the Internet or with the highway patrol isn't a bad idea; otherwise, just sit back, enjoy it, and consider it part of the journey. We learned all about shearing sheep one day while waiting at the front of the line for a guide car.

If paint or flying rocks are part of the construction, it's best to check your vehicle at the end of the construction area for any damage. Going back later when you discover a problem is usually not an option.

Rub-a-dub-dub

Keeping your home looking good on the outside can be challenging. Few places like the idea of you washing your vehicle on their premises—whether campgrounds or motels. So what to do?

We carried our own supplies, including a long-handled scrubber/soap-dispenser and were constantly on the lookout for potential locations where we could wash. We found a couple of motels and one campground where we were allowed to shine our baby up, but it was quite difficult to find appropriate places.

Most regular car washes can't accommodate oversize vehicles, but we did discover that many coin-op, "you wash it" places had over-height bays. Some even had platforms to stand on to make it easier to reach the top of the larger rigs. Truck stops also often have wash facilities. Ultimately we ended up using these types of facilities rather than trying to accomplish the wash job ourselves.

Souvenirs

> Take one picture each day throughout the year to remind you of that day's scenery. Every day provides at least one view that captures the essence of that day's travels.

No trip of a lifetime would be complete without a little souvenir shopping. You will definitely want to bring back some mementos, but size and portability become paramount over time.

Clothing in moderation is fun to remember places by, but those T-shirts can start taking over the closet quickly; small jewelry, however, can be tucked into lots of places.

We found that posters and art prints fit our interest area and were easy to handle. Most places can provide a sturdy tube to store them in—and they tuck nicely into corners. If there is a large souvenir you must have, you can always ship it home.

This could be the time to start a collection if you don't already have one. Charms, small spoons, key chains, or plates are all traditional areas of collecting, and you can add to your collection everywhere.

A postcard on which you've written your journal of that location's memories can be tucked into a shoebox, and it's fun to read when you return. Or you can mail them home, as we mentioned in Chapter 6.

One thing we wish we had done was to take one picture each day from the car as we drove along. Keeping a disposable camera just for those shots could be fun. It would remind you of each day's scenery throughout the year. You would remember the weather, the terrain, and the types of scenery. Every day we had at least one view that would have captured the essence of that day's travels. A little notepad in the glove box on which to jot down the date and location will help when you get the roll developed, and you could then transfer your notes to the back of the picture.

We have brochures from all the national parks we visited, along with lots of other small items we picked up along the way. We are still trying to figure out an interesting way to preserve and display those items, but they provide such great memories of all the fun we had.

Just remember that anything you buy or accumulate must go in your vehicle for the rest of the year—or be shipped home at some point. Size is of the essence. Happy shopping!

Chapter

Handling Emergencies

Get it out of your mind right now that this will be a "perfect" year. It won't be. Emergencies happen at home, and they will happen on the road. The real question is what emergency situations will happen to you—and how will you handle them?

Some early planning will help to mitigate the inconvenience of them and prepare you for how you might approach the situations. This chapter will discuss some of the planning, the things that happened to us, and how we handled them. Each person has to think through his or her own approach to emergencies. How do you handle them in your day-to-day life, and how would you cope with various scenarios on the road? Just remember that even the emergencies are part of this great adventure and its memories.

Emergency contact information

It's a sobering thought, but one that requires discussion: ***No one here knows you, nor will anyone miss you tonight.***

Although the chances of something happening are remote, a little planning for a potential emergency we think is time well spent.

Be sure to have your emergency contact information—probably someone at home with whom you stay in regular touch—and a copy of your medical insurance card in your vehicle with your car insurance information in case you are in a bad accident. If there is special medical information, be sure that it is also in the same

It is a good idea to have a regular system of touching base with someone every few days. A quick phone call or an e-mail would certainly suffice.

spot. The glove compartment is a good location.

During the day keep that same information on your person in case of a medical emergency or if something were to happen to both of you. We don't recommend carrying the vehicle description on your person. If someone were to assault you, they could grab your keys and wallet, and the vehicle description would make it easier to steal your vehicle with all your possessions. This is definitely not a pretty prospect.

As we mentioned earlier, be sure that your emergency contacts have the description of your vehicle: make, model, color, and license plate. They should also have stored on their computer a good digital photo of you and another of the vehicle that could be quickly e-mailed to a distant police department to help speed up any investigation.

A good tip comes from Anne McAlpin, in her book *Pack It Up!* She recommends that each of you carry a current photo of your traveling companion. That way if you become separated and need assistance, the police will have a good photo to help identify the missing person.

It would be a good idea to have a regular system of touching base with someone. We don't think it has to be every day, but every few days is probably smart. A quick phone call or an e-mail would certainly suffice.

We had absolutely no problems, but we did occasionally wonder what would happen if we were mugged and left in a ditch at some attraction. Who would miss us? When would they find us? Who would they call? How would they know which vehicle was ours and where it was?

Once you've done these things, we hope you never need to use them.

Medical issues

We found that a quick call to our insurance company before we left ended up being a smart move. We just let them know what we were doing and asked that our file be so noted. Insurance companies don't like surprises, and they may even give you special instructions on what to do if you have a problem on the road. Since you will be nowhere near your primary-care physicians, they will be of little use to you! The customer-service center will likely be your point of contact, so give them a "heads up" before you leave.

When I broke my ankle in the third month of the trip and sported a bright green cast for six weeks, the insurance company was fabulous. We were in a fairly remote area of Wisconsin at an attraction, taking pictures, when I fell into a lawn-covered hole and knew instantly that something bad had happened. An x-ray at a small clinic led to an evening visit to a hospital twenty miles away staffed by a wonderful orthopedic doctor who immediately embraced our dilemma. Two broken bones and the possibility of surgery loomed over us. The doctor felt that surgery was not a preferred option given our travels and set about trying to avoid that, but it did require ten days in a soft cast and a return to Sauk Prairie, Wisconsin—which of course was not exactly in our plans. We just made the best of it. We got a handicapped sticker, a set of crutches, some pain medications, and set off on a ten-day loop through Michigan.

Tip: If you do have to see a doctor and get a prescription, have it filled before you leave the state. Presenting a prescription from an out-of-state doctor does not work. We had a small supply of pain medication that the doctor had given us and didn't think anything about it, and we had quite a time getting more pills over a weekend in another state.

Meanwhile, we had called our insurance company and updated them on the situation. They took care of everything and even gave us our own personal representative, since this was not an ordinary circumstance. We made it easy for them to help us by cheerfully using their recommendations for "in-network" doctors as we moved along, once the initial treatment was behind us.

Back in Wisconsin ten days later, the soft cast was removed, and the doctor was not very happy with what he saw on the x-ray. Surgery again loomed. He wanted to try one more thing. He re-cast the leg and literally manipulated the bones into the position he wanted. Then the fun began. We left Sauk Prairie with x-rays and detailed instructions to the next—yet unknown—doctor along the way. I was to have it x-rayed again in a week, which put us in Columbus, Ohio.

We made another call to the insurance company for their recommendation of the next doctor, and then we initiated a very strange call to that doctor's office: "Hello, you don't know me, but we are traveling around the U.S. for a year and I broke my ankle in Wisconsin. I have my x-rays and the doctor's orders and need to see someone in your office next Tuesday. My insurance company referred me to you." The longest silence you can imagine followed. But after a few questions and a few times on hold, we got the job done. I think it was mostly curiosity that someone would actually do this and keep going that got me the appointment. The whole office knew the story when we arrived.

The care continued all the way into Connecticut with the same phone conversation repeating itself and the pile of x-rays and doctor's orders continuing to increase. By the time we went home for the holidays, I had been doing a couple of months worth of physical therapy on my own, following the doctor's orders, and the ankle was almost 100 percent back to normal.

The outcome could not have been better if I had been home the entire time. In fact, it was probably better because I had the time to focus on the physical therapy, which might not have happened in the rush of everyday life. See, even bad things can have good outcomes!

What did we sacrifice?

- We couldn't camp, as getting in and out of the van was difficult.
- We had to have a wheelchair for some sightseeing locations and some special transportation arrangements at others. You should have seen them loading me onto a luggage cart to board the ferry to Mackinac Island.
- We didn't do the walking tours we had planned in Chicago.
- We chose some different things to do that were less active (no golf, no hiking, etc.) for a few months.

What did we gain?

- Handicapped seats at Ohio State and University of Michigan home football games—Phil would not have gotten to see those games without the handicapped status.
- An appreciation for the importance of the Americans with Disabilities Act.
- Experience maneuvering a wheelchair, even on a bus; I never got really good with the crutches.
- A real sense of accomplishment that we didn't let it ruin our trip.
- More memories and good laughs about the whole experience.

Later in the trip, Phil had a semi-emergency with a suspicious mole. Another call to the insurance company found us an urgent-care clinic and a referral to a local surgeon. The mole was removed and analyzed as benign. We dodged another bullet and kept moving.

The upshot of all this is to be open and communicative with your insurance company, and they, in all likelihood, will do everything they can to help you.

Vehicle breakdowns and accidents

Since you will be traveling many thousands of miles in unfamiliar territory, the chance of having a vehicle emergency is much higher than any other type of emergency.

As for breakdowns, prevention is the best course. Buying a dependable vehicle and providing regular maintenance along the way will hopefully eliminate this hazard. Just in case, though, you should make sure that you get towing insurance for your RV or car. One tow could more than pay for the insurance, and who wants to be stranded in an unfamiliar location?

As for accidents, well, let's just say that August was not kind to us. Two weeks before the broken-ankle incident, we were rear-ended by an uninsured motorist in Minneapolis. This could have been a real horror story, but again, with open communication and great help from the insurance company, we worked through the issues.

We needed a non-standard new bumper for our wide-body van that had to come from the factory. But the factory had just closed for its annual *six-week* vacation! *Yikes!* Fortunately, the damage was such that, with a little hammering at the body shop, everything still worked—it just looked bad. So, what to do? We didn't envision staying in Minneapolis for six-plus weeks, and we didn't really want to come back that way either.

Another call to the insurance company solved everything. Through the wonders of technology, the shop that had done the estimate faxed their assessment and e-mailed their digital pictures to a repair facility chosen by the insurance company in the city where we estimated we could be in two months—Columbus, Ohio. That shop ordered the bumper when the factory opened. They contacted us when the parts were on their way, and we set up a time to do the work. Since by now I was sporting the mean, green cast and planning to see the next doctor also in Columbus, this became our home for a while.

But the surprises weren't over. It turned out that there was paint work to be done and that the van would be in the shop for two weeks. Well, we hadn't planned to spend two weeks in Columbus, especially since we had already been there a few days for the doctor's appointment, the Ohio State football game, and finalizing plans to drop the van and pick up a rental car. We had yet another decision to make.

> If an emergency at home does arise, don't automatically give up on your trip. Take a deep breath, garner you creativity, and think about the possible options.

We decided to pack up our little red rental car and plotted out a two-week loop through Kentucky, Tennessee, and West Virginia. We returned to Columbus and a brand-new-looking van. We covered some areas we had originally planned to do later in the trip, but this actually turned out to be better timing due to the weather. This is a good example of why you shouldn't plan ahead. Can you imagine the time—and frustration—we would have spent "undoing" plans that had been made months in advance?

Problems at home

The chance of an emergency arising at home or with your family is the same whether you're there or not.

Again, the real question is, how will you handle it? If something does arise, don't automatically give up on your trip. Take a deep breath, garner you creativity, and think about the possible options. In truth, your family probably really wants you to continue your journey, so consider the alternatives in that light.

Our own personal experience serves as an example. When we talked to my eighty-one-year-old mom one spring day, she just didn't seem herself. She finally admitted that she had been diagnosed with breast cancer and was trying to figure out what to do. So we started almost daily phone calls back and forth and initiated plans to fly home for a while. She really didn't want to tell us, much less interrupt the trip. But if we had been living somewhere else, the process would have been the same. We figured out when the surgery would be and who could be available to help out when and for how long. We looked at what airport locations we could reasonably get to for a flight home and what the airfares from different locations would be, and we considered what to do with the Rolling White House.

We left the van at a motel in Phoenix, Arizona near the airport where we stayed before flying home and when we returned. They had us park it near the office where they could keep an eye on it. We left a key with the manager and our cell-phone number in case of an emergency on that end.

Once home, we tended to Mom's needs and made arrangements for her care with other extended family members after we returned to the road ten days later. We had contacted professional help as a backup in case any of the family caregivers couldn't be with her as planned. She came through the surgery like a champ and was well on her way to a speedy recovery when we headed back out on the road.

Her encouragement of our finishing the trip was extremely important to us, and a good support system made it possible. Today, she is cancer-free and is still talking about our trip to her friends.

Safety

Your own life experiences and level of concern or comfort will dictate what you do in this area. We seldom felt unsafe during the trip, but we were careful not to put ourselves in obvious danger. We didn't wander dark streets at night, we didn't drive in unsafe areas at night, and we didn't act in ways that could make us easy targets.

Your motel or campground can help advise you on safety in the area, but your best defense is keeping your own senses and intuition working.

We always locked our vehicle, whether we were in it or not. We had an alarm system with a remote pager that was supposed to page us if the van was broken into. We found that the slightest bump would set the alarm/pager off. We finally quit using the pager when we got tired of running back to the van to see what had happened. We also found out the very first night not to set the alarm during the night. The first person up to use the bathroom set it off, to the delight, I'm sure, of the entire campground.

The one time when we felt we might be in danger was near dusk one evening when we made a wrong turn off a freeway and found ourselves in what was obviously a high-risk area. We had no detailed map of the area to guide us, so we just stayed on the main street and kept moving, even though we knew it was not the direction we wanted to go. We recommend you don't stop to ask for directions in these situations. We knew that we would eventually drive into a more stable area and could then get reoriented and back on our way to our destination.

Although we never had any issues when we were out walking, let your common sense prevail. Carry your cell phone and call 911 if necessary, or walk up to a home or business with lights on, or just keep calmly moving away from the danger. Call a cab if you are in the city and feel really uncomfortable. Better to spend a few dollars than risk a problem.

As for guns in your rig, we didn't, but you might be comfortable with that idea. Just be sure to know the laws in the areas where you are traveling and the inherent potential risks of having a weapon. We did have mace on board and kept it where we could get to it at any time. Fortunately, we never needed it.

Chapter 9

Coming Home

At some point near the end of your trip, you will realize that this wonderful thing you have done is actually going to come to an end. It is at this point that some people decide they really love this itinerant life, and they become what RVers call "full-timers." These are people who live on the road in their RVs without a permanent home base. If this happens to you, you'll find scores of books that talk about that lifestyle. Have fun, and happy travels!

But for most of us, this is truly a one-time event, and the prospect of returning to your former life will be met with both excitement and trepidation—excitement to see everyone again and to resume your former lifestyle with a new outlook and stories to last forever, but also with sadness that your carefree, simple, nomadic existence is about to end.

Don't rush

The tendency as you get close to home is to rush through your last few days or weeks. *Resist!* Stick to your non-plan and enjoy every last morsel even though you may be homesick and ready to return. In retrospect, it will all be over too soon.

You actually need to get mentally prepared for reentry. Just like being in a space capsule for a period of time, when you come back, it is disorienting. I know that sounds crazy, but people will call on you for all kinds of tasks and responsibilities that you haven't had for a long time. You probably haven't had to keep a calendar all year, but as you get closer to home, you will need one. Everyone will start calling or e-mailing you, trying to get you committed for this event or that, or asking can you make it home for this dinner or that ball game. *Resist!* They've gotten along without you for a year—another week isn't the end of the world.

Even though you will want to get home, the simplicity of your lifestyle on the road and your freedom to be a kid again are worth more than you realize. Savor the moments. Even consider lying. Tell people you will be home on a date later than you really expect to be there. That will help hold off the well-meaning friends and family and give you some time to get reoriented into your own routine.

Of course, if you sold your house before you left, finding a place to live will be your first order of business, probably while continuing to live in your vehicle. That will be motivation to get things moving! Maybe you've even spotted a few things on the Internet and have a realtor working for you.

Getting back into the swing of things

Almost as busy as the pre-leaving craziness is the post-trip craziness. Once people know you are home, they will expect to pick up just where they left off. And you will want some of that.

But things will be different. Your perspective on the world may have changed due to your adventure. You will be more knowledgeable about the USA than most people. Only two percent of the population has visited all the states. Your relationship with your travel companion will have changed, hopefully for the better, and you have all the experiences you have garnered to share with everyone.

All of that is good, but be sure to give yourself some time. You will have enough pressing matters to tend to, and you have become used to a different pace of life. Many times in those early months

Think about all you have learned this last year. No matter what your original goals were for your trip, your horizons have been broadened in way you couldn't possibly anticipate.

home, we would look at each other and long to be back on the road. Life was so much simpler then.

Depending on what you did with your house, you may be slipping right back into your old abode, or looking for a new place to live, or somewhere in between. At the very least, you will be unpacking boxes and integrating your personal items back into the home.

You may need to go buy a car if you sold yours, or you may be living in your RV for a while until you get a place to live and a car to drive. There are major decisions to be made on every front. But before you know it, everything will fall into place, and you will have your wonderful experiences to look back on.

The excitement of getting home is fun, no matter what issues you face. If you had renters in your home, plan on things not being perfect. Even the best renters will not leave things the way you would. After all, it has been their home with their style of living for the past year. It will help if you send a letter thirty days before they are to vacate the premises that lists your expectations of them if they wish to get their deposit back. In the appendix we've included the letter we sent to our renters in case you need a sample.

Newly reunited with our living room, we were amazed how many things we had. As we sat and gazed about, we thought, "Why do we need all this stuff? We got along perfectly fine without it for a year!" The house seemed huge, and all our possessions seemed heavy—almost a burden. That passed fairly quickly though. We do believe that we have done a better job since the trip of not accumulating "stuff." We are better at not buying new things and not holding on to things we don't need. It's one of the lessons of the road.

Tip: Don't make yourself nuts trying to get it all back in place in a week. You didn't get ready to go in a week, and you don't need to get back to normal in a week—or even two.

Our first order of business was to catch up with the grand-children. They all had changed so much and seemed so glad to see us, even though it had been only five months since we'd been home for the holidays. We decided that our friends could wait. We really just wanted to spend time hanging out with the little ones. That bonding is so precious.

Taking time to reflect

Once you have settled back into your routine, be sure to take some time to reflect on what you've accomplished. You have done some-thing that not many people can say they've actually made happen. Congratulations!

Think about all you have learned this last year. No matter what your goals were for your trip, you'll be surprised at how valuable the experience will be in normal conversation. Your horizons have been broadened in way you couldn't possibly anticipate.

Your relationship with your spouse or traveling partner will change. For us, it brought us closer and strengthened our under-standing of each other's backgrounds and sensibilities. Getting out of your daily routine brings up all kinds of opportunities to see the other person in situations and stresses that are new. How you each handle those events provides new insights into the other person. Your shared experiences and time just hanging out together will put a whole new spin on your life—hopefully a positive one.

There will be some unexpected consequences of your year away. We found that some friends had drifted away during the year. That could be good or bad, depending on your viewpoint. We found it took a while for people to remember we were home and put us back into their patterns too.

In fact, we have now been home for almost two years and we still run into people who say, "Gee, I didn't know you were back already! How was the trip?" or "Are you guys still traveling?"

To keep or not to keep the rig?

Since we had purchased our vehicle especially for this trip, we had a decision to make when we returned. Although we loved having it on the road with us, we didn't plan to do enough RV travel in the future to justify keeping it. Phil especially was ready to settle into a home life of golf, grandkids, and a great retirement.

If you enjoyed your rig and your travels, you may want to continue your adventurous lifestyle in shorter doses and decide to keep your vehicle. There are times we wished we had done that. So no matter how tired you are of seeing the inside of the thing, wait a little while to make the final decision.

The sale of the unit took longer than we anticipated, so we had an added expense when we returned home until it was sold. We tried most of the traditional routes: newspaper advertising, driving it around with a "For Sale" sign on it, consignment to the dealer, networking among our friends, and parking it on display at RV shows. All of those avenues created prospects, but none resulted in a sale.

As summer gave way to fall, and fall to winter, we quit advertising it locally and moved to the Internet. We placed both free and paid ads on all the large sites we could find. Again, we got lots of nibbles, and finally a family in Southern California found us. Many e-mails, pictures, questions, and negotiations back and forth and we had a deal. Sight unseen, the money was wired to our bank. He flew to Portland, we picked him up, he looked it over, we gave him instructions on the various systems, and away he drove into the winter sunset. We still correspond from time to time. The Rolling White House has a happy new home.

For those of you who might be interested in buying a used Class B, here are some numbers to help you. Based on the sale price, it had depreciated about 25 percent in the two years we owned it. We nearly tripled the mileage on it, going from 21,000 miles to almost 60,000 miles. By the time it was sold, it was about five years old and sold for about 55 percent of the cost of a new one. The Internet is a great place to check out values and actual asking prices. The NADA Guides (*www.nadaguides.com*) have complete information on all types of RVs, similar to the *Kelley Blue Book* for autos.

What next?

Since you are reading this, you know what was "next" for us. But what will you take from this experience?

You will be changed in some way from your road trip dream. But will it make a difference in what you do with your life? Only time will tell. You've had a whole year to grow in new directions that could potentially change the way you look at your lives, or maybe not. Whatever you do, the year will continue to interplay in your life. Even if all you do is enjoy recounting your experiences with each other, it will have been a year like no other. But don't discount the possibility of permanent change due to the trip. You may decide to relocate to someplace you visited. You may decide on a different way to practice your hobby, based on what you learned. You may decide to pursue something brand-new that you experienced on the trip. The possibilities are endless. Be open to them.

But don't be surprised if you settle back into your old life with your new knowledge and just enjoy the experience as the "great time-out" of your life. Remember the day that you decided to put *yourself* first for just a little while!

Part 2 | The Trip

What is it really like to be on the road, away from home, every day for a year?

It's not really important for you to retrace our steps, but what we think is important is to give you a feel for what it's like to travel for an extended period of time. Although our trip was in a camping van, your trip might be by boat or backpack. Whatever your mode of movement, the same principles apply.

This section will reveal a lot about the issues that we faced and how we handled them "on the fly." No matter how prepared you are for your adventure, each day will be endured or enjoyed based on how you react to all the scenarios you will face. And that is something we can't predict for you. It is also part of what makes this journey the trip of a lifetime.

So sit back, enjoy, and experience our road trip dream.

Chapter

Our Trip Should Not Be Your Trip

Way back in Chapter 1, we began our campaign to encourage you to make this your own trip. This book was conceived not as a travel guide but as a guide to travel—to help you turn *your* road trip dream into *your* reality. We encourage you to set your own goals for your trip and then to use our experiences as a guide to actually making it all happen.

This second part of the book is included not because we think what we did is important, but because many people who encouraged us to write this book also encouraged us to include a journal or travelogue so that you might get a feel for what it is really like to be on the road day after day, month after month. It is written through Carol's eyes, with occasional "Phil-osophies" thrown in.

Our website will be available to you to dig more deeply into our adventure and recording system if you would like, but the next few chapters will take you through some of our experiences, just as we recorded them during the trip. Sentence fragments and all. As you read through the chapters, bear in mind that it is truly a journal; some things will have already happened, some will be in anticipation of things to come, but all are excerpts of the original words recorded as we traveled along.

Remember, maintaining your flexibility and humor are the keystones to success in this endeavor—and these are our most important words of wisdom to impart to you.

We consider each of you who decide to do this our success stories, so please feel free to contact us with your stories or to ask questions. Our website and address are shown on the copyright page of the book. We'd love to hear from you.

Chapter

The Trial Run

Unless you are experienced RV travelers, you should head out for a few days or so to test your plan and your skills. We found that this little adventure taught us so much.

Tip: Don't go with anyone else. You need to figure out how just the two of you will handle all the tasks—and each other. It's too easy in a group to borrow skills and supplies from your friends and never really know how just the two of you will do.

We decided to visit some familiar territory here in the Northwest that we wouldn't cover on the trip, since we had already traveled through most of Oregon, Washington, Idaho, and Montana during other trips. We'll suggest a few things to see in those states, since our route doesn't cover them and we think they are pretty terrific states to visit.

Testing your plan

This is your big chance to see what works and what doesn't. Make sure that you take enough time to really check it all out and not just delay some things until you get back. Shop for groceries along the way. Do a load of laundry. Enjoy that wonderful experience of using a dump station. Test out all your electronic gadgets. Practice reading maps and navigating through a large city.

In camp (assuming you are taking something other than an SUV), practice using all the various systems. Run the air conditioner, even if you don't really need it. Make sure the furnace works. Heat up the hot water and do some dishes. Each of these seemingly simple tasks takes on new challenges in a confined space. For instance, if you are a cook who uses lots of pot and pans, you will soon discover that there is no place to set all of them and no place to stack them all to dry. Practice "one-pot" cooking lessons *before* you leave!

The biggest thing you'll learn is working with your partner. You'll find that each of you will be best at certain things, and you'll develop a routine for accomplishing them all. Try doing different tasks until you find a way that really works and is efficient. The first time you have to set up in the dark, you will appreciate your "well-oiled" machine.

Revise as you go

Although you will continue to revise all year long as you become more skilled and learn new ideas from other travelers, this is your last chance to add or delete major items before you head out. The more bugs you can work out now, the more time you'll have to enjoy the trip and not be fussing with getting everything organized and functioning.

We had a major issue with our mirrors that we didn't solve until we were a month or more into our trip. Some friends along the way who had RV experience helped us get the special mirrors we needed to see everything more easily. Phil also found that the seats weren't really comfortable for him over a several-hour drive. A lumbar pillow solved that problem.

Your list of challenges and laughs along the way will set the tone for your whole experience. We remember our very first night on the trial run. We wanted everything to be just perfect. We spent over an hour deciding between two camp-grounds. We finally chose the smaller one with treed sites and space around each

Learning to maneuver the van on narrow roads led us to Crown Point in the Columbia River Gorge, Oregon.

one. There were several "prime" sites still vacant when we finally made up our minds. We asked for "one of those along the back." They looked so inviting and the closest to the river. We should have known there was a reason they were still available. We got all set up, made our taco dinner, and enjoyed the evening along the river. When we went to bed everything seemed to be going just right. Then the freight trains started rolling. About twenty-five yards behind our site, hidden by those lovely trees, were the main tracks bound for Portland. It sounded like they were *in* our van, about every two hours.

OK, so we had a couple of new items to add to our list: (1) if the sites seem too good to be true, they probably are; and (2) always check for "amenities" outside the campground.

Hopefully this book will help you avoid some of our humorous mistakes. You'll get to make enough of your own. Happy travels!

The great Pacific Northwest

We are definitely prejudiced, but if you haven't traveled in the Northwest, we strongly recommend that you include some time in this area. From sophisticated cities to small towns, from sparkling coastlines to high-desert plains, from verdant forests to snow-covered mountains—this last frontier of the

All was quiet on the first night of our trial run—until the trains came rumbling through!

United States is truly unique. Since we have vacationed so often in these states, we spent virtually no time on our trip in these areas.

If your adventure includes our national parks, this part of the country has a lot of them. Crater Lake National Park in Oregon; Mt. Rainier, Olympic, and North Cascades in Washington; and Glacier National Park in western Montana are all spectacular. Most of these parks have lodges that date from Roosevelt's Works Progress Administration (WPA) days, and many have been lovingly restored. The most famous lodge in the area, though, is not in a park. Timberline

Lodge on the slopes of Mount Hood and near the incredible Columbia River Gorge in Oregon is not to be missed.

The outdoor activities in these states are unparalleled. I often tell friends, "Where else can you snow ski in the morning, water ski in the afternoon, and watch the sun set over the ocean?—all in the same day, summer or winter." Oregon would be the correct answer. In addition, the trails for hiking are boundless, including the Pacific Crest Trail running the length of both Oregon and Washington, and mountain-lake settings for camping throughout all of the states in the Northwest. If you have never tried river rafting, this is the place. Guided trips are provided on spectacular rivers in all four states. In addition, the San Juan Islands off Washington's coast provide sailing and boating opportunities you will never forget.

If your tastes run more toward urban settings, the cities of Portland and Seattle provide amenities found in every world-class city, but with their own unique touches. There is nothing more beautiful than Seattle on a clear day. Surrounded by water everywhere you look and with Mount Rainier (14,000-plus feet) and the Olympic Mountains punctuating the skyline, sipping your latte in the home of Starbucks and Microsoft while contemplating which of this city's great attractions to enjoy next can be a magical experience.

In contrast to its sprawling, traffic-congested northern neighbor, Portland straddles the Willamette River under the backdrop of Mount Hood as a jewel of urban planning. Its controversial urban-growth boundary, network of 180 miles of bike paths throughout the urban area, and still-developing light-rail system provide the model of how to develop a city for the next century. Portland is becoming a city of "cool." It is filled with trendy shops and restaurants throughout its neighborhoods, a vibrant livable downtown, and plenty of diverse arts and sports offerings to fill most every desire.

Beyond the big cities lies the real Northwest. Farming towns, fishing towns, timber towns, and recreation-oriented towns dot the landscape. The heritage of our pioneer and Native American forefathers can be explored at many locations. The Lewis and Clark Trail runs through each of the states with multiple attractions to learn about this first exploration of the area.

Indian reservations and historic museums are extensive, allowing a deeper understanding of their key role in the western expansion.

In addition to places mentioned above, some of our favorite spots include

- Cannon Beach on the Oregon coast
- The Columbia River Gorge between Oregon and Washington
- Joseph, Oregon, for its active arts community and bronze foundries
- Bend/Redmond, Oregon for the outdoor recreation, great weather, and small-town feel
- The winery areas near Newberg, Oregon, and Yakima, Washington
- Lake Chelan, Washington, for the boat ride down the lake
- Snoqualmie Falls, Washington
- Coeur d'Alene, Idaho, and the Coeur d'Alene resort
- Wallace, Idaho, for its historic downtown and silver-mining history
- Sun Valley, Idaho
- Big Fork, Montana, and Flathead Lake for their charm and natural beauty
- Lolo Pass (Highway 12) from Missoula, Montana, to Kooskia, Idaho

It doesn't really matter where you go in these beautiful states—just be sure to go and enjoy a feast for the eyes.

Chapter

The Sweet Smell of Summer

Week 1 | Oregon and Northern California

Our first night is emblazoned on our memory—we were so nervous about finding a place, getting set up, and not looking too stupid! Of course, the setting on the Rogue River and the lovely park we chose made it even more special. The owner promised to buy the champagne on our return trip a year from now!

The Oregon Caves were interesting. They are the largest marble caves in the country. Saw good size stalactites and stalagmites—g for ground, they are the ones growing up, c for ceiling; I could never remember which was which! The road up there is not for the faint of heart. The old lodge there is worth seeing—right out of the '40s.

From downtown Gold Beach we drove three miles inland out of the coastal fog, and the weather was beautiful. Not dressed for golf, but ready to seize the moment of good weather, we played in our jeans. We have never done that before. Salmon Run golf course is incredible—every hole is more spectacular than the last. It is a ball-eater, but a *must-play*, nonetheless. The wildflowers are beautiful, the wastelands vast, and the wildlife everywhere.

No trip to Northern California would be complete without at least one day in the Wine Country. Since we had been to Napa in years past, we decided to try the Sonoma Valley. Our plan was to go to the town of Sonoma, but we were ready for a break at Healdsburg and spent the day. Many of our favorite wineries are in this town—Rodney Strong, Clos du Bois, and Dry Creek, among others.

Phil-osophies

In 1959, I worked for a summer for Georgia-Pacific in Samoa, outside of Eureka, California. Pete and I were just punk kids, away from home for the summer, making a few bucks. The "old salts" thought we were amusing, if not crazy. We ate every meal at "the cookhouse" that was leased by GP to provide the workers' meals. We slept in a bunkhouse with characters that were hiding from every sin known to man.

Pete had told me that the cookhouse still exists, now as "The Samoa Cookhouse." We searched it out—and what a case of déjà vu. That entire summer flashed before my eyes. We had lunch where I had sat—although the tables were turned the other way—and the food was still great. We waddled out of there into the rain. I only remember five sunny days that whole summer—the waitress said nothing has changed with the weather.

I really wished my dad were still alive to relive that memory with him.

The Novato RV Park had been recommended to us by a couple in Grants Pass. (The networking amongst the RVers is unbelievable.) We weren't impressed at first because of the all-gravel and concrete spaces and the proximity to the freeway. We also had to "level" the van for the first time. Not as hard as I had thought. The "amenities" were great. An on-site deli that had every meal covered. People came from all around the area to get their sandwiches! The best pot stickers we have ever had! A windshield-washing service, a spotless laundry and shower facility, a nice pool, good Internet access, on-site planning for local attractions, and the morning newspaper readily at hand made us agree this was a great value—even at $29.25 a night (Good Sam Club rate, of course).

Had a nice respite at the St. Francis in San Francisco during "happy hour" at the Compass Rose Bar. A singer right out of the '40s, complete with suit and hat, singing great tunes. A tip on the cable cars: don't try to go from Fisherman's Wharf to Union Square—a one- to two-hour wait in prime time. Instead go from town to the Wharf—you can jump on most anywhere, anytime!

Our weekend plans in San Francisco had fallen through, so we had a couple days until we were due in Carmel. "Let's go a different way," Phil says—so, dutifully, I got the map out and sent us north on Highway 1. We fell into Monte Rio outside of Guerneville. Non-touristy, kind of funky, a totally delightful place on the banks of the Russian River. We found a small family motel with nice grounds, a nearby golf course, a *fabulous* restaurant up the road—we were there for the weekend!

Unfortunately, we had our first unpleasant experience here. We told the motel we were staying a second night, but they forgot to change our key card (a new system for them). They left the motel unattended and without an emergency number (isn't that against the law?) for four hours—and we were locked out of our room. Were we ever mad! It is a good thing we had the van, or I don't know what we would have done. We did manage to fill part of the evening with the local pig roast. They called him Elmer Fudd and he was yummy! A real value for $15 per person and all the Bud Light you could consume—and some folks consumed a lot!

Week 2 | Carmel and the U.S. Open

The condo we traded for two of our weeklong U.S. Open tickets is *awesome*! Not one block to *the* ocean, as we had thought, but one block to *Ocean*, the main street in Carmel! We are actually about eight short blocks from *the* ocean. We spent several hours there today—the weather was incredible! Definitely an "inner-city" experience—even in Carmel. We share the courtyard with a restaurant that is open for breakfast and lunch only—the fan on the roof, right by our bedroom, starts at 6:00 a.m.! Maybe I'll finally get up early and get some journal writing done!

Parking is very tight here—we have "landed" the van about four blocks from the condo and plan to leave it there until we leave! We've made two trips up there already today—think we may have completely unloaded the van into the Condo. We can walk about a half mile to the course—the other "non-Carmel" golf fans are having to park at Fort Ord and be bussed to the course. Spent our first day here walking the town—and getting my glasses fixed. (Phil sat on them in the van in Trinidad. Now we know why bringing an extra set of glasses was highly recommended! Had to order a new piece—it will be here Thursday.) Of course Phil chatted with everyone—and even managed to talk a couple of guys into driving us up the hill back to our condo!

The Open was really "a happening place." The USGA does a first-class job, and they charge a first-class price for everything too! They quit serving alcohol on the course at 4 p.m.—regardless of how long the play will continue! One day we were standing right by a garbage can and thought that since they were charging for everything else, we'd try charging a nickel to use the garbage can. We made a lot of people laugh, but collected no nickels. We decided we weren't charging enough to be taken seriously.

Wednesday night, our friends made reservations for all of us at Inn at Spanish Bay. *Wow!* As though the setting were not spectacular enough, the bagpipers came over the hill at sunset with those wonderful lilting tunes. Curtis Strange was also enjoying cocktails on the terrace. At dinner, we were seated next to Freddy Couples and his wife. To top it all off, the food was absolutely divine. It was actually hard to leave such a beautiful place.

Week 3 | Yosemite and the Gold Country

How could one week go screaming by so quickly? A funny thing about this trip, we have been surrounded by wonderful friends for most of two solid weeks, and now we will probably not see a soul we know for months!

Yosemite might be considered a religious experience for Phil. Phil Jr. had climbed El Capitan several years ago (it took five days), but we had no idea what that really meant until we were there. The age of instant communications made it all the more special for Phil, as he was able to reach Phil Jr. while we were awestruck in the Valley. Yosemite is a place not to be missed in a lifetime. We may take the grandchildren there. It is so breathtaking but is quickly being overrun with too many people. Let's hope they can maintain some balance.

Hiking with friends on the Pacific Crest Trail at over 8,000 feet near Reno, Nevada, where, even in June, we were tramping across snowfields

We reluctantly left Yosemite and chose the Gold Country route out of there, as the digital camera had died in Carmel and the only warranty service center in the United States happened to be in Sacramento. We dropped it there on our way to the High Sierra to visit yet another group of friends. Route 49 through the Gold Country is really something—another road not for the faint of heart. More suited for wagon trains than large vans. Phil did a great job of maneuvering the 10-mph hairpin turns.

Hiking the Pacific Crest Trail is awesome. It is something I have always wanted to do—so high above everything. We varied between about 7,900 and 8,200 feet. I thought I would die the first twenty minutes until my lungs got acclimated! We went about eight-plus miles and saw some of the most beautiful scenery. We tromped through snowfields, saw beautiful alpine flower fields, looked down at lakes that were themselves over 5,000 feet high, and saw an old gold mine left over from the 1860s.

Week 4 | Lake Tahoe and Nevada

Back to Sacramento to pick up the camera and replace our car keys—yes, we have managed to misplace one set of our keys already. One stop at the Dodge dealer, one stop at the "Viper" dealer (the alarm system), and one stop at the hardware store for all the van compartment keys and we were back in business. We now have a game plan (one set always stays in the van) and a hidden door key! Not everything on the road works out perfectly, and we would *really* be upset if we ended up with no keys! Which with our memories, is not out of the question! Off again to Lake Tahoe, the south shore this time. Our first KOA and our most expensive camping night to date: $32.

Phil-osophies
Carol, what is wrong with this picture? The campground is $32, and we have seen perfectly acceptable motels as low as $28! This supply/demand curve is out of whack! Oh, it is the babbling brook we wouldn't have at the motel. I still don't buy it! This campground is in the dirt and we don't have ESPN here.

Another thing that continues to amaze us is our inability to purchase gasoline economically! No matter where we decide to buy it, we invariably see it ten minutes later for 10 to 20 cents cheaper! We decided not to buy it in South Lake Tahoe (about $1.80 there) due to its high tourist-area appeal. We had plenty to get to our next destination, Carson City. We drove well into the city and everything seemed to be about $1.79 on up. We decided to stay here and started looking around for a place to stay. We did manage to find a great motel for $40, but we also saw gas as low as $1.51 after having just paid $1.79! On twenty-eight gallons, we could almost have paid for our $23.37 dinner—including wine! If this was the first time this had happened it would be one thing—but, unfortunately, it is not.

Carson City, the capital of Nevada, is a pretty little city nestled in the "foothills" at over 5,000 feet elevation. We both are a little under the weather, me from a cold, Phil from a sore shoulder suffered on the Pacific Crest Trail. We decide to just chill for a bit. We have had so little time to just stop and enjoy. Little time for reading—most of our reading is maps and guidebooks, getting ready for the next adventure, and of course, keeping the website updated. Our $40 motel has a nice pool and a large, decent room. Who knows how long we may be here.

A day of relaxing—*aaahhhhhh!* Well, not really relaxing—we decided to do some chores. We cleaned up the van, ran some laundry, had the tires rotated and balanced, had the oil changed (and the 24,000-mile service work done), had the propane filled, had the refrigerator checked. It wasn't cooling right today—not a major problem, probably "pilot error" in leveling. We enjoyed the fun Nevada State Museum, with an old mine replica in the basement and the old Carson City Mint upstairs. You should see the machine they used to stamp millions of silver dollars.

Our first great thunder-and-lightning storm this afternoon. It rained the biggest raindrops I've ever seen, and they felt really cold against the 104-degree air. The Rolling White House (Like the new name? Thanks to everyone who entered the contest to name her!) is spending the night plugged in—hopefully—at the dealership. They got us in at the last minute and weren't sure they could get everything done. Alas, we are carless tonight. We'll take a walk somewhere for dinner. Fortunately, we are very close to town and the dealership. We are actually enjoying the respite.

Well, the dealership did everything right, but once again pilot error took over. I forgot to turn the refrigerator to "electric," and by morning everything was room temperature. Out with the milk, meat, sour cream, etc. Another lesson in the books.

Wow, what a difference $185 worth of work on the RWH (Rolling White House) makes! We had the transmission serviced, among other things, and the car engine shifted so much better today, you can't believe it. After crossing 325 miles of desert today on the "Loneliest Highway in America" (official designation) and traversing three passes over 7,000 feet, we are thankful we had the work done. Who knows what may have lurked in those mountains and deserts.

Great Basin National Park is not easy to get to, but the views are breathtaking when you are there. The Lehman Caves put the Oregon Caves to shame. A thunderstorm rolled over and limited our hiking plans. They tell us that the drive to Wheeler Peak and the hiking there are the best, but the storm was centered up there and they didn't recommend it today.

Do you know what is significant about the Great Basin, which covers most of this area? I didn't. It drains internally. That is, it has no outlet to any ocean. All the water is either absorbed into the ground or drains into lakes where evaporation keeps everything in balance. That is your geography lesson for the day.

Week 5 | Salt Lake City and Sun Valley, Idaho

The scenery along Highway 93 from Ely to Wendover, Nevada, was like no other we have seen. You thread your way between two mountain ranges, some still with snowcaps, along this high-desert floor at about 5,000 feet. It is so desolate but peaceful, you can drive for thirty minutes or more and never see a car, a person, a house, or any signs of civilization.

From Wendover into Salt Lake City you go through the Bonneville Salt Flats, where most of the land-speed records have been set. I've never seen miles of white like this that isn't snow. Have great pics caught in the camera—which is dead again.

Salt Lake City is like a city "with its hair on fire"! Every road is torn up, signs make little sense, every block is under construction, and the locals are very weary of the confusion—and it is a year and a half until the Olympics. We are lucky to be here on a holiday weekend, as they have patched things up a bit for the celebration. We hear chaos reigns during the week.

What a day of contrasts Sunday has been—the Mormon Tabernacle Choir in the morning and a biker bar in Park City in the afternoon! I guess it just shows our flexibility and the contrasts in Utah. The choir was fantastic—over two hundred voices. Park City is the site of many of the Olympic events and is also under major construction. We were able to see the ski-jumping site, the slalom site, and the start of the luge construction. It is a beautiful little town. I don't think they really know what is in store for them in 2002.

Utah still has some of the strangest drinking laws. It ought to really confuse the Europeans for the Games! You can't order a drink unless you order food in a restaurant. If you only want a drink, you go to a private "club"—

You still have to share those special nights out, just like at home—but in new and beautiful settings like Sun Valley, Idaho.

think of it like a bar with a cover charge at all times! But you can't order a pitcher of margaritas in a restaurant. They bring a pitcher of the mix, and the shots of alcohol to go with it are served individually at a nominal fee ($1 where we were).

In spite of the Mormon-inspired drinking laws, we both thought Salt Lake City had a definite air of civility about it. No one was rude, in fact, everyone on the street acknowledged you. Their dress was classy compared to the average American city. If you saw an awful outfit, you knew immediately they were tourists. People actually wore dresses and suits to see the choir perform on Sunday, and the Sunday stroll still exists in Salt Lake

City. Phil was thrilled to see that shopkeepers actually closed down on Sunday. We had to go to a hotel to get lunch today.

In Sun Valley for the Fourth of July, we stumbled into a special surprise! Everyone warned us that we'd better have reservations somewhere, but as is our style, we didn't. Driving up there, I could tell we would be fine—the cars were streaming out of there the entire seventy-five miles up there and there were few cars going our direction. We had our choice of places to stay and decided we needed a treat. We stepped up for the Sun Valley Lodge, and it is worth every cent!

Upon checking in, they asked if we wanted tickets to the Ice Show and Fireworks, so of course we said yes. There was a nominal fee, but we thought it would be fun. Little did we know that this was no local gig! Katarina Witt, Jozef Sabovcik, and Sasha Cohen were skating! It was wonderful, followed by fireworks that were choreographed to "Stars and Stripes Forever."

This place is a Norman Rockwell painting. The only thing missing are the parasols and bustles. There are well-behaved children feeding the white swans in the pond, families having picnics on the lawn, bicycles everywhere, and service that is gracious at every turn. As we were casting about for what to do for dinner, we walked by the Rams Head Inn—and spied the fresh trout on the menu. I said, "We'll never get in there! It is 4 p.m. on July 4th. This place is busy." But once again, Phil prevailed, and we had a lovely table on the patio with piano music and a view of the pond. The tab for dinner with wine and tip: $55. Experience: priceless!

Since the lodge is not full, Phil has negotiated a second night here for us for $100! We are off to ride bikes, play in the pool, and explore the little town of Ketchum!

Week 6 | Grand Teton and Yellowstone National Parks

Jackson Hole, Wyoming, our third famous ski resort in less than a week—and not a drop of snow to be found! It definitely retains the flavor of the Old West—but in a very "yuppified" manner. Great stores for fabulous Western wear. If you ever need to appear in *City Slickers*, this is your place to shop! Really wonderful things.

Our lack of planning almost caught up with us here. After finding our first three choices full, we got the last space at the KOA in Teton Village! It caused us to say, "Yikes—maybe we better get our act together in these popular parks." So we promptly made reservations for the next four nights here and in Yellowstone. I think once we get through this area, we can go back to our whimsical ways!

The Wort Hotel proved to be our favorite. The Silver Dollar Bar and Grille has an interesting history. They had a massive fire in 1980, but the semicircular bar was saved. It has embedded in it 2,065 uncirculated 1921 silver dollars. They were bought directly from the Denver mint in 1949. They are, however, worn. That is because there is no covering over them. You can actually lean your elbows right on them. Some have tried to remove them from their black plastic surrounding, unsuccessfully. When they were originally embedded, the plastic was drilled out slightly smaller than the dollars. The dollars were frozen, causing shrinkage (stay with me—this is basic physics!), and the plastic was heated, causing, yes, expansion. Then the frozen dollars were set in and the whole thing was allowed to "cure," causing a very tight fit!

So what did we do in Jackson besides eat, drink, and shop? We mostly looked at the breathtaking scenery. We did go white-water rafting on the Snake—not nearly as rollicking a ride as Oregon rivers, but it was still fun. We hiked this afternoon along the edge of Jackson Lake near where we are staying at Coulter Bay. We had a delightful conversation with a professional photographer and his wife from Colorado. They were photographing wildlife in the park and had been waiting patiently for some specific shots for over a week. He was retired from IBM with a golden parachute and now following his passion—we loved it!

Onward to Yellowstone. What a testimony to nature. You can see her best and the worst all within the park. The fire of 1988 is still very much in evidence, all over the park. Some places are haunting with their stark sticks still stretching to the sky; other areas are hopeful in their regeneration; and still other places are totally devoid of fire penetration. Almost without reason as to what happened where.

The rivers, streams, and waterfalls make you think this is "normal" geography, and then you round the next corner and know that this is one of the strangest places on earth. There is more thermal activity than all other places combined. Beautiful springs, tall and small geysers, weird colors, pots of mud plopping and steaming, noxious sulfur smells, steam wafting in your face, and people everywhere enjoying what nature has provided.

It seems the wildlife cause the most traffic problems. You'd think these fools had never seen a deer or elk! Maybe they haven't. They stop their cars in the middle of the road and shoot pictures from the window! Get off the road, get your derriere out of your car, and walk fifty feet to take your disposable-camera picture! Unbelievable!

We took a three-mile walk today to view the Morning Glory pool. One of the most famous, and unfortunately, one of the most vandalized. Due to people throwing things into the vent, the water has cooled and allowed the beautiful blue color to begin to fade at the edges as different bacteria have begun to grow. What a shame. Old Faithful, however, is still in good form, and the Park Service is doing a good job of trying to keep the park accessible yet not overrun. This is no small task.

Lodging in the national parks is quite interesting. All types, from primitive to rather elegant, are available. It takes a bit of delving to figure out what is what. We stayed at the only RV Park in Yellowstone (adequate, but surely not the nicest we've stayed in), but also a cabin at Mammoth Hot Springs that would be the pride of any Army barracks! Since the Army ran the park in the early 1900s and Mammoth is the HQ of the park, I'm sure these were Army housing! You can figure that anything under $100 is going to be basic, with the prices going to several hundred a night for the most desirable locations, like the Old Faithful Inn. Some of the campgrounds allow RVs to dry camp (no hookups, generators allowed during certain hours). None of the reference books do a very good job of explaining all this. Hopefully, as we visit more national parks, we'll get this figured out!

Mammoth has thousands of little critters called pigwhistles. They look like a cross between a chipmunk and a small weasel. They whistle like birds and will take things from your cabin or car given a split second to do so!

"All doors closed at all times" is the motto here! They are very friendly and quite cute.

The big debate leaving Mammoth was whether to take the Beartooth highway into Billings or go the "safer" route through Livingston. The Beartooth is supposed to be spectacular—but scary—and very high—almost 11,000 feet. We decided to suck it up and go the Beartooth. I drove since we have decided I do better on these kinds of roads if I'm in control! What a breathtaking choice! The road really wasn't that bad—easy to say when you're driving!—but the scenery was like nothing we've ever seen before.

You are high above the tree line, looking down at the glaciers and eye-to-eye with the tops of very rugged mountains. There are alpine meadows strewn with boulders left by the Ice Age and the bluest nosegays of flowers you have ever seen. The sky was so blue, but the air so thin. I was actually a little light-headed. They were doing some repaving right at the summit. We were sitting in the car for about twenty minutes, taking in the view, when the cell phone rings! We couldn't believe it. Here we were, on top of the world, miles from anything—and we had cell coverage! The world really is getting small. It was daughter Andrea and grandchildren Nick and Megan, looking for Grammie!

Friday took us to the Custer Battlefield. We spent all afternoon there. The park-ranger talks about the battle were wonderful. This guy should make a video to be used in the schools. He really made the whole thing come alive. As he pointed to various places in the valley, you could almost hear the Indians in their camp and see the Army on the hills. We then got the audio tour and drove the entire battlefield. Never has a piece of history been so alive for either of us.

Our National Parks pass that cost $50 has now crossed the break-even point—and we still have ten months to go!

Week 7 | Wyoming and North and South Dakota

There are so many things we are interested in, and yet, we find ourselves everyday choosing how to spend our time. We are on the go from mid-morning (after breakfast, showers, e-mail, repacking/disconnecting the van) to early evening. We try to stop by 4 or 5 p.m., but still cannot do everything we would like to do.

Everyday we meet people from every walk of life from all over the United States. Everyone is so nice. They want to share their experiences and any information they have about your next stop. Today we learned that the main road to Mount Rushmore is closed! But a family in the Devil's Tower KOA where we are staying had just gone through there and had the route scoped out on how to go! They even gave us their map—highlighted with the changes!

We really did the tourist thing last night and watched *Close Encounters of the Third Kind*. You may remember that Devil's Tower played a prominent role in that movie. The KOA showed it outdoors at dusk—it was kind of eerie looking up at the Rock as the movie played. Plus it was a full moon, so this giant rock was really lit up.

Can you imagine Phil at the Great North American RV Rally? We actually had a good time talking to the folks and picking up a few supplies. We had lost our pressure-reducing valve, and a hose-connection piece had developed a leak. Plus we found this neat foldup table that is just right for those locations without picnic tables—or for extra cocktail room! We spent most of the day there looking at the booths—hopefully helped the Pleasure-Way guy sell a unit to a couple from Colorado!—and eating and listening to the music. We made it out of there without Phil buying a larger unit.

We've been in Spearfish, South Dakota, for a couple of days now. Really a neat little town. Took time to get some laundry and dry cleaning done, pictures developed, grocery shopping, etc. We took a beautiful drive yesterday afternoon up Spearfish Canyon—another *wow* place.

Beautiful campsites are everywhere. We loved our view of Devil's Tower in Wyoming.

The road continues to Lead (the oldest continuous-operation gold mine in the Western Hemisphere), Deadwood, and on to Sturgis. Deadwood is the most idyllic, but it has been ruined by too many tourists and too many gambling halls. It has a great setting, neat old buildings, cowboys shooting it up in the streets, and a general fun atmosphere. We saw the location where Wild Bill Hickox met his demise while playing cards, holding a pair of aces, a pair of 8's, and a lone 9—now called the dead man's hand! We wanted to take a look at Sturgis before the Harleys ride into town on the 7th of August. They are expecting up to a half million bikers that week—we wanted to be nowhere near here by then!

The town of Medora at the entrance to Teddy Roosevelt National Park is quite basic but provides a real Old West feeling to the area. Most of the town is owned by the Medora Foundation and is well maintained. We heard people talking about the "Medora Musical" and inquired about it. Now in its thirty-fifth year, this professionally done production is staged in a beautiful outdoor amphitheater, facing the hills. They have a variety of entertaining acts, but what impressed us the most was their reenactment of the Rough Riders, led by Roosevelt, charging the hill in the 1898 battle of San Juan (Spanish-American War). The set actually rolled back and the hills beyond revealed a fort. The boys on horseback and on foot "charged the hill," cannons exploded in the night hills, guns fired, soldiers dropped. It was spectacularly moving. After the battle was over, the soldier on a white horse brought back the flag from the fort (followed all the way by a spotlight in the night). Definitely an evening well spent—yet another thing we just stumbled into!

Phil-osophies

Who ever heard of a place where they don't get USA Today*!? I mean, nowhere. After checking and checking—we went to three different towns, becoming more and more frustrated—someone actually had the guts to tell me that* USA Today *is not delivered* anywhere *in northern North Dakota. Are these people un-American, or what?*

I have to comment on their use of the word *river* around here. We would not even consider most of them a decent *creek*! They meander everywhere and barely contain water at this time of year.

But maybe they make up for it with their rain. The rain is very well behaved here—it deluges quickly and moves on! Usually it happens in the evening or at night—also convenient, doesn't ruin the days! At 6 p.m. the night of the Medora Musical, it was raining like crazy—we thought the production would surely be canceled, but by 7 p.m., it was done and the sun was back out. By 8 p.m., most everything was dry—but the ushers handed us a wipe anyway, just in case the seat was still wet.

On the way back to South Dakota, we had front-row seats to a huge weather cell moving through. Beautiful blue sky and puffy white clouds edged with pink on both sides of this ominous black cloud that towered high into the sky. For a while we thought we were headed right for it, but the road turned, the storm moved, and we mostly missed each other. We got about five minutes of the edge of it, but even that was scary—we experienced high winds that blew us around, huge raindrops, and some pretty-good-sized hail. The lightning was quite a ways away but still provided a spectacular show.

Week 8 | South Dakota

We're off to Mount Rushmore and Crazy Horse today. Everyone was talking about the new entrance and facilities. Some liked it, others didn't. We thought it was awe-inspiring, but we hadn't seen it before. As you walk up from the parking lot, you go through a granite entry with flags of every state, with the four guys right ahead of you. People said you used to be able to get closer and it was less commercialized. We took a tour with a ranger—these guys and gals are good! Saw the studio where Borglum and his men worked and heard the story of the monument, complete with demonstrations of the tools, etc. It is amazing that no one was killed and that it was ever finished as far as it was. Borglum's original concept was never completed, as the rock below the busts was not granite and could not be carved. The whole monument took fourteen years to complete, at a total cost of under a million dollars!

Crazy Horse Memorial, which has been under private development since 1949, refuses to take any government help, but visitors are "contributing" $8 per person at the gate.

"Phil, Phil! What are you doing with your bare feet on that piece of paper?"

"Oh, Carol, glad you caught up with me. This is Tony White Thunder of the Lakota tribe, and he is going to make me a pair of those cool beaded moccasins."

"Really? Why, pray tell?"

"I am really into this Indian stuff and I think it will be a great trip memento and we can pass them on to the kids."

"Uh-huh, and how much has Phil White Wampum promised Tony White Thunder for this?" You don't want to know. What's next, a headdress with cool feathers?

Oh, I have my camera back! Seems to be working. I'll get some new pictures up on the website soon!

Today was interesting. We visited the Needles highway, the pigtails, Custer State Park, and the Black Hills Playhouse in the evening. All just driving and looking on very narrow roads, but the scenery was really neat. The pigtails are bridges that are built round and round like a pig's tail to lift you up in a small space. Quite ingenious. One tunnel on the Needles highway was only eight-foot-seven-inches wide. Our rig is eight-foot-two-inches. It was actually kind of fun squeezing through there. Had lunch and went on a walk around Sylvan Lake. There are huge granite rocks lifting right out of the water all along part of the shore. Lots of activity there—swimming, paddleboats, canoes, etc. We tried to stay at the Sylvan Lake Lodge, but they were full. They got us into another nice lodge, though, the State Game Lodge. It turned out better, as the Game Lodge is closer to the Playhouse and you don't have to go over that Needles highway at night! Dinner was great—trout and walleye pike!

Phil thinks it is downright hospitable of South Dakota to name a town after him!

Custer is an interesting park in that it is totally self-sustaining. They actually sell 400 to 500 head of buffalo each year.

They have one of the largest, most-productive (over 90 percent of the females calve each year), and best herds in the country and sell them for slaughter as well as to other individuals to start or supplant their herds. This revenue covers about one-third of the park expenses. The rest is paid for through entrance fees, a percentage from the concessions, including the four beautiful lodges in the park, and camping fees. They say they run it like a business, even though they report to the State Parks Commission—what a novel idea!

Off to the Badlands. It will be interesting to see if the 35mm camera was able to capture the beauty of these hills. The digital pictures just don't do it justice. This is another one of those places that you just have to say, "Why this, why here?" The coloring of the hills varies from beige, rose, steel blue, sea-foam green, brilliant gold-yellow, and rusty brown. Incredible against the bright blue sky. We went through late in the afternoon, and the shadowing really made them pop out.

On into Wall for the night so we could see the famous Wall Drug the next day. There are signs literally all over the world saying how many miles to Wall Drug—hundreds of them in Montana, Wyoming, and South Dakota. What a piece of Americana this place is! All that is really in Wall, South Dakota, is Wall Drug, which takes up several blocks.

We're starting to get into the Great Plains now. Fields are everywhere—wheat, sunflowers (for the oil and seeds), and corn, mostly. Farm implements lumbering down the highways to the next field to be harvested. "Contract harvesters" who bring their own equipment, people, etc., now do much of the work. Schoolteachers make up many of the crews.

The state capital of South Dakota, Pierre (*peer*—we quickly learned the correct pronunciation!), and the wide Missouri River appeared out of the middle of the fields. It is a lovely town of about 20,000 on the banks of the river, which has been beautifully made into a park.

We found our best value of the trip in the Capitol Inn Motel—too hot to camp with no trees! It was right downtown by the Capitol and the park. It had a nice outdoor swimming pool in the courtyard with grass all around, a guest laundry (becoming a very important feature to us!), nice well-maintained rooms, electrical hookups for the van, continental breakfast, great AC—*and* they let us wash the RWH at no charge! Most campgrounds and motels won't let you do that, and of course it won't go through a conventional car wash. The poor thing has not been washed in over 6,000 miles! It was really dirty! We got our swimsuits on and suds her up, even as the heat again climbed into the 90s. We then promptly jumped into the pool to cool off! The Rolling White House is white again! The price for this bit of heaven? $35 a night plus tax! Mark it down—best value!

Week 9 | Minnesota

Off for eastern South Dakota—seems like we have been in South Dakota for a long time. I just checked—we have! Eleven days, and we have two more nights here!

After a nice visit with our friends in Brookings, South Dakota, we took the back way into Minneapolis. What wonderful little towns along the way! Finally found out what that dark-green, short, broad-leafed crop was that is everywhere between the cornfields—soybeans.

The start of our visit in Minneapolis is not good. We were hit during rush-hour traffic as we were looking for a motel or campground down near the Mall of America. Luckily, Phil had his foot on the brake and we were able to stop before hitting the car ahead of us. It took all day today to get everything lined up on that. Turned out that the other driver had let his insurance lapse. We understand he paid it today, but it doesn't look good that the company will consider him "covered" yesterday. We will find out the damages tomorrow. Looks like we'll be in the Twin Cities a bit longer than we planned. Oh, we are both OK and the RWH is fine—just a new bumper, wheel cover, and a little paint.

Even driving in Minneapolis in the evening when the cars have gone home is more than we could endure. We had planned to eat downtown, but parking and maneuvering were difficult. We decided it was too much trouble.

Got the estimate on the van today—not too bad, so life will go on! The bummer is the factory is closed for summer vacation for six weeks, so we have to figure out where to have the parts shipped when they start up again!

We're taking a city tour tomorrow. Driving here is scary—too many free-ways, all under construction, and people going like bats out of you know where! Spotted St. Paul Cathedral as we came into town. This is truly a cathe-dral—like the kind you see in Europe. It is massive and beautiful. Built between 1911 and 1915, it is awe-inspiring. Crisp bright stained glass, mosaics that were made at the Vatican, an altar reminiscent of St. Peter's in Rome. It was actually patterned after that church, I found out later. The dome alone is 196 feet high. From ground to the top of the cross on the copper roof is 307 feet, an imposing site from all over St. Paul.

Good news! Farmer's Insurance has come forward and said they will cover this accident! Apparently the insured paid his lapsed insurance—and they backdated it! But now we have to start over with them. We are off on a city tour of Minneapolis-St. Paul today, so we will deal with them Monday.

What a great tour! We should have done this the first day, then we could have gone back to some things that were really interesting. The rivalry between the two cities is quite real. The tour guide characterized it as frater-nal twins—St. Paul, the steady conservative "if it ain't broke don't fix it" atti-tude, and Minneapolis, the floozy sister who wants everything new and shiny all the time. You can see it in everything about the cities. We liked St. Paul and thought they were really moving forward with some great projects. St. Paul is the home of Charles Schulz—of *Peanuts* fame—and they have done a cute thing with Snoopy statues all over town with various themes.

Phil-osophies

Our tour really gave me an appreciation for the cleanliness of Portland and the development of our waterfront. Most everything in Minneapolis looked like it was in need of some maintenance—and water! Although the flowers on the lampposts were nice, the parks, sidewalks, etc., were all just a little "worn" looking. They did do an ambitious thing within the city. Every waterway (lake, stream, etc.) is bounded by public park land—and there are a lot of them even within the city. Therefore you don't have houses or commercial buildings right on the waterfront. It does look nice from that aspect—they just need more maintenance!

Off for the only RV campground that we've seen rated at 10-10-10 (park-restrooms-scenic). It is out in the middle of nowhere—Hinckley, Minnesota. The first thing we noticed was that Bill Cosby was coming to their amphitheater. (Clear out here?) We took another look at the map and it turns out that Hinckley is one hour from Minneapolis–St. Paul, one hour from St. Cloud, and one hour from Duluth—over 80 percent of the state's population! This place was incredible. A 500-site RV park with its own clubhouse, beautiful pool, grocery, etc. A casino (Indian) that was as big and nice as anything in Vegas, two hotels, a wonderful 18-hole golf course, several restaurants, and a 24-hour shuttle service that ran every fifteen minutes throughout the park. Our only complaint was that the trees haven't grown up in the RV park yet—and we felt a little "exposed."

Our next stop was to settle in a cabin or nice RV park along one of the 10,000 famous lakes for a couple of days. The Brainerd area had been recommended as having a lot of nice places of those types. Little did we know there was a twenty-state baseball tournament in the area. We couldn't find anything, anywhere—not even a cheap motel! Drove on toward Grand Rapids and finally found an RV site. We were pooped out! We are not used to going till 8 p.m. before stopping! We got a recommendation for dinner, and what a people-watching place this was! The Forty Club in Aitkin, Minnesota, a big formal wedding party kicking up their heels, and it was jammed with other locals, tourists, etc. We had a great prime-rib dinner and just enjoyed being around a crazy bunch of people for a while!

Sunday morning dawned rainy, so we decided to abandon the idea of a few days in the area and headed toward International Falls and Voyageurs National Park. Another week under our belt. . . .

Week 10 | Minnesota

Cattails! Can you say *cattails*! I've never seen so many in my life! They are everywhere—around every lake, by every road. They should be the Minnesota state flower!

International Falls, Minnesota—somewhere near the edge of the earth, I'm sure. Nothing is here, including reliable cell service, but you can imagine the dog sleds and snowmobiles charging down the streets when it is minus-30F! Just a few miles out of town, life gets better quickly. The fishing resorts along Rainy Lake at the edge of Voyageurs National Park are wonderful and plentiful. The only way to see Voyageurs is by boat. There are no roads—only water, islands, and cattails! Since we didn't tow a boat with us, we needed to figure a way to see the park. It seems there is only one place to stay in the park, the twelve-room Kettle Falls Hotel. We don't have reservations and the Minneapolis paper did a big spread on them in today's paper. What do you think our chances are? "Give 'em a call, what can it hurt?" I said to Phil.

As I write this, I'm sitting on a lovely screened porch in the heart of Voyageurs National Park. Kettle Falls Hotel was built in the early 1900s, long before Voyageurs was a park, and it remains true to the era. It was remodeled in the mid-1980s—larger rooms, shared baths (yes, I actually got Phil in a shared bathroom), and the simplicity of another time. People arrive by canoe, houseboat, pontoon boats, or any other watercraft to enjoy the simple hospitality and family feel—oh, and of course, fishing. Everyone fishes in Minnesota, and the walleye are wonderful!

Grand Portage is where the Indians "portaged" their canoes eight and a half miles from the Great Lakes into the Northern waterways and eventually as far as the West Coast. It became an important "rendezvous" spot between the voyageurs, who traded the Indians for the fur pelts, and the trading companies (Hudson's Bay, Northwest Trading, etc.), who paid the voyageurs and took the pelts to the East Coast and often on to Europe.

The Grand Portage National Monument was great! The guides took us on a first-person, present-tense account of their lives in the fort. We heard from the French chef, Henri, about how he cooked eight- to twelve-course meals for the "partners" (owners of the companies) and also provided a few scraps for the "low-life" voyageurs. "You know, they are uneducated and have no manners," Henri recounted. Another lady, who tended the skins, allowed Phil to dress the part of a partner and explained the class system, the various types of pelts, and other interesting stories of the time.

Isle Royale is an enigma of a national park to us. It is very remote, a small island, nothing really to see, except wilderness—I thought that's what the

Nature Conservancy protected. We had a nice day there. About a two-and-a-half-hour ferry ride each way, and the "day-trippers" get about three hours on the island. A nice lunch overlooking the bay and a fun nature walk with Ranger Mike and we were back on the boat! There must have been some hard lobbying by Michigan to make this a national park—maybe a "monument," but a full-fledged "park"? We're at a loss.

Grand Marais had been recommended as a great small-town escape—and we agree. A lady at the campground bathroom was lamenting, "No Wal-Mart, no Kmart, and no fast-food restaurants, what's so great about this place?" I told her those exact things were what's great about this place. I don't think she got it!

The Angry Trout—great name!—had been recommended to us as a "must-do." We walked from the campground to town and thoroughly enjoyed this cute little restaurant right on the bay. After a really tough night with mosquitoes in Grand Portage, we were glad to get through the night without many bites! I discovered a "leak" in the screen by Phil's head—duct tape to the rescue, and we were mosquito-free tonight—but I think other things bite here too! A few serious bites from flies have taught me to be wary of everything that flies!

The lighthouse and the whole waterfront here make this a great getaway location. Nice shops, great galleries, and a beach with Adirondack chairs everywhere! We thought we were in New England already!

At the Angry Trout, we had talked with a couple who said Bayfield, Wisconsin, was one of their favorite places. It belongs on everyone's "must-visit" list. We've decided to make this our first "vacation" spot. We need some downtime. Unfortunately, they need a new representative at the visitor center—he would scare the most hardy away, barking orders about what people can and cannot do and what is and is not available. Fortunately, we ignored him.

Ranger Mike intrigues schoolchildren and adults alike with his nature walk at Isle Royale National Park.

Generally, we have found visitor centers to be a great resource to an area, and we knew that lodging here on a weekend was going to be tight. We had even resigned ourselves to traveling away from here and coming back during the week. We managed to secure a room on our own for Sunday through Tuesday, but tonight, Saturday, was a problem. We were still regrouping when the lady from our Sunday-Tuesday reservation tracked us down—thank goodness for caller ID—and said she had a cabin that was being unexpectedly vacated (accident in the family) and would we like it for tonight! What a sweetheart!

We also secured reservations for a few of the neat things to do around here—a fabulous golf course tomorrow, a half-day sail to the Apostle Islands on Monday, and a "fiddle" concert on Tuesday. I thought we were going to just chill here—seems we have a hard time doing that! But Suzi, the owner at the condo/motel, is going to make sure our laundry gets done tomorrow in the motel laundry, can you believe it? She wants to make sure we enjoy our time in Bayfield! Great PR! She wouldn't take any money for doing several loads for us *and* folding it. We left her a little something sweet, but nothing could be as sweet as she was.

Week 11 | Wisconsin

On the morning of our half-day sailboat trip through the Islands, we got to the dock at the appointed hour only to find there had been an overbooking problem. A salesman, who had more clients show up than he had booked, was very apologetic and asked if we could possibly go the next day. We, of course, having nothing else to do, said sure. He then offered to pay for our trip ($90) if we would do that. We assured him that, although this was a kind offer, it wasn't necessary. The next morning, he was right there with the check for our captain. The sailing trip was breathtaking and the weather better than the previous day when we were supposed to go!

The real unexpected treat, however, was Big Top Chautauqua (*sha-TOK-wa*). They have entertainment all summer—under the big top. We opted for fiddler Natalie McMaster. She was *fabulous*! From Cape Breton Island, Nova

Scotia, she has it all. A great fiddling talent, beautiful, witty, entertaining (you should see her jig while she plays!)—the *best* concert I have ever seen, bar none. If you ever get a chance to see her, *run* to get the tickets! We're not particularly fans of that type of music, but the whole show was magnificent! She played, danced, sang, talked, and gyrated for two and a half hours. She must have been falling-down tired but still signed CDs for fans afterward.

A great "time-out" in a wonderful town, but it is time to move on. Green Bay and Lambeau Field beckon. Phil is like a little kid, he is so excited just to see this icon. No home games coming up, so we have to be satisfied with a tour and a look at the Packers Hall of Fame.

It is everything Phil had hoped for. We saw the field, heard the history, sat in the press box and sky boxes, toured the well-done Packer Hall of Fame, and of course, visited the "Pro Shop" for a souvenir! We even went to Bart Starr's Steakhouse for dinner—yum!

Just when you think you've seen the absolute cutest place ever, you find something even more quaint. Door County is all its reputation claims. Surrounded by Green Bay on one side and Lake Michigan on the other, this still mostly rural area oozes charm and class. The Lake Michigan side (Highway 57) is the more laid-back side. Less developed, fewer resorts, but lovely sand beaches, makes for a relaxing time to just explore. The Green Bay side (Highway 42) is the more upscale cousin. Around every bend is another town that is more special than the last. Everything is there from fabulous art galleries to funky shops, from quaint cabins to upscale resorts, from hamburger joints to the finest cuisine, from cherry orchards to cherry pie, from bicycles to paddle-boats. These forty-plus miles of beach-front locale have something for everyone. When was the last time you saw clothes hanging neatly on a clothesline or saw a drive-in movie theater that is still operational and is well-maintained? What a refreshing view of life!

Of course, you have to have a traditional Door County fish boil, complete with the cooking ritual, topped off with homemade cherry pie. It is a not-to-be-missed experience. We chose the White Gull Inn in Fish Creek for our fish boil. They really do a terrific job.

Week 12 | **Wisconsin**

We have finally torn ourselves out of Door County, only because the weather cooled and was cloudy today, or I'm sure we would still be there!

We're sure that many of our friends and family never thought we would make it this long, but we're here to report that this is more fun than we've had since we were kids! Every day is a great adventure and we are learning so much—about history, about people, about culture in our country, and about why everyone sees things so differently around the country.

How do we find the places to go and things to see? We have been very impressed with the tourist booklets that every state and locale puts together. You've just got to be willing to plan on the fly. We would have missed so much if we had developed a rigid plan ahead of time. The other great source of information is the people you meet—locals, tourists, it doesn't matter—as everyone has ideas of what you should see or where you should go. Some of our best tips and educational experiences have come from casual conversation waiting, eating, checking in, grocery shopping, and doing the laundry. Everything is an opportunity to learn something!

We are off to the town of Kohler—as in plumbing fixtures. Around the turn of the century, Mr. Kohler bought a large tract of land three miles from Sheboygan and moved his factory there. As workers' houses started building up willy-nilly, he decided that there needed to be some master planning to keep a nice community feel to the area. He hired a planner from the East, and Kohler became one of the first master-planned cities in the country. It still has a wonderful feel, and the Kohlers continue to direct much of the development today. The Midwest's only five-star resort is in Kohler—the American Club. It is a lovely old building that was originally housing for the immigrants

Look! I got a souvenir from one of my favorite teams at their wonderful visitor center in Green Bay, Wisconsin.

brought over to work in the factory. They lived there, went to school to learn English, and learned their skills there and in the factory. The basement museum has examples of all the products over the years. It is really fun to see some of the stuff from the '40s and '50s. Did you know that the first dishwasher was actually built into a deep sink compartment and was designed and built by Kohler?

By the time we finished looking around the center, a fierce storm had moved in—flood warnings, thunder, lightning, and driving rain. Uh-oh, what do we do now? You could hardly see in front of your face, and the thunder and lightning were really intimidating—very loud and close all around us—and it was raining sideways. Milwaukee is only an hour away—but in this mess? Going back to the Baymont Inn where we stayed last night was an easy decision. By 8 p.m. it was all over, but I think we made a wise choice.

Phil-osophies

People in the Midwest are so friendly! Everywhere we go people extend themselves to you. They are easy to talk to, friendly, have a good sense of humor. We'll see if that holds true when we get to some of the bigger cities like Chicago, Detroit, etc.

Well, you all know by now that the Frank Lloyd Wright House was not meant to be! Phil assures me we *will* get back there. He was such a character, and I love his architectural style. Hopefully, I'll be getting around well enough by the time we come back to see the doctor after Labor Day that we can go back there then. The doctor was wonderful to an old lady who turned her ankle in a hole in the grass trying to get "the perfect picture." A young man who graduated medical school in '92, he is an orthopedic doctor, specializing in hands and feet, with a specialty in sports medicine. I really have a lot of confidence in him. He seemed to have the latest techniques and wanted to try letting my ankle heal without surgery. He said that most breaks of this type will take care of themselves. He said doctors don't like for patients to move around like we need to, but he jumped right in when he heard what we were doing and said we'd figure out a way to make it work. After coming back to make sure it is healing OK, he is sending all my x-rays, his notes, and his action plan with us to give to some unknown doctor down the line. Let's hope it will work!

Right now, we're off to Chicago to explore that city—probably mostly by car!—and to see the Bears play at Soldier Field. We haven't decided whether I'll be able to do that or not; Phil may have to try to sell my ticket there.

Everyone told us it was two and a half to three hours to Chicago—and six hours later we reached our hotel! An accident had us stopped cold for about thirty minutes. But I had a nice conversation with granddaughter Megan, who called while we were stuck in traffic—good timing! Then we didn't factor in Friday traffic (by now the rush hour was starting to develop), and finally, because of all the delays, we were now stuck in traffic going to Soldier Field for the game. Of course, we made reservations at a hotel within walking distance of the field—which certainly seemed logical at the time!

When we got to the hotel, the parking was all in a parking garage that accommodated up to seven-foot-high vehicles—and we're eight-foot-six! Fortunately a $20 bill slipped to the garage attendant allowed us to park in the loading zone in front of the hotel—all night! We weren't sure we'd have a vehicle in the morning. Since we were so much later getting to town, Phil really had to hustle to the game. I got to order dinner from a nearby restaurant that delivered to the hotel. Chinese food and the newspaper made a nice quiet evening with my ankle elevated!

One of the things we wanted to see in Chicago—we dumped the idea of the architectural walking tour!—was the *T. Rex* named Sue that was discovered in South Dakota in the Black Hills in 1990. The Field Museum paid $8.4 million at auction for her from the farmer whose land she was found on. The woman who discovered her, named Sue Hendrickson, hence the name, got nothing out of the deal. Doesn't seem quite fair! She is the largest and most complete *T. Rex* ever found. She is absolutely awesome! Forty-two feet long, twelve feet tall at the hip, and weighed about seven tons alive. Her fossilized bones weigh more than 3,000 pounds. They couldn't mount the actual skull due to its weight. It is displayed separately with a cast head mounted with the rest of the actual skeleton.

We seem to have a hard time in large cities. The traffic is so fast and confusing that we really don't enjoy them like we could. Add to that my new limited mobility and you have a recipe that says, "Get outta town now!" We both agreed we'd come back sometime—fly in, get a downtown hotel, and really see the sites.

Off to Michigan as our week comes to an end. We're anxious to get there, as I'm two days from being out of my hormone pills. There hasn't been a Rite Aid since Idaho. We knew it was going to be close making it from Idaho to Michigan, but we really didn't want to move the prescription to another pharmacy and then try to move it back. Too much chance for a problem. There are Rite Aids most everywhere from here on out. It really is slick—you can get a refill anywhere. Their computer systems are actually networked together, so they can see all your prescriptions, no matter which store you go into! Neat, don't you think?

Week 13 | Michigan

The tall ships were in town in South Haven. It would have been interesting to see them, but it was getting late and we had to find a hotel somewhere. At one point the Wal-Mart parking lot was becoming an option—even with my foot! Once again, Phil's gift of gab paid off. We were about to head for Grand Rapids but decided to stop for gas. The gal in the mini-mart heard Phil's plight and said, "How much do you want to pay for a motel?" Phil told her $50 to $70. She picked up the phone and had a room for us! A decent place that we would never have seen just driving around. Bless her. It was not in the guidebook.

Spent Sunday just lollygaging up the coast. The little town of Manistee was really cute. The whole length of their downtown, about ten to twelve blocks, was lined with petunias along both curbs and the parking strips—really pretty. We are now in Traverse City, and it is time to get the car serviced again. We will visit with some people on Tuesday that we met in the Bahamas last January. It was to be a golfing outing—guess I'll be driving the beer cart! I've got to call and make my doctor appointment back in

Wisconsin tomorrow, and then we can plan our return trip and see what we can fit in between now and then.

Traverse City is another picture-perfect Great Lakes town. Every time we think we've seen "the most perfect town," we find another that also fits the description. Traverse City sits on sparkling Lake Michigan. There is a peninsula that divides Traverse Bay into East and West. Our friends live on the peninsula overlooking East Traverse Bay. What a treat to see them again! She was a real sweetheart and a trooper the next day. We had a real adventure trying to get a handicapped sticker for the van, and she ran us all around town getting the job done. Thanks to her, we can now park in the handicapped zones—it really helps!

The real laugh is that since we were in Michigan, we had to have a Michigan doctor sign the form saying we could have one. The doctor's authorization from Wisconsin was no good. We finally went to an Urgent Care Clinic and got the required signature. I asked the lady at the Secretary of State why it had to be a Michigan doctor since the stickers are good in any state. She had no good explanation for that!

The next day we were off to Mackinac Island. It was another adventure on crutches! We parked right up front at the ferry terminal with our handicapped sticker, and they rather unceremoniously loaded me onto a cargo cart to get on and off the ferry—a very steep ramp! Did I feel silly—but it worked great!

Our friend was right—if you like the smell of horse manure mixed with fudge, you'll love Mackinac Island! Mackinac has no motorized vehicles—except a fire truck, an ambulance, and a utility truck for power, phones, etc. It was very quiet the day we were there. We found it quite pleasant to walk (hobble) around and look at things. We had to take a private carriage to see the island, as the group tours required too many on/off and changes of vehicle. We had a nice old gent who has been working on the island forever and knew all the history of the houses and mansions. If we come back, we would like to stay at the Grand Hotel. The grounds are beautiful and the ambiance is from another era. Coats and ties are still required after 6 p.m.

Friday brought our second-longest travel day of the trip, 302 miles from Mackinaw City to Ann Arbor. Phil is like a little kid. He is so excited about seeing a University of Michigan game in the "Big House" with 110,000 people. We have secured a wheelchair and handicapped seating for the game. We made the drive in about four and a half hours, including lunch! We arrived in a muggy hot Ann Arbor. Even the locals are complaining about how hot it has been!

Game day dawned overcast and muggy. We took the city bus service right from the hotel. The handicapped loading was fast and efficient—they put the ramp out, wheeled me in, strapped me down, and away we went. People were at the stadium to help direct handicapped—they had a lot of seats! All seats were in the end zone, but they were roomy. *Was it hot!* I think half of the 110,000 people were outside the stadium in the shade at any given time! It was a fun time anyway. And Phil got to see a game in the Big House. To him, that was priceless!

Phil-osophies

West Coast sports fans have a huge advantage over their East Coast counter-parts! The Sunday papers here don't have the scores and the blow-by-blow from late games on the West Coast, and if there is a late-afternoon or evening game you want to watch from the West Coast, you'll be up at midnight still seeing the end of it!

Week 14 | Michigan and back to Wisconsin

Have you *ever* seen *all* the handicapped parking spots full? Well, naturally, when I need one at the Henry Ford Museum in Dearborn, they're all full. They had at least twenty of them! Unbelievable! I suppose Labor Day weekend a lot of people were escaping the heat and humidity in this great museum.

If it had wheels and even if it didn't, it is in this tribute to the change that the automobile made to American life, mixed in with some of old Henry's passions. Thomas Edison, his good friend, has a prominent place here, along with such curiosities as the chair that Abraham Lincoln sat in when John Wilkes Booth shot him—complete with blood stains!—and one of the two hundred original copies of the Declaration of Independence. They are the only ones ever made from the original document.

Ford was quite an innovator and businessman. He failed twice before making a go of the auto business, but he just kept believing this was going to be big, and eventually he was right. He was within $200 of being broke the third time when he got his first sale. One of the interesting stories that is documented in the minutes of a board meeting in the 1920s is that Henry was having a difficult time keeping employees due to the difficult working conditions and pay of $5 a day. It was costing Henry a fortune to keep hiring and training employees, many only lasting a few days. The company, by now, was making good money and Henry figured if he shared some of the riches with his employees, they would not only be more loyal, but they would be able to afford the product they were making. So he convinced the board to double their wages to $10 a day. He was right on both counts, and never again did he have trouble keeping employees!

Labor Day was a travel day back toward Sauk City for my Wednesday doctor's appointment. This doctor is great! He is so straightforward, honest, thorough, and personable. He took a bunch of x-rays and didn't like what he saw at first. The "spacing" around the ankle wasn't even. So he recast it and turned the foot in and re-x-rayed it. The space around the bones was now in alignment, so more x-rays in a week, but no surgery will be necessary. Just this lovely green cast for six more weeks! It is going to be a long fall! But I'm getting around on my crutches better, and we have snagged more handicapped seats for the Buckeye game in Columbus, Ohio, in a couple of weeks! Phil likes this, as all the other tickets were sold out!

We called Taliesin—they *will* be giving us a personal tour. We'll be going down there in the morning. Meanwhile, we love Sauk City! I'm going to go get a manicure and pedicure—on one leg, but a toenail-cut and new polish on the casted one! Phil was afraid to try to do it!

I got a pampered afternoon. The girls at the local salon, Allure, were great! I ended up with a mani/pedi and a haircut! I feel like a new woman—and a girl again, not a tomboy! My nails have been a mess! I had given up on them, but Tamara gave them new life—and "Berry Berry Broadway" on my toes and fingers looks fabulous! Even peeking out of the green cast!

Taliesin was wonderful! I was cursing Frank Lloyd Wright a bit for his use of the sandstone on all the walkways and floors. It was beautiful, but uneven is *not* good when you are on crutches. We actually got to go through parts of the house not open to the public because it eliminated many of the level changes. This is a very serene place, and the architectural interest is beyond description. Wright's love of nature and his bringing that into his buildings is very much in evidence here. Some feel this is his greatest work. It was a life-long project that evolved through time and disasters (three fires over the years). The restoration perspective was fascinating. Wright saw this as a lab-oratory project, so he tried many different techniques, some of which have caused nightmares from a maintenance standpoint. The materials he used are very interesting. He was quite poor most of his life, save his vast art col-lections, which he regularly sold off to accomplish other goals. Many of the pieces, both rare and trivial, are still in the house. It was his favorite place to come throughout his life. Most of the materials are scavenged, or quite com-mon, and they were reused as much as possible after the fires. Nonetheless, this is truly a place of uncommon beauty and a wonderful legacy to a man of uncommon talent, not to mention quirkiness!

Oh, and Happy Fiftieth Birthday to my sis tomorrow—September 8. Can't believe it! Hope you have a great party this weekend. We'll be thinking of you!

We did find Moline's shining star, the John Deere Pavilion. Yes, we are hard up for entertainment! Actually, it was pretty interesting. After driving through hundreds of miles of corn and soybean fields, you begin to get curi-ous as to how they plant and harvest all these crops. Tractors, harvesters, specialized equipment, old and new, were all displayed in their trademark bright green. Several people commented that my bright green cast, drab green shorts, and mint green shirt really fit in with the displays!

These crutches are a drag! They were having a street fair, but after stump-ing around the John Deere display, I had no energy for the street fair. It was lunchtime, so I found a comfy bench at the pavilion overlooking the fair, and Phil went foraging for lunch for us!

The end of another week of travel. It has been two weeks, two days since the crutches came into our life. We are off to Ohio, via Springfield, Illinois, and Indianapolis, Indiana.

Chapter 13

There's Nothing Like the Fall

Week 15 | Illinois and Ohio

I had my first driving experience of more than an hour since the accident—I really enjoyed it! I finally felt like I was contributing something, rather than poor Phil doing everything! We are off for Springfield, Illinois, where Abraham Lincoln lived his adult life—for about twenty years—before going to the White House.

There was lots to see, starting with the New Salem Monument outside of town where he lived before getting married. This is where he studied to be a lawyer, got his first political experience, and made his first home. In Springfield are his old law offices, the original state capitol (where the Lincoln-Douglas debates took place), and the home that he and Mary bought for $1,500 and lived in as they raised their family. It was handicapped-accessible (they had wheelchairs to loan, as the site covers several blocks and a number of period homes) and quite interesting.

The most imposing site, though, was Lincoln's tomb on the edge of town. Right in the middle of an otherwise normal cemetery rises this very fitting memorial to one of our greatest presidents. Lincoln's assassination and the loss of her children nearly did Mary in. The last part of her life was lived in unhappiness.

On to Columbus, Ohio, where we are putting down "roots" for about a week. We have a doctor's appointment on Wednesday, the Amish country on Thursday or Friday, a Buckeye game on Saturday, and the Rolling White House gets fixed starting on Monday. We'll go to Cincinnati while that is happening and then off to Akron, where I was born, when we get the rig back. We have lots of errands to be done while we're here, but we'll still try to take in some of the sites. This is a big city of about 700,000, not including the suburbs. Just got back from the Buckeye game. Ohio State won on a beautiful, sunny fall afternoon. We had great seats, down near the field in the corner of the end zone. Phil said handicapped sections are like watching from your own patio, with 96,000 of your closest friends! The game was good, the bands were wonderful, and the cheerleaders—especially Miami of Ohio—were fun to watch.

Phil-osophies

So, you think the roads are bad back home in Washington County? Be thankful! The roads throughout the Midwest and East are horrible. It is because of the constant freeze-thaw in the winter that causes their breakdown, and they are constantly repairing some part of every road! You'll have a mile or two of decent road (last year's repair), several miles of horrible, bumpy road (next year's repair), and then several miles of construction. It seems to be a three- to four-year cycle of constant work everywhere we go. Plus, every major city seems to be building new freeways at breakneck speed. Since they can't pave during the winter, they really hit it hard during this time of year. What a mess! The lanes are narrow and people drive like maniacs. We just try to stay out of their way!

This week really flew by! You can feel fall in the air—cooler nights, leaves rustling around your feet, and bright sunny but cooler days. The doctor's report was good. Probably two more weeks in the cast, and then a removable boot and the beginning of getting back on my feet! Both of them!

We went to the body shop that is doing the van repairs. The parts are still in transit, but they seemed hopeful they would be here when needed. We will give them the van on Monday, and they need it for eight to ten days! Not the three to four that the guy in Wisconsin said. We called the insurance company just to check it out, and we expect to hear from them on Monday. So, needless to say, we have had to alter our plans a bit. It appears we will have a lot more time with our rental car than we thought. We think we will do not only

Cincinnati but also go down into Kentucky and catch the Smoky Mountains, Blue Ridge Parkway, and who knows what else!

Sunday took us to the Amish area. Not as famous as Lancaster, Pennsylvania, but Ohio's Amish area is the largest in the world. One thing none of the literature told us—everything is closed on Sunday! We had a hard time finding a place to eat lunch!

As we headed back toward Columbus, we came upon the Longaberger Basket Company. They make exquisite baskets that get handed down from one generation to the next. This is another quality-run company that is proud to show off their plant, headquarters, and wares. You can even make your own basket under the guidance of the professionals. You just amble on up to the "horse" (the apparatus that holds the basket as it is made) and weave away! Their main sales channel is through "home party" representatives.

We can't believe another week has slipped away. Next week the van gets fixed. It will take over a week due to paint-drying times on the rear door, etc. And we are off in a rental car to see Cincinnati, Kentucky, Eastern Tennessee, a bit of West Virginia, and whatever else we decide along the way! We'll make a loop, ending up back in Columbus. Yes, we know, this isn't on our itinerary this fall, and it will really foul up those mileage estimates for the contest, but what's a mother to do?

Week 16 | Cincinnati, Ohio, and Kentucky

Cincinnati is where my mom spent much of her early adult life, and she has fond memories of this place and that time. It is now a large metropolitan city, about the size of Portland with 360,000 people. We'll be off to see some of her memories today and record on film what we can of the old and the new. We are staying across the Ohio River in Covington, Kentucky, with a nice view of the city.

This is Olympic Games time, and we have been thoroughly enjoying watching them in the evenings. Even though they are tape-delayed, we are so busy during the day that we don't hear what is going on. It seems live to us!

Cincy—the "Pigopolis," so named from their early reputation as a major meat-packing and -processing city—is right on the Ohio River. Just as St. Paul has their cute Snoopys all over town and Chicago has their cows, Cincinnati has their pigs. They are cute and theme-appropriate for their various locations. They have even crossed the river into Covington, Kentucky, a part of the metro area.

Cincinnati reminds us a lot of Portland. The city is bounded by hills and the river. The skyscrapers nestle in a small area, and the center of town has a block-size square where things are "happening." Many bridges cross the river, and parks abound around town. The two big contrasts both have to do with cars. They lack any type of mass transit, other than a trolley that runs around the downtown and nearby Covington and Newport and some buses. There is no transit mall, no light rail, no subway, no planning. As a result, freeways and gridlock abound everywhere. For a city similar in size to Portland, they have many more freeways running everywhere and more under construction. We need to be thankful for what planning and light rail has done for Portland.

Downtown we saw Fountain Square and enjoyed a yummy lunch, soaking up the fall sunshine, watching the people go by. Phil wandered off—he does that a lot now with my limited mobility—and ambled into a men's store. What else with his years as a men's clothier! He was shocked to see his old vendor Nick Freeman, of H. Freeman Clothiers, doing a trunk show! They had a good chat, and Nick had to tell everyone in the store about Phil's store and his fishing flies in the lapels. Everyone seems to remember that about Phillip Stewart! Phil and I have a running joke that no matter where we travel in the world, we *always* run into someone that he knows—without fail. We had commented a month or so ago that he hadn't run into anyone yet. We wondered how much longer it would take.

Oh, I've forgotten to mention this jazzy little car that Enterprise gave us. It is a fire-engine red Grand Prix with dual exhaust. This baby moves—talk about a contrast from the van! This thing is like driving a go-cart!

Little did we know what we were in for on our short drive to Louisville. I'm now convinced we don't know what rain is in Oregon! We had to pull off the freeway just south of town and wait for the storm to pass. We absolutely could not see, and the trucks were still barreling down the highway at 65 mph. It was too scary for us in our go-cart! After pulling off the road for a while, the drive was sunny and beautiful all the way into town. But a storm warning was posted for Louisville for the evening, and sure enough, a big old thunderstorm rolled through for about twenty minutes. There was no damage here, but three dead and a hundred-plus injured up in Ohio, right where we just came from! Our luck with the weather has been something else.

Horse Country. We have arrived. Churchill Downs, horse farms, and antebellum mansions. Louisville is a charming city too. We decided to use our day here to see the home of the Kentucky Derby and the home of Louisville Slugger bats. Neither attraction disappointed. The museums attached to both were extremely well done.

The walking—or in my case, the wheelchair—tour of Churchill Downs was almost like being there for the race. You could feel the pageantry and excitement in the air.

The bat factory was really interesting—I know you all think we have a very weird taste in what we enjoy seeing! They make only wood bats here—all Louisville Slugger brand. The production has gone from seven million a year to 600,000 a year since the advent of the aluminum bat. They still make 75 percent of all the wooden bats and provide bats for most of the major-league players. You can try hitting a ball "pitched" at the speed of a major-league pitcher!

We picked a back road through the bluegrass horse country to Lexington. Here we find such luxury, such beauty, and such wealth. It has a historic downtown that has been thoughtfully preserved. Friendly people, a caring community, and lots to see make Lexington one of our favorite cities so far. Lexington is about the same size as Louisville, but it has the feel of a town rather than a big city.

The arts are alive and well in Lexington. There is a lot of unimaginable wealth in the area, so fund-raisers and nonprofit endeavors are everywhere. They even have

These two "old mares" put out to pasture at Churchill Downs in Louisville, Kentucky—one four-legged; one an incapacitated, two-legged type!

a nonprofit racetrack! Keeneland is beautiful, and all the profits go to charity. They also don't believe in gambling. You'll see no casinos in this area—also no billboards. They do have a curious distinction between "gambling" and "betting." You see, betting on the horses is not gambling. It is a gentleman's sport, like golf or polo.

The next morning, we were off for a tour of the horse farms and Keeneland Racetrack. We were lucky enough to witness the end of a three-day horse auction of yearlings. What beautiful animals! These farms are incredible. The barns look like houses and are cleaner than most homes! They spend well over $1 million on a barn that will hold ten to twenty horses. They have huge stalls, climate-controlled birthing stalls, chandeliers, and special rubberized floors that are easy on the horses' feet. A farm will typically have several of these "barns." With barns of this caliber, you can imagine what the houses look like!

Keeneland Race Track has a much more intimate feel than Churchill Downs. Ivy-covered stone walls, small courtyards, and beautiful trees and flowers characterize this setting. They race only about fifteen days in the spring and fall. The rest of the time it is a country club for the three hundred owners, whose stock in the track is handed down from one generation to the next. There are no stock dividends, and all profits go to charity. How lovely!

Week 17 | Great Smoky Mountains and Ohio

Over the Cumberland Gap, you actually don't go over it anymore, you go through it—in a shiny new tunnel. They want to return the actual Gap to the way it was in Daniel Boone's day and make it a wilderness trail once again.

Off to the Great Smoky Mountains. We went through Gatlinburg. I should have known this is the most visited of all the national parks—over 60,000 cars per day during the summer! All the way from I-40 to the park is like a three-ring circus. You can't believe all the motels, restaurants, tacky shops, amusement parks, and theaters with live music stretching for twenty-eight miles to the park. This is middle America at its worst!

Today is a cloudy, rainy day, which really dampens the beauty of the mountains. Most of the time you couldn't even see them! The trees are starting to turn, and when we could see, the view was breathtaking. Another couple of weeks and this range will be ablaze. We didn't even go to Cades Cove or Clingman's Dome, as there was nothing to see but clouds! This is really the first time on the whole trip that weather has spoiled an activity.

On to Asheville. I finally got to drive the hot rod. Phil had had enough. We've driven almost 1,000 miles since Columbus, and he has driven all of it! Heavy fog, rain, and a winding road with lots of tunnels made this stretch challenging.

Asheville, North Carolina, is a town of 60,000 that looks like 100,000 or more. We've tucked into a motel near the Biltmore Estate, which we will explore tomorrow.

It's the largest private residence in the United States, built by George Washington Vanderbilt in the 1890s. A lot of the mansion has been restored and is open for viewing, but much of it has yet to be done. There are thirty-four bedrooms, forty-three bathrooms (all with hot and cold water, as original), an indoor pool, an all-glass-roofed garden room, a pipe organ, a bachelor wing, a dining room that seats sixty-five, and so much priceless artwork—especially tapestries—that you can't take it all in. They have a good tape-guided self-tour that lets you enjoy each room to its fullest. The grounds still comprise hundreds of acres, but originally there were many thousand. The beautiful formal gardens (even now between seasons), a massive greenhouse, a winery, stables, and a new hotel with two-hundred-plus rooms are all worthy of exploration. The restaurant is housed in the stables adjoining the house through the portico. A totally pleasant room where you actually sit in what were the stalls in cozy booths, or at more spacious tables for groups.

Talk about a confusing town to live in! Bristol is in both Tennessee and Virginia. There is actually a line running down the middle of Main Street that separates the two states. They have different laws, different licensing, and two local governments. What a strange deal! We found a Super 8 on the Virginia side and collapsed.

Today we are off for one of the highlights of the trip, The Greenbrier in White Sulphur Springs, West Virginia. I have read about it in many magazines as being a most gentile, fabulous place. If we could secure a room, we knew the tab would be steep, but hopefully, it would live up to The Green-brier reputation. From the Super 8 to the super deluxe, we were not disap-pointed. Phil was almost hoping we couldn't stay. It was so elegant, and we looked like bums!

The young man at the desk, though, wasn't going to let him go. He wanted us to come back when we could stay and golf the three championship courses and enjoy every amenity you can imagine. He wanted to make sure we got to "taste" The Greenbrier for just tonight. I'm sure the staff/guest ratio is at least one-to-one. He found us a small suite for the price of a basic room. This place had his-and-hers closets, one and a half baths, a dining area, and a spacious size overall. He got us dinner reservations—it is a "meals included" tab, and all gratuities are included in the $22 per person "service fee"—and directed us with a few ideas of what to do.

You only have to be there for a few minutes before you feel like you've been there forever. Everyone seems to know your name and wants to make sure that your every need is answered—and some you didn't think of! The place is spectacular. Like the Biltmore, the gardens were spectacular and immaculately groomed, but you could stay here, unlike the Biltmore. Croquet courts, falconry, equestrian, tennis, a wonderful spa, outdoor pool, and deluxe shops make up just a few of the things to do.

Our favorite thing, however, was the coat-and-tie-required in all public areas after 6:30 p.m. It lends an air of civility to everything that is without compare. The dining room had piano and violin music, and dancing was available—for those with two good legs!—in several venues. The drinks were strong, the service impeccable, the food to die for.

Although Phil had a hard time making the transition from the Super 8, once he got into the swing of things, I almost couldn't drag him out the next day! The tab for one night in this little piece of Southern Heaven? Count out six big ones and leave with fabulous memories and a vow to return.

Friday was a great day! The van looks fantastic, and my cast has come off! The doctor x-rayed, poked, turned, had me walk, and pronounced he was progressing me directly to the plastic aircast, bypassing the boot step! Crutches—just as long as I feel I need them—and a bunch of exercises to get the mobility back. The foot is hard and still swollen, but he assures me that the proper rehab work will get rid of that. Find another doctor in about a month for a check, and I should be on my way back to normal! You can't imagine how wonderful it is to be on two feet again! Even if it is somewhat slow going. I have actually done some short walks without the crutches already. The aircast really supports it well.

Finally, we are getting out of Columbus! It feels like we have been here for a month! We are headed toward Canton and Akron for the weekend.

The Pro Football Hall of Fame was calling Phil's name. We had to make a pilgrimage there. They were having a big anniversary promo—half-price admission, discounts at the gift shop, a free disposable camera and "grab bag" gift for everyone—and interesting exhibits. Phil was in heaven. I tagged along on my new foot and crutches "assist" but found I wasn't quite as strong as I thought! Part way through, we had to call for a wheelchair—my foot had had it!

Sunday was the trip down memory lane—a visit to where I was born. It was too weird! We found the house and I was taking pictures (we knew the people weren't home—no lights, and the paper was still on the porch) when I struck up a conversation with the neighbor. I told him I had lived there from '47 to '53. He said, "Balzhiser, you must be Carol!" *Can you believe it!* He was born the same year as me and is still living in the same house. He'd bought it from his parents!

Phil celebrates a great fall afternoon at one of his highlights of the trip in Canton, Ohio.

From there, we were off to the Rock and Roll Hall of Fame in Cleveland. It has all kinds of memorabilia, great music, and a wonderful group of displays detailing the development of rock and roll—everything from the gospel influence, to the blues, to country, to Motown, to England, and right on through the decades, including grunge and hip-hop, which aren't *really* rock and roll in my mind! We closed the place down!

Week 18 | Upstate New York and New Hampshire

Finally, we are out of the state of Ohio. I thought we were going to be there forever! It felt like we were in a whirlpool, waiting to be spit out! We briefly hurled through Pennsylvania on our way to upstate New York. Of course our first stop had to be Niagara Falls. It is kind of a grimy little town everywhere except right at the Falls area. Had we known, we definitely would have stayed on the Canadian side. I think the exchange rate has killed the American-side tourist trade. All the nice hotels and the best views are from the Canadian side. Each time you cross the border, though, they get you for $2.50! And it is all like one big town!

We managed to bypass all the hawkers of "tours"—they were every-where—and went straight to the state park on the American side of the Falls. They have a nice visitor center and all kinds of choices in ways to see the Falls. One warning: Don't bother with your Visa card here. They only take cash! And they charge for everything: parking, $5; elevator, $1; lunch, $12; people mover to the Falls, $4.50 each; *Maid of the Mist*, $17 for two—oops, we only had $15 cash left, but smooth-talking Phil got us in for our measly $15! I don't know how he does it!

The real highlight, though, was the *Maid of the Mist*. You have to do that! It takes you right up to the base of the falls, thundering 1.5 million cubic feet of water per second. The power is awesome! That tug must have some power just to hold the boat there while the mist gets all over everyone in their bright-blue souvenir rain suits, flashing their point-and-shoot cameras into that massive wall of mist! It was an incredible experience that you can't imagine just standing on the shore.

Our first camping evening in almost six weeks. The fall colors have arrived in New York, and we were enjoying every turn with new landscapes to thrill the eyes. We pulled into a nice park in the Lakes region and got hooked up. It took some time, and we were laughing at how much we had forgotten in just six weeks! We used to be able to do this in less than ten minutes!

Now here is an episode that had us rolling on the floor. The space we were assigned didn't have a water hookup, so we decided to move to the space next to us. There was hardly anyone in the whole park. Since we had the electric cord already hooked up and had the water ready to be hooked up, Phil said, "Just leave them. I'll handle the connections while you maneuver the van." About this time, two couples—from Roseburg, Oregon!—happened by on their evening walk and inquired of Phil, as he is holding onto the two cables connected to the van and as I am moving it along the road, "Are you out walking your van this evening?!" I swear, this is true! We should have replied, "Yes, but we have to keep it on a very short leash!" but we were laughing too hard. Had a nice conversation with them about "home." I think they finally decided we weren't fools.

Phil-osophies

Wouldn't you just know it! I have supported and followed those darn Ducks, Beavers, and PSU Vikings, too. They've broken my heart—all of them— time after time, season after season. So what happens? Of course, the year I leave town and can't even watch them on TV most of the time, and they are all *nationally ranked! If they show one of their games here in the East, it starts at 10:30 p.m. or so—and I'm asleep before the first quarter is over! It just isn't fair.*

We're off to New Hampshire, through the mountains and all the fall foliage. The eyes can only absorb so much over many days. We had a lot of rain and moments of beautiful sunshine. The patchwork quilt of colors from scarlet to burgundy, from sunshine yellow to brilliant orange, from dark umber to light tan, from mint green to dark forest green made for an afternoon of mouth-gaping views. The white bark of the birch trees lined the quilt with random threads amongst the color. Nothing in the West comes anywhere close to these views.

We caught up with a friend from home in the White Mountains of New Hampshire. We saw a lot of the sights we had been told about—Franconia Notch, the Old Man of the Mountain, Mount Washington, the Mount Washington Hotel—really a neat restoration, another one of those great steps back in time—with the beautiful fall foliage in the background.

Week 19 | Maine, Boston, and the Cape

Even though it is the middle of October, the popular destinations are still full on the weekends. We headed into Maine and the Acadia National Park area on a weekend, and we couldn't find housing within fifty miles of the popular areas (Bar Harbor, Ellsworth, etc.), so we stopped at Bangor before we got into a problem. Once again, the visitor-center people were very helpful in giving us current, up-to-date information. We were calling motels as we drove along. Even Bangor was very full. We found a place with the two rooms we needed— our friend was with us too, remember! We asked directions and the very exit we needed was directly in front of us. We couldn't believe it, nor could the lady at the motel! Once again, we fell into a good solution right in front of us.

The weekend was beautiful. The fall colors still magnificent. Acadia National Park is absolutely wondrous! It has it all. It has wilderness, glorious views, water, and landscapes of beauty. The weather turned cold, quickly, as we reached Cadillac Mountain, the highest point in the park, and it actually descended freezing rain upon us. We took a few pictures and headed for lower ground!

Portland, Maine, was waiting for us, but it was several hours away. We enjoyed being in "Portland" again, but we were off for Boston. After a huge backup at the toll booth (all the "leaf peepers" were heading back to the city after the big Columbus Day weekend—what a mess!), we arrived in the heart of Boston's Brookline area. It was a wonderful haven from which to explore a great city.

You can really see what the newscasters are talking about. The further south we went, the less the color. The Boston area was not yet in "full color," but it was in "full traffic nightmares"! They have this thing called the "Big Dig" going on, where they are redoing all the downtown freeways and redoing some of the subway system. Streets stop mid-block, signs lead to nowhere, lane directions change on a whim, and confused people are coping with the locals who whiz in and out with little regard to the confusion.

Nonetheless, Boston is still a great city. The brownstones of the Back Bay, the sparkling water everywhere you turn, a world-class public-transportation system (the T), wonderful downtown parks, historic preservation side-by-side with modern buildings, great shopping, and delicious food of every possible type make this an incredible place to visit. We had a hard time choosing between Italian and the ever-present seafood!

Phil had never seen many of the historic locations in Boston (Eric: Remember when we walked the Freedom Trail?), so we decided to brave the traffic again. We were spinning around down there in hysterics—remember, this is in the middle of the Big Dig—windows open waving people down to ask where we were, wrong way on one-ways, through red lights, through stop signs, our friend finally blowing kisses to motorists to let us across three lanes of traffic! But we eventually saw lots of things and ended in the North End with a parking space right in the heart of the area. My parking karma came through again!

We had had enough of the crazy city and headed for Cape Cod for a few days. We decided that Hyannis was a good central location to work from and went on the hunt for a great motel value now that the off-season was here. How about $39 a night with indoor and outdoor pools, a whirlpool for my ankle, right in downtown Hyannis, continental breakfast, and a nice clean well-decorated room! Not to mention we had sunny weather in the 70s!

We were there three days and the weather was so spectacular you can't believe it. One day we headed for the beach just to hang out in the sun. We even braved the water! We had a fun Italian picnic in the sand and just absorbed those last rays of summer—*mmmmmmmmm!*

The three of us spent a whole day out at Nantucket. We flew there, fifteen minutes versus one and a half hours on the ferry! There were such great views on such a beautiful day. Strict architectural controls make the whole island very homogeneous in look. The day couldn't be beat. We grabbed a great sandwich and headed, on foot, to the nearest beach. My ankle held up pretty well, about a half mile each way. We sat on the dock and talked to the locals, basked in the sun, and enjoyed the beautiful views. We had a great discussion with "the man with the big balls"! He owns and rents out buoys that the boats tie up to in the harbor in the summer. They have to be removed in the fall, as the harbor ices over and would drag the buoys out to sea. He has a barge with a hoist on it to grab them out of the water. Fascinating guy.

Week 20 | **Massachusetts and Rhode Island**

The Minutemen marching across Lexington Green to meet the Red Coats. Paul Revere riding out from Boston to warn the troops. The march on the North Bridge—and the shot heard 'round the world. "Do not fire unless fired upon, but if they intend to have war, let it begin here."

And with those skirmishes in April of 1875, the Revolutionary War had begun, and it would last for eight long years, as the young settlers fought for, first, representation in England—remember "Taxation without representation"—and later for their independence. Even after independence was declared on July 4, 1776, that was far from the end of the conflict. Many did not want independence—only representation.

Walking around Lexington and Concord and through the Minuteman National Historic Site really makes it all come alive. The actual locations and many of the buildings are well-preserved or restored. The Minutemen were much like our National Guard. They trained in each town and stood at the ready "in a minute" but were not part of the regular Army.

We had missed Plymouth, so we headed back over to the coast to see where the Pilgrims landed. Plymouth Rock was a major disappointment—just a puny little rock with "1620" on it, encased in a monument. It could be any rock! We did enjoy the town of Plymouth, though, and rode the narrated trolley to see all the sites around town. The highlight was the Plimoth (original spelling) Plantation. It is a reconstruction of how it was in 1627, with character actors in role. They will talk to you about anything from 1627—but don't ask them about anything after that—'cause they don't know! The dialects, the houses, the problems they had, their politics, cooking, keeping house, and so forth, were all demonstrated in good detail.

We had wanted to go to Martha's Vineyard while on the Cape, but we ran out of time. So we decided, heck, the weather is improving, let's go back there. The next morning dawned rainy, but soon it stopped and we enjoyed a cloudy but comfortable day at the Vineyard. It was very different from Nantucket—more eclectic, not so perfect and homogeneous. Lots of wealth here also. It was more developed—six towns—and offered more things to see.

We took a really fun, funky island tour on an old pink school bus. Our guide was a fun young guy, whom we could actually understand, unlike our Nantucket guide!

Heading for state number twenty-eight, Rhode Island. It was a short trip from the Cape into Providence. It's hard to get adjusted to these small states! Blink and you could miss a whole state! Rhode Island is only forty-eight miles long and thirty-seven miles wide! It is time for van service again. We need an oil change and transmission service—every 12,000 miles on the transmission seems a bit much, but our weight must be tough on it! The Dodge dealer down in Newport could take us, so we headed there after visiting the AAA office in Providence to make arrangements to take the train to Washington D.C. next weekend to see family—son and daughter-in-law Eric and Kristen, and granddaughter Megan. We are really looking forward to seeing them!

We love Rhode Island! The weather has been gorgeous, which helps, but this state is really pretty. Lots of rocky outcroppings and lots of water everywhere. Newport is really a classy—and expensive—town. Weather is in the 70s with a good wind. We had to go sailing! We went out on a 72-foot schooner—and did it move! Lots of wind in her sails—we were clipping along at about eighteen knots—heeled over and moving! What a glorious afternoon!

The Guilded Age of the late 1800s. The Vanderbilts, the Astors, the Morgans, and others—what a time that must have been. Newport has more "cottages" of that era than most any place. These were fabulous mansions that were just summer cottages for the rich and famous. Many are now museums, but many are still in private ownership. We bought a multi-mansion ticket and saw a couple one day and had to go back the next to see the rest. The opulence is just mind-boggling. The parties these places have seen! It is a lifestyle I can't even begin to relate to.

We loved Newport—one of our favorite places, so far. But we did have to move on—we have to be ready for the doctor again on Thursday in Stamford, Connecticut, and the train early on Friday to go see Eric and Kristen and Megan! Much more to see between now and then. Fortunately these states are small and the distances between things small. Off to Mystic, Connecticut, for tomorrow. Pizza anyone?

Week 21 | Connecticut

We've got to do some modification to our "normal" schedule. It's getting dark earlier, and we don't like to travel in the dark when we don't know where we're going—it's bad enough in the daylight! Arrived in Mystic in the dark and fell into the nearest motel that looked reasonable. We'll see the town earlier tomorrow and move on during the daylight! Guess we can't fiddle around in the morning until noon.

We just can't get over how breathtaking the scenery is here. Whether we are on the freeway or in a little town along the water, the views are captivating. Wonderful rock formations, water that glistens like diamonds, leaves of every color—it makes just driving along a sensual pleasure. Add a little "oldies" on the radio and you have a perfect day! Of course, the sunshine and 70-degree days don't hurt either.

Mystic is everything I remember from the Julia Roberts movie. There are boats, old and new, large and small, everywhere, a crowded, darling downtown—and of course, Mystic Pizza. We've got to go there for lunch! "A little slice of heaven"—it was indeed that, and movie pictures and articles don the walls. Walked along and just enjoyed yet another glorious fall day—rigging on the boats slapping in the gentle breeze, people laughing and calling to each other along the sidewalks. Everyone seemed glad that the tourists had finally left and they could once again enjoy their Mystic town on the bay.

We enjoyed a beautiful fall afternoon in Mystic, Connecticut, where Julia Roberts filmed her breakout movie Mystic Pizza.

We had a hankering for a late-season ice-cream cone and wandered into the Bridge Ice Cream parlor, right at the edge of the bridge, and had the most awesome homemade ice cream you'll ever taste. Maybe because we do that so seldom, it always tastes so good!

Headed out for Springfield, Massachusetts, on one of Connecticut's scenic byways—

Route 169. It was a great afternoon drive. We had a real heart-stopper, as a clueless driver almost pulled out right into us. How could you possibly miss the Rolling White House coming down the road? He slammed on his brakes, I swerved, and disaster was avoided by inches! Where is the darn horn on this thing? Couldn't find it when I really needed it!

Phil-osophies

As a basketball player myself all these years, I couldn't pass up the chance to see the Basketball Hall of Fame. Great memorabilia from all the college and pro greats. The Hall of Fame is located in Springfield, because that is where basketball was invented as a winter activity when the kids couldn't play outside.

They are building a much-needed new Hall of Fame next door to open in 2001. For one of the richest sports in history, the existing building and the exhibits were pretty tired-looking and in need of a new facility, even though I had great memories looking at everything.

Looked like a long way on the map from Springfield to our next destination, Stamford, Connecticut, down on the coast. Less than two hours and we were there. About the time we get used to these little states, we'll be back in the big ones! We'll stay here until Friday morning, when we'll be up early, on the train before eight o'clock and headed for Washington D.C. to see the family.

Did our usual "slow-down" activities—laundry, pictures developed, needed odds and ends, and another doctor appointment. He says the ankle is "ahead of schedule"; the flexibility I have regained through diligent exercise has paid off, and I need to wean myself from the aircast and get on with life! Good news again! Full strength won't be back for another four months or so, but I can start golfing, biking, rowing, and so on, within the next month. Another couple of months and I can do impact and lateral movement activities—tennis, jogging, etc. Anybody need a pair of crutches?

One day we went to Westport, Connecticut, to see the house Phil lived in when he was six, in 1948. He knew it was on King's Highway and that the owner's name was Chapman, but he couldn't remember where it was. A man we were talking to in Eddie Bauer suggested we go to the town clerk at city hall and look at the records. We found a mortgage deed from when Mr. and Mrs. Chapman bought the house that had the legal description on it. From that, the records clerk helped us narrow down where it was. Map in hand, we were off to find the house.

Phil recognized it right away as we drove along. Being his normal shy self, he pulled into the driveway, walked up to the door, introduced himself and his story, and made an instant friend. We thoroughly enjoyed meeting the family and hearing what they knew about the house, and they enjoyed Phil's memories of it.

Off to Washington D.C. tomorrow and stopping in New York City for several days on the way back—including Halloween. That should be a treat! We're not taking the PC on the train, so we'll be out of touch for a week or so!

Week 22 | Washington D.C.

What a great week! It was nice to not have "the shell on our back"! We left the Rolling White House in Connecticut and turned to other forms of transportation—trains, subways, city buses, tour buses, cabs, feet, and ferries! Sometimes I was looking pretty longingly at those new racy scooters zipping around! Even with my trusty "aircast" on, my ankle still needed ice many nights. We walked our feet off in two great cities!

Fantastic fall weather greeted us at Union Station in Washington D.C. The train station has been redone, and it is worth a trip to just gaze around. You can tell that this was once a very elegant mode of transportation.

My son Eric gave me specific instructions on where to meet them. I had a "senior moment," and we ended up at the Museum of American Art instead of the Museum of American History. A mistake anyone could make, right? Not only were they not there—surprise—but the museum was closed for renovation. Thank goodness for cell phones! A second attempt yielded better results, and we had a great afternoon at the museum—gowns of the first ladies (granddaughter Megan and I oohed and aahed), war stuff (Eric's favorite), and things from every generation of our history. Hunger struck and we found a fun Irish pub and had "black and tans" (half Guinness and half

Bass Ale; they actually stay separated—something about different specific weights, per Eric) along with our dinner.

The next day we got tickets for one of the "hop on, hop off" tour buses and started our trek around the town. All the monuments—Washington, Jefferson, Lincoln, and Vietnam. At Arlington, we saw the Kennedy graves, the changing of the guard and a special wreath ceremony at the Tomb of the Unknowns, and the Robert E. Lee estate from which Arlington was created as an embarrassment to General Lee (laying the dead at his "feet"). Eric and Phil hiked to the Iwo Jima statue just outside the cemetery.

The subway system here is fabulous, clean, bright, safe, well-marked, fast, frequent, and reasonably priced. We really enjoyed using it. Hotels are expensive, and the room taxes are almost 15 percent extra! Weekends are cheaper than during the week.

Back on the train for New York City! We definitely need more time here, so we will come back as we drive through the area in a couple of weeks.

The Big Apple! What a crazy place! So much activity, so many people. But I can see why people love living here. There is so much to do and see. We stayed at the New York Athletic Club, a reciprocal club with our home club, the Multnomah Athletic Club.

We had decided we wanted to try to see *Regis Live!* while we were there, so we got up early to "stand by." I had gotten the info from the Web that they started taking standbys at 8:30, but you needed to get in line earlier. So we were out of the hotel in the nippy morning air to 67th and Columbus, ABC, at 7:15 a.m. We were numbers 25 and 26. Naturally, they took up to number 24 that day! They gave us tickets for Wednesday, which was some consolation, but we were whining to the gals there, so suddenly they produced two tickets to *The View!* That had been our first choice, but tickets appeared hard to come by according to the Web—plan on waiting six-plus weeks! We were thrilled, so off we went to get some coffee and find the studio a few blocks away. Indeed, people in that line had been waiting a long time for their tickets. Another coup!

Broadway Theater was also part of our plan, so we lined up for the "cheap tickets" at Times Square starting at three o'clock each day for that evening's productions. Most are half-price, and we had great seats! We saw *Fosse* and *Swing*—both are dance musicals and both were fantastic. Such energy and style! For *Swing*, we were only about six or seven rows back, in the center. We could almost feel the sweat! For *Fosse*, we were a little to one side, but still they were great tickets. This is another "cash only" deal. Fortunately, there is a very busy ATM close-by.

Halloween in New York City! They really get into this holiday in the East. Houses everywhere have been decorated, elaborately, for weeks. It has been really fun to see them all over the Northeast. New York is, of course, crazy all the time, but Halloween gives them the opportunity to be really nutty! Greenwich Village has a big parade in the evening. We watched it on TV, as we were off to the theater.

Speaking of parades, we were there for the New York Yankee victory parade. As the winner of the World Series, they got to enjoy a full-blown "ticker-tape" parade. People began gathering early in the morning—very early!—for the 10 a.m. parade. Kids skipped school (at the urging of Mayor Rudy Guiliano—can you believe that!), commuters detoured for a late work start, the buses were packed. Everyone wanted to be there, and they were. We watched from several locations during the day.

It was the best weather of our three days in New York for our ride out to the Statue. No rain while we were there, but very cold and windy, except for this day. It was fairly warm, sunny most of the time, but definitely fall; brisk air and leaves swirling around us everywhere—better than garbage, which is what I remember from my last trip here! Actually, we thought the city was cleaner and friendlier than twenty years ago. People actually stopped and asked us on a couple of occasions if they could help us find something!

We got back to Stamford on the train on Wednesday night, wondering how our meager duffel bags could have gotten three times as heavy, and we didn't buy anything! And oh, my poor ankle! We were really tired. In fact, we spent the whole next day just recuperating. We didn't leave our motel until 2 p.m., and that was only because we were starving!

Another week almost gone, and we're off for New Jersey and Pennsylvania. For the first time on the trip, we haven't even looked at the map or thought about what we want to do next—we were so busy in New York. I guess we'll make it up as we go along!

Week 23 | New Jersey and Pennsylvania

New Jersey—what's to see there? A couple of battlefields near Morristown, and Atlantic City, but we're not gamblers, so that doesn't have a lot of appeal. We did get off the interstate and drove through some of the small towns between Morristown and Bedminster on our way to Princeton. Lovely estates and nice towns all along Route 202.

We got caught in Friday-evening traffic on 202/206—what a pain! Naturally it was dark when we got to Princeton, and we were all spun around trying to find the motel area. A little frustration on both of our parts! We ended up at the Novatel, a European chain that provided us a wonderful room for $80 in a city of $100-plus hotels! You could really feel the European influence in the rooms and lobby. It was one of the nicest places we've stayed for the money. We enjoyed having room service and watching the Louis Ruykeyser special at Carnegie Hall. Most places we stay, there is no restaurant, so this was a treat.

We had to spend a little time exploring Princeton. It's a charming, upscale town of 12,000, and the campus runs right along the downtown area. It was game day, so most people were there and the downtown was pretty empty, just no place to park—thank goodness for the "handicapped" sticker. We're going to miss that starting next month!

Decided that the Philadelphia area had lots to see, so we headed for King of Prussia, which seemed to be pretty central to all the things we wanted to see. We've checked into an Apple Inn, near a huge shopping center, and plan to use this as a base for the next several days as we do the battlefields and downtown Philly.

We loved Philly! Not only does it have so much history from the American Revolution, it has done a good job of integrating the modern alongside the history. It does seem a little bizarre to cross several blocks of cobblestones as you enter the freeway, but it holds speeding down! The Independence

National Historic Park contains the Liberty Bell, Constitution Hall, and many other historic buildings, most still intact from the late 1700s! In Independence Hall, you can see the actual room where Washington was appointed commander in chief of the Continental Army and where the Declaration of Independence was adopted and the Constitution was drafted. You can almost see George sitting in his chair (the original), cajoling his fellow citizens into compromise, as he presided over the constitutional convention.

Until the new pavilion is completed, you can still touch the actual Liberty Bell. It is in very poor condition and people touching it is making it worse, so they are moving it to a new hall and removing it from the reach of people. Kind of too bad, but future generations need to be able to see this symbol of our independence.

Again, we took advantage of the "hop on, hop off" trolley tour and saw all the sights around town including the only U.S. Post Office not to fly the American flag. Because it is in the historic district from before we had our current flag, they can't fly it! The "B. Free" Franklin Post Office from the 1760s! Good bit of trivia!

On leaving downtown, we decided we would try to find "The Main Line" area, Philly's society area of wonderful homes. We had some vague instructions on where it was. We were enjoying our ride through Fairmount Park and saw a sign to one of the mansions, so thinking we were in the right area, we took the next exit. Within three blocks, we were in the worst ghetto you can imagine. It was scary! Lots of one-way streets, thugs everywhere, and we were running out of light! Yikes! All we wanted to do was to get out of there—*fast!* Fortunately we found a main street and just headed in the general direction we had come from! In about ten minutes we found our way out! *Whew!*

We couldn't leave Philly without a pilgrimage to the home of the Philly steak sandwich at 9th and Passyunk, Pat's Famous Philly Steaks. It is right near downtown and on the edge of the Italian section and on the narrowest street you can imagine, people parking everywhere to walk up to the take-out counter. Then there is Geno's across the street, the competition, also attracting a large lunchtime crowd. Quite a scene. The drive through the Italian section as we headed for the freeway was something. Vegetable stands, boxes, crates, garbage, trinket shops, and bakeries lining the street to the point where you almost couldn't navigate the roadway! A lively atmosphere to say the least! Oh, the Philly steaks? *Yum!*

We had a tip that we needed to head for Cape May, then on to Atlantic City. Cape May is at the very southern tip of New Jersey, and it's a quaint, Victorian-era town that was also a favorite, along with Newport, Rhode Island, of the East Coast socialites. We found a wonderful oceanfront location with a balcony with rocking chairs to watch the sunset. Yes, I know the sun sets in the west, and you face east on the Atlantic Ocean, but Cape May is at the southern tip of the state, and you can actually see the sun set also. It was one of the most spectacular we have seen—red, red fireball, followed by crimson clouds.

Election Night 2000 in Cape May—we stayed up until almost midnight. What a roller-coaster, and we still don't know the outcome. Phil and I feel really weird. Neither of us has missed an election for many decades. We were hoping our ballots would be forwarded to Andrea along with our other mail, but, alas, it didn't happen. The first all-mail Oregon election in history and we missed it. Some say we were lucky, as the Oregon ballot was massive!

We took the scenic route to Atlantic City, through lots of small towns on tiny spits of land and along the coast with lots of wetlands. We ran into our first detour due to the weight of our van. We estimate it is between four and five tons. A bridge between the land spits was undergoing some repair and was limited to three and a half tons. We had to turn around and take a different route into Atlantic City.

The Monopoly City. Get your board out—all the streets are here! We made our way to the Boardwalk area and looked for a hotel without all-garage parking. We were heading for the Tropicana or the Holiday Inn, both right on the Boardwalk. We saw the big garages and looked a little further—turns out both could have accommodated us in surface parking that wasn't obvious at first glance. We landed at the Days Inn and for $79 a night have a wonderful boardwalk-front, ocean-view room with parking for the van!

We expected to not like Atlantic City, since we are not gamblers, but we were pleasantly surprised. Walking down the boardwalk in the evening was very enjoyable. We felt safe and the weather was great. We actually went into the Tropicana and gambled $15 and had about thirty minutes of fun! The people-watching was great!

Phil-osophies

As you can guess, we travel with a portable bar. We do enjoy our cocktails in the evening—big surprise, huh? What has been amazing is the purchase of alcohol around the country. Each state seems to have its own twist on how you accomplish this feat. I think we already talked about Utah, a total mystery in liquor laws. In Michigan we encountered "diluted" alcohol. Just that—certain stores sell it diluted and other stores sell the "real" stuff. They don't seem to mind the difference there—hmmmm. Then you have the "everything, everywhere" states. They stop just short of selling it in your local McDonald's. Then you have your "big-box" states. Stores bigger than Home Depot that sell every liquor you can imagine. How about freeway exits that go only to the liquor store? It's true! We also have encountered various permutations on the "confusing" ideogram. Pennsylvania has one of the more interesting twists. Wine and spirit stores that can sell nothing that doesn't have alcohol in it—not tonic, not soda. But also no beer—that is a separate bureaucracy with separate outlets. They can sell anything else they want, but only beer for alcohol! But they can't be a "grocery store." A convenience store is OK, but grocery stores can't sell beer or any other spirits! What a country!

On our way back into Philly, we had to cross a toll bridge. Normally, we pay just like a car, because we only have two axles and are less than twenty feet long. This is the first bridge we have encountered that charges by weight once you are over three tons—regardless of axles. So what we thought was an outrageous $3 toll for a fairly short bridge turned into a really outrageous charge of $9 for a two-axle vehicle—$4.50 per axle over three tons! The bridge tender didn't even ask us our weight. He knew we were overweight!

Lancaster, the Amish Country, is very rural, very relaxing, at least at this time of year! We found the best shops and crafts in two towns with funny names, Bird-in-Hand and Intercourse. I'm sure there are lots of jokes about the latter. We found many wonderful handicrafts and managed to make a few Christmas purchases before leaving town. We had a very interesting conversation with a "modern" Mennonite owner of a quilt shop about the Amish people and the Mennonites. She describes herself as somewhat modern but still conservative. She spoke of her mother as being "more plain" and her grandmother as "very plain." There are differences in educational views, technology views, business views, as well as the religious differences. She was very open, and we appreciated and enjoyed her candor and helping us understand more about their culture.

Week 24 | Maryland and back to Washington D.C.

Even though the fall colors are really over, we are still enjoying the aftermath of true fall colors. Robust burgundies, deep forest greens, thick luscious rusts, tawny golds, dark browns, and tree barks from powder gray to almost jet black. You can really see where the designers get their inspiration for "fall" colors. It doesn't come from the vivid palette of a few weeks ago, it definitely comes from these yummy leftovers of the now-neglected forest beauty. Mix this palette with a little sun, a little rain, and some clouds, and you have a sight every bit as breathtaking as the much more acclaimed "fall colors."

Tune up those fifes and drums—we're marching on to Gettysburg. The town is right in the middle of the battlefield and the National Military Park. The battlefield stretches for many miles, so before you get your audiotape to head out there, they recommend their "Electric Map" presentation. It costs a few dollars, but it is worth it. We've never seen anything quite like it. You sit in a tiered auditorium with a map of the battlefield on the floor below you. They narrate, with sound effects, the entire three-day battle. As they describe the various battle positions occupied by the Confederates and the Union, appropriate colored lights illuminate on the map. It was a very effective way to show us novices what happened.

Off to Baltimore on Sunday. We like to explore large cities on the weekends. It is so much easier to get around, park, and see things without the workday crowds around. We didn't know what to expect in Baltimore and really just focused on their renovated harbor area. They make extensive use of water taxis to get to the various places around the U-shaped harbor. For $5, you can ride them anywhere, all day long. We decided that would be a fun way to see things, and we "hopped on, hopped off" several times to enjoy the sights. This was a beautiful fall Sunday with lots of people enjoying their city—street jugglers out, music along the promenade, and people sitting outside at the many restaurants all along each area. The skyline is beautiful, and this part of the town is vibrant and enjoyable.

What a nice place Annapolis is! Water all around. It sits on a little peninsula in Chesapeake Bay. It has a small downtown that really exists to support the Naval Academy. There is a beautiful view of the Academy as you come down the hill and across a bridge into town. The sun was shining, the midshipmen were out in their sailboats, and the buildings struck an imposing stance along the shore.

We found the post office among all the quaint buildings downtown—more of those darn "roundabouts." We picked up our swimsuits that we had left in Newport, Rhode Island, on the back of the bathroom door in our room. I knew when I saw them on the door that it was a bad place, and sure enough, we left them hanging right there.

We are going to finish up our week back in Washington D.C. We'll be there for several days, so we have gotten an "all suites" place for $99. That is less than most of the regular hotels and the cheapest price we could find close-in! It is wonderful—two TVs (I don't have to watch sports all the time!), a full kitchen (we're loving fixing our own meals), and a real living room. I didn't realize how much I missed it all.

Today we fell into a very special celebration, the 200th Anniversary of the White House. They had a party with the Marine Corps Band, guest appearances by Thomas Jefferson, John Adams, and Calvin Coolidge, and punch and cookies. It was really fun! We have to come back tomorrow. We missed the tour times. They are only from 10 to 12, Tuesday through Saturday.

Our final stop for the day was Ford's Theater where Lincoln was assassinated, and the house across the street where he actually died the next morning. We couldn't see the theater due to rehearsals for the upcoming production of *The Christmas Carol*. But we're going to try again tomorrow—they say we can see it before noon. The museum has all kinds of artifacts from that fateful night. It is still chilling.

So much to see and we haven't even started on the rest of the Smithsonian Museums. Mama Mia! Our tootsies and backs are killing us, two long days in town in a row! We were off early to see Ford's Theater and the White House before noon. Both were worth getting going early to see.

The White House really is beautifully decorated. There are 132 rooms just in the main house, without the east and west wings! It is six stories, two below ground and four above. Every day they roll back the Oriental rugs (which are exquisite!), put up the ropes and runners, and then take it all down again three hours later! What other country in the world can you tromp through the home of the leader! Wonderful!

After a bite of lunch at a deli, we were off for the Washington Monument. We found out that they give out tickets for this at 8:30 a.m. each day until they are gone, and of course, they were gone. We groaned. "But wait! Not everyone is showing up today for their appointed time." (Why not? It is a beautiful day!) "So we've started this standby line over here." Ten minutes later we were in the elevator to the top! And what a view it is! We really enjoyed seeing everything from a bird's-eye view.

Week 25 | More Washington D.C. and Thanksgiving

Those darn Ducks—what's wrong with them? Oh well, there's always next year. It was fun sitting in our apartment here watching the game in a real living room, smelling dinner cooking in our real kitchen! It's amazing how the little things can become so endearing!

It is really cold here. We've been worried about the Rolling White House freezing. The water in our tanks could be a problem, and probably other things we should worry about too, but we don't know what they are! So far, no problems, other than the olive oil had turned to a semisolid gel when Phil went to get it! I needed it for the beef stroganoff.

Today we headed out in the van to go to Bethesda and the Washington Cathedral, but it started snowing as we headed up the Beltway! Yikes! We promptly turned around and headed south again. By the time we got back to Alexandria, the sun was out, so we decided to see the George Washington Masonic Memorial—very impressive—and another Frank Lloyd Wright house, the Pope-Leighey house in Alexandria.

Phil-osophies

We were downtown enjoying the city when I spied the MCI Center, home of the Washington Wizards—a terrible team—but they were playing our hometown Trail Blazers tonight! Sure enough, tickets were available—in the nose-bleed section—but we were in! We had dinner and got to the game, and by five minutes before game time, the place was still mostly empty. I said to Carol, "It must be the in thing to arrive at halftime." Sure enough, the place filled up during the second half. The Blazers won handily.

The neatest thing, though, was the Metro after the game. The station is right under the MCI Center, so you never even go outside, and just waiting for the game to get out are dozens of Metro trains going every which way—some were express routes, some normal. What a way to handle a crowd!

Tuesday finally took us to the Washington Cathedral on the Metro and bus—we weren't chancing the driving again! It was started in 1907 and wasn't completed until 1990, but it is spectacular, the sixth-largest cathedral in the world. It is Gothic architecture and is worthy of gawking for hours. The stained-glass windows are incredible, including one memorializing the Apollo 11 crew. It contains an actual moon rock—very beautiful.

Well, we've been in our apartment hotel, the Washington Suites, for six days now—the longest we have been anywhere since Carmel. It has been really wonderful to have a base to work out of during our visit in this area. But we have to move on to our holiday destination, the Lansdowne Resort in Leesburg, Virginia.

The Lansdowne is gorgeous. It is new, not old like I had thought, but on rolling hills. Very pleasant, if it weren't so cold—the high today was 38. It is going to have to warm a lot for us to play golf on Friday as we have planned. The restaurant looks really nice for our Turkey Day tomorrow.

No sightseeing, no hustling off somewhere—just pure relaxation! We went to the spa and enjoyed the pool and whirlpool. We watched some football, talked to the family, did a little mending, took a little snooze, enjoyed our Thanksgiving cocktails, read the newspaper by the lobby fireplace, and enjoyed the scenery. Dinner was delicious. We definitely took time to count our blessings.

Friday dawned cold, crisp, and clear. There were frost delays on the golf course, but by our noon tee time there were lots of folks out braving the elements. We were bundled up good and had a cart with wind gear on, so it was really very enjoyable. First golfing since the broken ankle, and it held up very well. We both played decent, not great, but OK for our first outing in months!

We are off early tomorrow for Newark, Delaware. The Portland State Vikings are playing in a conference playoff game against the University of Delaware Blue Hens. It should be interesting—more cold weather predicted.

Week 26 | Delaware and Virginia

Half a year down as of this week! We can't believe it—the time will fly by when we come back refreshed after the holidays and back into the good weather in the southern states. Before we know it, it will be June and the Great American Adventure will be over! We've visited over half the states, but we have about two-thirds of the national parks left, as most of them are in the South and Southwest. Clinton just added a new one this week in Colorado that we'll be sure to add to our list.

Well, Portland State University disappointed us today in Delaware. We braved the cold to watch them lose—badly. But it was fun. Only a few PSU fans there, so we were small but loud! Mostly players' parents. A group of fans noticed our Oregon plates on the van at halftime—we were warming up with straight scotch! They asked us when we'd had to leave to get here. They thought it was pretty funny when we said the first of June!

What a glorious day! Shenandoah National Park was sparkling in its winter best. The ice on the road was gone, thankfully, and the sun shone all afternoon. The lodges and visitor centers were closed, but this park is really about scenery anyway. We almost had the park to ourselves. We only saw about a dozen cars along the way. Frequent overviews of the Shenandoah Valley, the Blue Ridge Mountains, tiny hamlets, and a river that meanders through it all, the Shenandoah, made for a relaxing ride.

Monticello, Thomas Jefferson's home, was our destination in Charlottesville. As Phil said, it really creates an intimate feeling about a person when you wander through their home and hear all about how the person lived there. Jefferson was no exception. You definitely felt the difference in lifestyle between this home and Mount Vernon, George Washington's home. Jefferson was much more an aristocrat, and his home reflected that. He was a very intelligent, scholarly man and adapted many European trends in his home.

The Jefferson Hotel in Richmond, built in the 1700s, is incredible. A huge Tiffany-glass dome, many stained-glass windows, and marble columns make this a truly classic showcase. Virginia's only five-star hotel, and the restaurant is also five-star. We chose a small seventy-room inn down the street called the Linden Row Inn. Only three-star, but cozy, quaint, huge rooms, great staff, and much more affordable at $89 a night including breakfast, wine and cheese in the evening, newspapers, and other nice amenities. They have a courtyard that would be fabulous in the summer. We did walk down to the Jefferson for dinner—absolutely wonderful. We had an alcove that was cozy and romantic. The food was excellent.

Thomas Jefferson designed their State House, which isn't as impressive from the outside as many around the country, but it is very interesting inside. He wanted a peaked roof, but a dome in all his works was his trademark, so he did an internal dome, under the peaked roof but not visible from outside the building. It is lighted by two sets of skylights. A life-sized marble statue of George Washington is in the rotunda. It weighs 36,000 pounds—the floor had to be reinforced for it—and the detail is so lifelike. The sculptor spent several days with Washington, watching his movements, talking to him, taking measurements, and making a mask of his face while he lay on the kitchen table. Can you just imagine the father of our country on the kitchen table with quills sticking out of his nostrils and mouth so he could breathe! It's quite an incredible work of art.

Onward to Williamsburg. If there were one place you could take your kids or grandkids to learn about Colonial days, this would be it. It is expensive—$30 per person per day; multi-day packages are available—but it is authentically reconstructed. The money to purchase and rebuild the town came from John D. Rockefeller initially. Some buildings are original, but the reconstruction has been painstakingly done, even down to cutting and milling their own lumber, making their own nails, and using only tools of the era. It is a totally self-contained town with all the businesses of the time. Thankfully, within the historic area, only things you would find during the 1700s are available for sale and to eat. Really cool!

One of the highlights was seeing George Washington speak to the locals (us) about his recent trip to the First Continental Congress and the resolutions that came out of that. His "report" was mostly on the issue of taxation without representation. He then fielded questions ranging from his earlier experiences leading in wartime, to his teeth, to his affair with a married neighbor. This guy was good! He couldn't be stumped or ruffled!

Chapter 14

Winter Comes to the South

Week 27 | Virginia and North Carolina

Snow! Our archenemy! The forecast shows a storm coming right through here this afternoon! What to do? Stay put? Try to outrun it? They are so accurate with their weather reports in the East. We have to take this seriously!

We want to see the Carter's Grove Plantation on our way to the Hampton Roads area (Norfolk, Virginia Beach, Newport News), so we're headed out rather early to see the plantation and get to Virginia Beach ahead of the snow, hopefully. It was cold at Carter's Grove and spitting a little snow, but it is a beautiful mansion on the James River, all decked out for Christmas. I love the way they decorate here. They use lots of fruits and vegetables, greenery of every kind, and just a little ribbon or commercial decorative items. They had a large tree that was strung with lots of popcorn and handmade ornaments—quite lovely.

By the time we got near Newport News, it was snowing and raining but not sticking. Just twenty-five more miles to Virginia Beach. Will we make it? By the time we arrive, it is snowing sideways but still not sticking. It's about 1:30 in the afternoon, so as the temperature starts to drop, it will stick. We have found a great condo/hotel for $45, right on the beach! It is great for storm-watching. Because we have a full kitchen (and a big Jacuzzi tub!), we ventured to the grocery. We don't know how long we'll be here! We got enough for dinner tonight, breakfast and lunch tomorrow, and we are tucked in to watch it snow.

By bedtime the snow was still blowing sideways, and it was now sticking on the beach and boardwalk. All around town there were people in trouble.

Many people just pulled off the roads and holed up. They handle snow here just about as well as we do in Portland! We left our drapes open in the bedroom, and the morning dawned strikingly sunny, crisp, and clear. The snow was gone at the beach, but the roads around were still a problem. The schools were closed, accidents, the usual.

By noon, all seemed well, so we ventured forth, heading for the Outer Banks and Cape Hatteras. What a wonderful drive with clear roads, but the snow was still on lawns, trees, and parking lots. By the time we reached Kitty Hawk, there was no evidence of snow—and indeed, none fell in this area—and the temperatures were more moderate. We stopped to see the Wilbur and Orville Wright Monument.

Cape Hatteras National Seashore is really pretty, but you can't see the shore for most of the way—bummer. We got into Hatteras (the town) about dark and found the only hotel that was open! They gave us the names of two restaurants, but neither were open! Rather than drive back ten miles to the previous town, we got into the van and found leftover meatloaf from last night, a loaf of bread, a can of clam chowder, mandarin-orange slices, plates, bowls, silverware, and napkins. Soup and sandwiches made a great dinner, cooked in the microwave in our room! The Rolling White House is so handy sometimes!

Another gorgeous day in the making. It is sunny and a little warmer than the last couple of days. The Cape Hatteras Lighthouse is one of the most famous in the United States and the tallest at 208 feet. It is the one with the black spiral painting going up it. I'm sure in the summer this is a hopping place, but today it is almost closed. If not for the car ferry (free!), I'm sure it would be closed!

One of our travel books had written up a little town called Beaufort, North Carolina, that was right on our way after the ferry, so we decided to stop there and were not disappointed. We found the Beaufort Inn. A cute place right on the waterfront with a wonderful hot tub. Since we had been driving and sitting for a couple of days, we decided to take off on foot to explore the town. It has over two hundred restored houses from the late 1700s and 1800s. A nice waterfront downtown, all decked out for Christmas, really added to its charm. Pretty wreaths surrounded each gas streetlight all up and down the main street.

Off to Raleigh to line up our van repairs while we are home. Our generator still doesn't work since the accident in Minneapolis, and the RWH needs some service work. We easily found a good place that will keep it secure while we are gone. That was way too easy!

The Governor's Mansion, in downtown Raleigh, was having its Christmas Open House, and we just blended in with the crowds. The most interesting thing was the use of tobacco leaves in the decorations. They really looked great! That reminds me—I mentioned to an Oregon friend, transplanted to Rocky Mount, North Carolina, that it seems like a lot of people here smoke. She laughed and said in her best, fake, Southern accent, "Shhuugg, that's the smell of money burnin'. We love it here!" We are already learning that the South is, indeed, a different country!

We are embarking on our last week before the holidays. We're getting anxious to get home and see Portland again. We're missing the kids and grandkids and all our friends. The calendar is getting full. But you know what, we're already planning what we'll do when we get back here after the holidays. I think the traveling is in our blood!

Week 28 | Getting ready to go home for the holidays

We've been "on the road" for over half a year. Pretty unbelievable!

Most everything has gone generally according to our original plan. The budget, overall, is about right on—over in some categories (food and motels) and under in others (gasoline and RV hookups). We have stayed at least one night in each of the thirty-two states we have visited, except Vermont, and we have seen all of the national parks (thirteen) that we had planned. We will see all forty-three of the parks in the lower forty-eight states. In addition, we have seen twenty-nine other national monuments, historic parks, seashores, and so on. It's been the experience of a lifetime. We will carry these memories forever.

The Pinehurst/Southern Pines area is a golfer's mecca and a bargain at this time of year! Of course, we had to go to see the Pinehurst courses, clubhouse, and resort. The little community of Pinehurst is like a small Carmel, only with tall pine trees instead of the windblown ones there. It has very nice shops and is within walking distance of the resort hotel, the Carolina. Within less than an hour's drive, there are close to one hundred golf courses. We asked around and decided on Talamore. A challenging track, the weather was biting cold, but not windy or raining, so it was bearable.

We went to the Carolina for dinner and it was magical. The decorations were awesome, and the local Hospital Ball was happening there that evening, so the arriving outfits were something to behold. I've never seen so many beautiful furs of every type. The dining room was formal and fabulous. They had a combo for dancing and we had our first dance since "the ankle." Did OK. The menu was prix fixe and the choices were almost too hard to decide. Everything was absolutely delicious, as you would expect, and for some unknown reason, our waitress, who was a sassy gal and really fun, "comped" one of our dinners. What a shock! We couldn't have eaten at the Holiday Inn for what we paid!

Today was our day to clean up the van, choose what we were bringing home, mail a box of "stuff" we weren't going to need anymore (and some gifts), and just relax a bit. Tomorrow, we will deliver the RWH to Capital City RV Repair. They will keep it safe and make it all ready for our next six months. The people here at the Baymont Inn are going to pick us up where we drop the van and deliver us to the airport. So it looks like we're getting ready to go!

Have a wonderful Christmas everyone. We'll check back in with you when we return from the holidays.

Weeks 29–32 | Home sweet home

Can you say *whirlwind*? How about *homeless*? Maybe even *totally unsettled*? After seeing over seventy-five friends and relatives, attending twenty-four get-togethers, getting to thirteen doctor/dentist/personal-service appointments, renting one of our investment houses right before we left town, making two trips to have the Volvo worked on and putting 1,800-plus miles on it, buying all the Christmas presents (and birthdays for the next six months!), changing housing locations seven times, and still celebrating the holidays—we are ready to get back out on the road! It is way too confusing at home, especially when you have no home! This all took place in twenty-eight days!

It was, of course, fun to see many of our friends after having seen basically no one we knew for six months, but we feel badly that we couldn't fit everyone in our limited time. Many people have promised to meet us on the road this winter and spring, so we'll hopefully see more people as we travel the southern states. All in all, not much has changed while we were gone. A few new buildings in town, a few new happenings with people's lives, but mostly "the beat goes on."

We actually got to stay in our own house for a couple of nights, as our renters went home for the holidays. Very weird to be in your house with your furniture and someone else's "stuff." "Why did she move that there?" "My, that plant has sure grown!" and "What happened in the courtyard?"

We apparently had a leak in our water line between the house and the street, which caused a plumber to have to tear up a portion of our courtyard to replace it and the landscaper to redo some plants. It still wasn't finished when we left.

And, of course, there was the dead battery in our awaiting car the night we arrived home in an ice storm. My friend had just parked it there a few hours before, and it had been fine! We were exhausted. Rather than try to get AAA in the middle of an ice storm, we just checked into the nearest motel and waited until the next day to deal with it. It's always something. It matters not whether you are home or away; you always have to have a little rain—or ice—before the rainbow.

Week 33 | South Carolina

Well, we're almost back in the swing of things. We got the van on Thursday and headed for Wilmington, North Carolina. We got back into the "big-rig" driving mode fairly easily, but my navigation skills were a bit rusty. I kept spacing out when I should have been looking and directing! A few missed turns and exits and I'm doing better now.

We've nestled in at the Grand Strand, the Myrtle Beach area. We decided that the high-rises in town looked too much like a cross between Disneyland

and Las Vegas (even though the $35 prices were enticing), so we ended up south of town at the Litchfield Golf Resort at Litchfield Beach for a mere $50 a night, still a real bargain. A little more spread out, but with lots of units and three golf courses in the complex. We played the Litchfield Country Club course today and finished just as the rain started. The golf gods were with us.

We fired up the new two-way radios my sister gave us for Christmas and tried them out. They work well. Maybe now I can keep track of Phil when he wanders off!

Everyone has said that Charleston is not to be missed, and they were right! Under 100,000 people, historic preservation going on since the 1920s, a height restriction on buildings, and a wonderful Southern hospitality all make for a lovely experience.

The AAA book indicated that the hotel prices were high even in the winter. We once again stopped at the local visitor-information center, and again, they knew where the secrets were! We wanted to stay in the historic district so we could walk and explore, because the streets are very narrow and confusing. She found us a wonderful historic Days Inn for $59, right in the heart of everything. We have really come to depend on the visitor centers, as they are usually very helpful and know what is going on.

We signed up for a walking tour the next day with a guide named Butler—her first name. Turns out she was a cute, knowledgeable Charlestonian with a lovely Southern accent. Butler is a family name, and she also named her daughter Butler. It really fit her. We had a great morning learning about the history of the area. She pointed us to a few more things to see and we were off on our own. We had a fabulous lunch at 82 Queen Street—She Crab Soup to die for! We had to walk our lunch off, so we went shopping, of course! Bought a couple of souvenirs, a sweet-grass basket for $40 from a street vendor, and a couple of watercolor prints. We saw some sweet-grass baskets later in a gallery for over $200! They are really lovely.

What a day! It is moving toward 70 and sunny! We're just rolling down the road toward Hilton Head. We need another golf fix. We arrive on the island to wonderful weather, but what is that out there? By the time we decide on a hotel and get to our room to see our ocean view, the fog had moved in and was just sitting there! We are at the Hilton Resort at Hilton Head—more great deals abound!

Phil-osophies

I saw this old, interesting-looking store on Main Street in Beaufort, South Carolina—Lipsitz. I had to check it out. It was a real throwback. The owner is eighty-plus years old and was born upstairs. The store has been here, in this building, for 125 years, and I think some of the inventory has been there at least that long! There is stuff everywhere and papers stacked in every table, nook, and cranny, you name it. But the old guy and his wife know where everything is. She sized me up immediately (XL), found out what I wanted (a long-sleeved polo shirt in cotton), rummaged through some drawers, and voilà, she had the perfect shirt, for $14! A real American institution. I loved it!

We did have a shock, though. We wanted to go out to the Sea Pines Community, but they charge $5 just to *drive* out there! After recovering from that idea, Phil says, "We have to do it. We can't come this far and not see Harbortown and the famous golf course there." So we get our five bucks out and head to the gate. Phil shoves the money out the window and the guard says, "Can't take that from you, sir." "Why not?" queries Phil. "You're a camping vehicle—not allowed in Sea Pines." Phil, not ready to give up, replies, "No, we're just a normal-sized van. We're not a motorhome" (*with disdain*). Unswerving, the guard looks us over again and confidently replies, "You've got LP gas on board and sewer disposal. You're a camping vehicle. Can't let you in." Busted. Can you believe that! The Sea Pines covenants outlaw *all* camping vehicles, regardless of size, even to drive through! Speaking of snooty!

Week 34 | Georgia

Savannah—the city obsessed with *In the Garden of Good and Evil*. Their tourism has increased 67 percent since the book/movie. It is a lovely city along the Savannah River that has been working on preserving its treasures of old homes and buildings. But it may be too little, too late. They are a pale comparison to their northerly cousin, Charleston, which has been at it since the '20s and has a really sparkling gem to show for it. Savannah does have a wonderful series of "squares" (parks) every few blocks throughout the mostly residential downtown area.

So *why* did I always believe that the capital of Georgia was Augusta? I understand it was at one time, but not when I was learning that stuff! This strikes me as a town that can't decide what it wants to be. Millions have been spent on the waterfront, which is lovely, but a mere one block away, the main street, Broad, is almost dead. A wonderful wide parkway running down the center of the street, nice old buildings, pretty lampposts, but absolutely nothing going on—and it goes downhill from there. One exception is the Summerhill area where, back in the early 1900s, many resort hotels were built in the area on the hill for the wealthy Southerners. It was from this development that the Augusta Country Club was built. It is now practically in the middle of town.

Everyone told us to skip Atlanta. There is nothing there and it is a big, dangerous town. But we both wanted to see it. It is one of the major cities in this country. We decided to check out Stone Mountain on our way and ended up staying there. It is only about forty-five minutes out of town and lovely. The Stone Mountain Inn was available for $69 a night. It is a lovely older inn with nice grounds and a view of Stone Mountain itself, the largest hunk of granite in the world!

We found our way to the MARTA Park and Ride to go downtown. It is about fifteen to twenty minutes from Stone Mountain, but the lot we entered was full. We could see a practically empty lot that was cordoned off. We found a MARTA employee who was just going off shift and asked him the drill. A nice young man, he said, "I'll show you how to get there, but I'll have to ride with you—it's complicated." I was more than a little nervous about this idea, but we let him in the van. He was right about it being convoluted, but he got us to the other side of the fence. It took about ten minutes more driving to get in from the freeway side of the lot—very strange system here! We thanked him, and he hopped over the barriers and went on his way home. Can you believe our luck in finding nice people! MARTA was another good system, taking us everywhere we wanted to go.

After a night in Americus, the world headquarters of Habitat for Humanity, we were off to Plains, Georgia, and Jimmy Carter's homeland. The entire city has been made into a National Historic Site. This includes his school, the hospital he was born in, his boyhood home, the train station where his campaign HQ was housed, the peanut warehouse, Billy's gas station, and the houses they lived in then and now. It is charming, old-fashioned, and a true piece of Americana. He still teaches Sunday school at the Baptist Church. Nothing has changed about Jimmy Carter.

Several hours on the road, past the swamps, through all kinds of small towns, and we arrive at the Golden Isles—Brunswick, Sea Island, St. Simon Island, and Jeykell Island. Jeykell Island is where some early millionaires bought an island for $10,000 and created their own enclave. Names like Rockefeller, DuPont, and others built the Jeykell Island Club and invited only their friends to attend. The basis of our current Federal Reserve policy was created here, and the first transcontinental telephone call from Alexander Graham Bell to Thomas Watson in San Francisco with the president in Washington D.C.—three-way calling in those days!?—was completed from here in 1915. Much of the compound has been restored to its original elegance. The "cottages" they owned weren't as opulent as those in Newport, Rhode Island, but still very substantial homes. Most of this started in the late 1800s and continued into the 1940s, when the island was sold to the state of Georgia for a park.

I really felt old the other day. We were somewhere and a father was explaining to his ten- or twelve-year-old son about something that happened in the '60s. (I can't remember what it was—another sign of my advancing age!) I was mentally nodding along with his explanation—like it happened yesterday—and the kid says, "Yeah, I know, Dad, we learned about that in *history* class!" Oh my goodness, how can that be?!

Week 35 | Florida, finally

I think we have returned to the land of sun! It is so nice here in St. Augustine, not quite shorts weather, but getting close. The palm trees are swaying, the sun is shining, and everyone is out enjoying this day.

We enjoyed a full day of sightseeing from one of the "hop on, hop off" trolleys with great narration about the city. Henry Flagler was the mover and shaker behind this town. He was a VP at Standard Oil working for Rockefeller when he got "burnout" and came to see his doctor in St. Augustine—and fell in love with it. He envisioned a railroad connection from the north, clear through to St. Augustine to bring his wealthy friends to this lovely area. He far exceeded his own vision, bringing the railroad all the way to Key West and opening up Florida for development.

First he built the elegant Ponce de Leon Hotel in the late 1700s, which is now Flagler College, a four-year liberal-arts college, which is a breathtaking Spanish-style building. The "cafeteria" seats 750 people at mahogany tables with priceless Tiffany-glass windows all around them! It is an absolutely glorious room. Tiffany was hired to do all the interiors of the hotel. But Flagler wasn't satisfied with just this hotel, as you had to be on the "social register" to stay there. He wanted to build a separate hotel for the "entourages" of his friends and others who came to town. So, across the street, he built another hotel of more modest means. But he also built what today would be called a spa—really the first spa in this country—with a huge indoor pool, Turkish baths, steam rooms, a bicycle track, and other amenities. Pretty soon, his rich friends were staying there instead of at his more expensive hotel next door.

Phil-osophies

Before we left the Saint Augustine area, I really wanted to see the International Golf Hall of Fame, which is sponsored by the PGA. I've seen clips of it on TV and wanted to check out all the tributes. The "front nine" showed the history of golf, and the "back nine" showed today's golf—complete with a swing-analysis booth and a putting contest that provided "live" TV coverage, a "winners" interview (Carol beat me and got the interview!), and your name in lights—or Carol's name in lights, in this case. Outside there is a replica of the 17th hole at the TPC at Saw-grass, which is a charity hole-in-one trial. At least I got a nice poster for my attempt!

A clear, cool day dawns for our first outing with Phil's brother, Tom, who has joined us for a few days. We spent the whole day at Cape Canaveral. We went on the "behind-the-scenes tour" that showed the launchpads and many things Tom was familiar with. I don't remember this being so expensive—$50 per person for both the museum and the tour. The next morning we went to the Astronauts Hall of Fame, a really cool place, with lots of hands-on things to do, in addition to the Hall of Fame. We took a flight to Mars in a simulator. Phil tried the weightlessness of the moon and crawled inside a Mercury Space Capsule. We all passed on the four Gs of pressure like going into space.

Off to Orlando and a nice, if cool, afternoon at Sea World. We got to see Shamu, the waterskiing expo, the dolphins and the manatees, among other things. Tom really liked it all. The last day, we headed for Epcot, but not until the afternoon, as we were all getting tired and wanted to stay for dinner, the parade, and the fireworks. It rained on us, but we had fun anyway. We didn't get to do the GM Test Track ride, as it doesn't run in the rain, but we saw most everything else. We had dinner in Italy—Tom's choice—and great seats for the fireworks. The next morning, we put a tired but happy Tom on the airplane back to Portland. We headed out of this rain and clouds—south, to the beach!

Week 36 | Florida

A peak at the sun, but more rain going through! Palm Beach is absolutely incredible. Our eyes are popping out of our head at every turn! We found a wonderful small hotel right in the heart of Palm Beach, the Heart of Palm Beach Inn—even the name is cute! We didn't think we could afford to stay in town, but we quickly found that even the "cheap" places away from town were $150-plus for a nothing place. We found this place for $159 right in the heart of everything! We've been so lucky, but the AAA book and cell phone are a big help once you scope out an area. We can't wait to explore the Breakers, the Flagler Mansion/Museum, and the shops on Worth Street tomorrow.

The rain came down, drowning our plans to head out for dinner. However, we enjoyed a wonderful home-cooked dinner of beef stew at the restaurant "in-house" at the hotel. Very intimate, lovely atmosphere. The rain really raised the humidity factor—crank up that air conditioning!

The morning dawned humid but beautiful. We went for a nice walk along the ocean; peaking through the gates of these fabulous homes was great fun. We saw part of a house that had just been moved onto the site, a beautiful two-story Mediterranean, with two more pieces yet to arrive. It was floated down the Atlantic on a barge, put on an elaborate "dolly" system, and moved across the sand to its oceanfront site. The other two pieces are due to arrive this week. The local paper says the owner has $10 million into this venture so far.

Highway A1A is the way to go, but slowly! You can go along the coast, by all the beautiful homes and high-rise condo towers, all the way to Miami. We drove through a huge rain cloud around Boca Ratan, but by Fort Lauderdale it was gone. It is amazing to us how many thousands of units there are all along this area, both waterfront and off the water. Money just seems to drip off every tree here!

Miami is a scary place. Everywhere from the outskirts of Fort Lauderdale into Miami the poverty was evident. Miles of houses with bars on all the windows and doors and high iron fences with sharp tops. What a way to live! Fortunately, we landed in Miami Lakes to visit with our friends. An oasis in this crazy town!

It is another national-park day, Biscayne and Everglades. They are quite close together. We got some chores done—it's that time again—and headed for the parks on a glorious day—high 70s, light breeze. Biscayne is almost all water. We signed up for a boat cruise tomorrow morning, went on a ranger talk about the mangroves and other plant life, and headed for the Everglades. We signed up for the "backcountry boat tour" tomorrow afternoon, enjoyed the visitor center, and went on a hike on the Anhinga Trail. Wow! The trail is actually a boardwalk

At Cape Canaveral, Phil and his brother Tom contemplate heading out on a real adventure!

out into the "glades"—lots of birds, turtles, and of course, alligators. We got to see a rare sight—baby alligators, about 8 inches long, six days old, about twenty of them. Only one of them will live to maturity, if they are lucky. The mom was basking in the sun and totaling ignoring her offspring. They are usually born in October or November—these were way off sync!

Got up and going early for us. 9:30 check-in for our Biscayne cruise, and it was cancelled due to boat problems! Bummer. So we regrouped and decided to try to get a place at the Flamingo Lodge out in the Everglades Park. Luck strikes again and we got a bay-view room. By the time we got to the park gate, the "Lodge Full" sign was out. We squeaked by again. It is a pretty drive out there. The Everglades are not at all like I had expected. Open, broad expanses of grass fields, with occasional "hammocks" (raised land areas about a foot above the grass river) of mahogany, pine, palms, cypress, and the ever-present four types of mangroves, but no swamps, trees with hanging moss, etc. The Everglades is really a huge river that flows out of Lake Ockochobee with seawater flowing in from the gulf, making "brackish" water, a combination of fresh and salt waters. The "river" is a hundred miles long, two hundred miles wide, and an average of five feet deep, filled with grass! Many factors are threatening this one-of-a-kind environment, but man is the root of most problems—development, recreation, fertilizers, etc.

Week 37 | Florida, still

Why do people go clear to the Caribbean? This place is incredible! I'm sure the summers are awful—mosquitoes, humidity—but the water is so clear and just an azure blue that is beautiful. And always a nice breeze.

The Keys are a collection of 126 islands connected by 42 bridges. They say that 15 percent of the highway is over water, and the views are spectacular from each bridge. The RV parks are incredible, mostly huge and right on the water, but they cram them in so close together it really takes away from the beauty. We ended up in Key West at a park right in the heart of town. Absolutely no atmosphere, but you could walk everywhere in a few minutes, and the people were great, the bathrooms clean and nice. At night, we fell to sleep to the sound of steel drums wafting up from the waterfront restaurants. We also enjoyed a couple of nights at a funky place in Islamorada, the La Jolla

Resort. It was perfect. Accommodations are quite expensive at this time of year. The RV park was $49 a night—the KOAs, etc., were $65 to $70!—and Key West hotels started at $150 and went on up.

Key West is a happening place. Every night they celebrate sunset with a huge party in the town square, Mallory Square. Jugglers, high-wire acts, human statues, dancers, singers, bands, animal tricks—you name it, it's here! Everywhere in Key West you can walk around with drinks in hand, and most people do! The open-air restaurants are a trip—parrots on shoulders, dogs roaming around, cats, chickens (no kidding—they're everywhere in town), and the wildest assortment of people you can imagine. The waterfront has every type of watercraft—huge private yachts and sailboats, party barges, commercial fishing vessels, sunset cruise boats, dinghies from boats anchored offshore, massive cruise liners, catamarans—a real menagerie! A couple of days here were all we could take. We had to retreat to more calm locales!

Oh, our day trip out to Dry Tortugas National Park was fabulous. I was concerned about seeing that park, as it seemed so remote, sixty-seven miles off the coast of Key West with no accommodations, water, food, etc. But once we were in Key West, there were a number of choices to see the park. We chose a catamaran trip, the *Fast Cat*, two and a half hours each way and about four hours at the Park. They fed us breakfast, lunch, and a snack, gave us a guided tour of the fort (the major artifact in the park), provided us with snorkel equipment, and treated us to a really fun trip.

A leisurely trip back up the Keys with a stop at a highly rated state park, John Pennekamp, and we found ourselves saying, we can make it back to Florida City. Then we figured we could make it to Naples, no, let's go to Marco Island—and so our trip continues to be a happenstance! A stop at the Big Cypress Visitor Center out in the middle of nowhere gave us a break. We found a great KOA at Marco Island and settled in for the night after a nice walk around the park. A water-exercise class was our first calling the next morning. The weather, the birds, and the nice people made for a very enjoyable experience. There were a few mosquitoes—and they all found me!

We ambled along up the coast while we searched out our next beautiful spot. I was reading the AAA book and found out that Sarasota is the home of the Ringling Brothers circus and that there is a museum there about the circus and Mr. Ringling's mansion. So off we go. Most of the museum is a regular museum with a large collection of the artwork he accumulated during his lifetime. A beautiful Italianate building with perfect gardens houses his collection. In another building is the circus collection. Old costumes, old circus wagons elegantly restored, pictures, posters, and a scale-model replica of a "big top" circus were the highlights here.

I think we went over the highest spot in Florida. The soaring bridge connecting to St. Petersburg from the south is breathtaking—definitely higher than anything around!

Just a little farther up the beach due to horrible traffic, we settled into a little motel right on the Gulf at Belleair Beach, the Belleair Beach Resort. A great value at $84. It is right on the beach with a very nice pool and well-kept beach area—complete with shuffleboard (everywhere in Florida), a nice grassy area, a picnic area with BBQs and lounge chairs facing the Gulf—really perfect. We found some neat shells here too. The motel referred us to a great spot for dinner, Guppy's. It reminded us of the kind of place you would find in Portland. It made us homesick, and the food was great.

We have really been just doddling along and decided we needed to make some time or we'll never make New Orleans for Mardi Gras. Finally we got out of the Clearwater area and headed for the interstate to make time toward Tallahassee. We camped along the way in an RV park with lots of trees with hanging Spanish moss—really pretty.

We are off to Tallahassee in the rain and headed to the coast and a night at a KOA at Alligator Point. Although cooler than down south—we actually ran the heater in the van—this coastline is really pretty and not nearly as crowded as other places we've been. This is how Florida must have been years ago—white-sand beaches against clear blue waters with hardly any people or highrises interrupting the birds or the waves. The road runs right along the water most of the way—very scenic. At about Destin, the scenery changed to more dunes, the first we've seen since the Outer Banks. Just before Pensacola we traveled about fifteen miles through the Gulf Islands National Seashore—very isolated and beautiful. The azure blue waters and sugar-fine sand were back.

Week 38 | Alabama

Well, as of today we are one time zone closer to home! We probably will be on Central Time for the next couple of months. From Pensacola, you can cover four states in four hours—Florida, Alabama, Mississippi, and Louisiana! I never realized how narrow the seacoast areas of Alabama and Mississippi are. We could have been in New Orleans tonight, but we are saving that for a few days and are going to explore Alabama and Mississippi instead.

Before we left Flori-*da*, though, we had to be reminded of the "da" just one more time. As we left Pensacola, over the large bridge—but not that long—was a highway sign that read "Long Bridge, Check Gas." Da!!

We decided to take in the Jefferson Davis Memorial Library and house. The library is new and well done. We learned a lot about Jefferson Davis. He had some tremendous strengths and some serious weaknesses. The house, Beauvoir, was where he spent the end of his life, a beautiful place right on the water.

We hung around another night and went to one of the casinos that was very much like Las Vegas. Phil is having a suspicious mole on his neck removed tomorrow. We couldn't believe we actually found someone who could do it on short notice.

Rain greeted us on our way to Mobile. We wanted to see the Bellingrath Gardens. It is supposed to be one of the top five gardens in the United States. They are on a beautiful old plantation that was developed by one of the founders of Coca-Cola. Once again luck was with us. By the time we stopped for lunch and got down to the gardens, the rain stopped and we were able to enjoy the daffodils, tulips, camellias, tulip trees, and many other beautiful blooms. Bellingrath is known for its azaleas, and there were thousands, but they weren't quite in bloom yet. They must be beautiful in full bloom.

A beautiful day and we're off to Selma, the home of the voting-rights campaign in the South. It seems unbelievable to us that just thirty-five short years ago, black people couldn't vote. We saw the entire route of the march from Selma to Montgomery in the '60s. It is kind of sad that the people of

Selma haven't organized the legacy of the march as well as the march itself. The Voting Rights Museum could really tell a story, but instead it is an odd collection of pictures with no theme or story and not done very well at that. The various locations around town that sparked much of the history are difficult to seek out. There are four different museums that are loosely associated with the movement, but there is no coordination to tell the story. In addition, the visitor center, which could play a role, is located far from the action. Nothing much has changed in Selma since the '60s. That could be a real advantage in putting together a historic view of the events.

Phil's last birthday that starts with a 5! His wish is for a day of golf—what else! We are right in the heart of the Robert Trent Jones Golf Trail, an undertaking by the State of Alabama Retirement System. They have built eight sites with three courses at each site, a total of 378 golf holes, all designed by Robert Trent Jones Sr. and all designed to be affordable resort play. $55 per person is the top price, and the course we played was fabulous. Rated at 124, but a really tough course, just a few miles from Montgomery. They have a lodge with ninety rooms on the premises, and we thoroughly enjoyed our stay there. We were surprised how quiet it was, considering the weather is quite good this time of year. Their prime months are March and April before the humidity and bugs set in.

Week 39 | Mardi Gras

The end of the trip is coming close enough into view that we are beginning to talk about "when we're back in Portland." The most common themes are getting our golf games in shape, working out regularly, being with friends again, and just being in one place for more than two days!

We just encountered our first "shutout." We drove up to Tuscaloosa today to see "Bear" Bryant Stadium at the U of Alabama and the "Bear" Bryant Museum. They were both closed up tight. Phil was really ticked off, as the museum signage said it was supposed to be open, just like the AAA book said! Oh well, can't win 'em all. It was an extra hour out of our way— bummer.

Off to Mardi Gras after a stopover in Meridian for the night. We have no reservations until tomorrow night, so we will stop short of New Orleans. We found lots of rooms available in Slidell and van service into the city, about twenty-five miles. Tonight is the last night for parades (Lundi Gras), so we will head down there. It is pouring here, but they say there is no rain in town, and there isn't.

I can hardly describe all that goes on here. Just about anything you can imagine, you'll see somewhere in the French Quarter. The parades are actually outside that area. They skim the edge on Canal Street. It is probably a good thing, as there are over one million people here for this. Having the parades on St. Charles Street helps spread out the crowds, but you can't imagine the intensity of the masses everywhere. The crowds, however, were orderly. Lots of police presence, but it was unneeded from what we saw. Their main functions appeared to be to give directions, drink coffee, and keep cars out.

The floats were huge and well done. They are all sponsored by krewes, or carnival "clubs" that are long steeped in tradition here. They have kings, queens, courts, and balls, and millions are spent on the twelve-day event. We saw some of the previous queens' gowns and trains on display at Bellingrath Gardens. The docent there said some of these outfits cost upwards of $20,000, and the cost is born by the families of the "royalty." We didn't see any of this on the streets, but we got to enjoy a lot of it on TV.

Out on the streets, the most impressive thing, besides the crazy people, was the litter. Thousands and thousands of bead necklaces are thrown, along with carnival toys, doubloons, Mardi Gras cups of every type, and anything else that can be hurled at the crowds! They are thrown from balconies, off floats, amongst the revelers, off ladders—you name it! At the end of the day, much of the thrown material, along with plates, beer cups, food, glass bottles, bags of garbage from restaurants, cardboard boxes, and, I'm sure, small children and drunks, ends up on the street! It's amazing that all of this seems to coexist and everybody has a great time.

On Mardi Gras day, we got a different look. After some time in the French quarter, we headed down St. Charles Street to meet up with the daughters of Phil's friend. The girls go to school here and live just off

St. Charles. We walked and walked and walked, but we finally got to their place in the garden district. In this part of town the locals set up camp in the streets with all kinds of food, tents, more beer, and ladders for getting a good view and the ability to grab the best "throws" from the floats. The girls and their friends took good care of us old geezers, even feeding us and getting us back to our hotel at the end of the day.

Well, we just shipped $35 worth of Mardi Gras paraphernalia home for our party next year. Start preparing your costumes and favorite Southern food now! We'll even have a walking parade, weather permitting!

We wanted to make it to Natchez so we would only have a couple of hours into Monroe tomorrow, so even though it was getting late, we got back on the road. Just north of Baton Rouge, it started to rain again . . . and thunder and lightning . . . and more really hard rain . . . and getting dark . . . and more rain . . . and lightning that lit up the whole sky . . . and really, really hard rain . . . and fog . . . and more rain. We were so glad to see Natchez and a Days Inn right on the highway. We had pizza delivery to our room—we'd had enough!

Week 40 | Mississippi and Tennessee

A rainy drive found us in Monroe, a town of about 50,000, and Phil's friend greeted us right at the freeway exit. He, thankfully, guided us to their lovely home and the beginning of a great weekend visit with them. We loaded up our gear in their Suburban and we were all off for "the cabin." Good-bye to the RWH for a few days!

What a neat place, just what a cabin should be—a big fireplace, animal heads high on the walls, wood surrounding you everywhere, a big family kitchen, very cozy, yet roomy. It is tucked on the edge of a lake—or was it a bayou?—with tall trees forming a canopy around it, adding to the cozy feeling. We nestled in here for lots of laughs, catching up on our lives, good food and drink, and the ever-present poking and stoking of the fire. *Ahhhhhhh.* . . .

The evening brought a bustling house full of visitors who all joined us for huge steaks, drinks of every kind, cigars, and fun conversation between the generations. It was a wonderful evening. It was especially interesting to us to understand a little about the political and racial climate of the South. There are some very real reasons why these states are consistently at the low end of the educational and economic statistics.

The Natchez Spring Pilgrimage starts Wednesday, so we're going to head to Jackson first, then back down to Natchez to enjoy some of their lovely mansions while they are open to the public. Then we've got to get moving. We're getting behind on our schedule!

We have seen some really beautiful state capitols, but Jackson's may be the best yet. After a $19 million restoration in the 1980s, this place is fantastic! The stained glass, the marble columns, and a rotunda that is open from the basement right through to the top with extremely detailed paintings and artwork all make for a memorable building. Even the two chambers have huge stained-glass skylights in them.

Natchez turned out perfectly. Today was the beginning of the Pilgrimage, but the crowds have not yet arrived. We had no trouble getting tickets or a place to stay. I was flipping through the AAA book, looking for a dinner spot, when I spied the Monmouth Plantation. "Dinner in the elegant surroundings of the dining room, single seating at 7:30. Explore the grounds." This sounded really interesting, but it *is* Pilgrimage. Oh well, I'll call and check anyway. Sure enough, there were two spots left at the table! Scored again!

We got our good clothes out and arrived at 6:30 for cocktails in the study. Too cold for the garden and veranda—darn! There were nice people from all around the country. We met a super couple from Seattle, where he is a published travel writer! Big score! He gave me some really good pointers about my book and agreed to review the book for me when I get it done! I won't be losing *that* business card.

We went on the "Peach Tour." They rotate the houses from day to day and have them laid out so they are easy to find, even though they are spread all over the area. These places are so interesting. Some are completely restored B&Bs, others are in the restoration process, and one we visited was never finished—nor will it be. That was really a shame, as it is the largest octagonal home in the country and so pretty from the outside.

Oxford is a breath of fresh air! The college town where Ole Miss is located and a wonderful town. The campus is beautiful, and the little downtown square, set around the county courthouse, had the best shops and restaurants we've seen in the South. We had lunch at a recommendation from one of our travel guides, and it was delicious—no fried foods, real fresh ground pepper, and interesting preparations. There was still too much salt—they salt everything to death down here. I hope one of us doesn't have a heart attack! We spent too much time and too much money here, but we got a couple of birthday presents for later this year.

We found a place to stay not far from our adventure for the next day, Graceland. I thought Graceland would be the ultimate in tackiness, but it was really pretty well done. In addition to the actual mansion, you get to tour his airplane, his personal effects, and a museum with a bunch of his cars. All his gold/platinum records and trophies are on display. His gravesite, along with those of his parents and grandma, are right on the grounds. It was interesting and really gave us a new appreciation for Elvis and his life. He looks like a saint compared to most of the recording artists today! Most people don't know how generous he was—some would say flagrant—with his money. He helped a lot of charities in the Memphis area.

The afternoon brought us to downtown Memphis and an evening of music on Beale Street. They are trying valiantly to keep their downtown together, but the many boarded-up or vacant properties right on the trolley line don't bode well. The Peabody Hotel is expanding and they have created Peabody Place near the hotel, perhaps in hopes of keeping things alive.

We hopped the trolley and headed for the National Civil Rights Museum located in the old motel (The Lorraine) where Martin Luther King Jr. was assassinated. It was a fascinating experience made even more so because we were definitely in the minority in this venue. It is amazing all the civil-rights initiatives that have gone on, dating back to the Thirteenth to Fifteenth Amendments to the Constitution. There are very well done displays with enough interactive exhibits to give you a real feel of the times. The bus where Rosa Parks refused to get up for a white person is there, with a figure of Rosa sitting there and the bus driver yelling at her. You are right on the bus experiencing all this—chilling. The actual room where Martin Luther King was staying when he was shot and a good explanation of what led up to the killing. You can look across the street and see where the assassin fired the bullet. A very moving experience.

Week 41 | Arkansas and Missouri

Hot Springs National Park in Hot Springs, Arkansas, is a very different park. It is the smallest national park, consisting of a few hundred acres surrounding the edge of the town. The springs were deemed worthy of protecting long before the idea of national parks took shape. As transportation improved and the word of the healing powers of the forty-seven hot springs spread, people began flocking to the area for all kinds of "cures."

Hot Springs is a cute town. With 850,000 gallons gushing forth each day, the water runs freely in many locations around town, and they encourage locals and tourists alike to fill their jugs with the naturally pure water. They do nothing to treat it. After all, it has been in the ground about 4,000 years from falling rainwater to bubbling spring water.

We nestled into the Historic Arlington Hotel, which has its own operating bathhouse. The bathing routine takes place in equipment that may be original to the reconstructed hotel from the 1920s. A whirlpool bath where the attendant actually bathes you, a sitz bath, a steam and then the hot packs and body wrap, followed by a needle shower, and finally, a relaxing massage. You leave there a total mushball! All this for about $45! This is not for the overly modest, though. They are whipping those sheets and towels on and off you at every station!

Up the road is Eureka Springs, which is built in a crevice. The houses and roads cling to the sides of the hills on both sides, and the downtown straddles a one-street-wide valley. Trains originally brought the people here to "take the waters." Like Hot Springs, many luxury hotels sprang up, and horse-drawn trolleys moved people from the train to their hotel. Only a few of the hotels have survived. The most famous is the Crescent, high on the hill overlooking the town in a crevice. Well-marked walking tours are much more effective for seeing this town—the horse-drawn carriages haven't started running yet—of tiny streets and wonderful restored Victorian homes. Most have no backyards at all, as they cling to their perches. Little parks surprise you at every turn, where each of the still-bubbling springs forms the basis for a park. The shops and restaurants are homey and friendly. Since the tourist season hasn't really started, most people had time on their hands and were willing to share some conversation about the town or their business with us.

The next morning dawned rainy—bummer—as we still had more exploring to do. We decided to push on for Branson. It was a rainy drive through the beautiful Ozark Mountains. Branson is a town of only about 3,400 people, and we're sure they have at least that many hotel rooms! This place is amazing. It is built in the rolling foothills of the Ozarks. We had a difficult time finding a motel that had any level parking for the RWH. The prices here at this time of year are eye-popping, starting at less than $30 a night. However, it is really too early to be here, as many of the shows haven't started up yet.

Once we settled into our Comfort Inn with level parking, we headed to the ticket desk and decided on three shows. We'll see "Country Tonite" this evening, Pierce Arrow tomorrow afternoon, and the Platters tomorrow evening. Each show ran about $25 a ticket. We know there are deals to be had—if you want to listen to a pitch. We decided to just enjoy the shows without the "sideshows," but we saw many seniors clutching their coupons! We are definitely "juniors" in this town!

Phil and I realized today that we haven't given you any "stories from the road" for a while. You know, those funny things that happen along the way that just crack you up. Today we encountered one of those twilight-zone kind of experiences.

Upon arriving in Poplar Bluffs, Missouri, on our way to Nashville, Tennessee, we surveyed "motel row" up and down and decided that the three-story—you'll see the significance of that soon—Pear Tree Inn looked pretty nice, and they were advertising $39.99 rooms. We have learned that these are the teaser rates for some unknown room that no one would want to stay in! So we figured that a king room would probably be in the mid-$40s—still good. Phil goes in and gives them his usual pitch—whatever that is, I've been afraid to find out—but he comes back out with a laugh in the air. "We have a new twist tonight," he explains. "First-floor rooms are $51, second-floor, $45, and third-floor, $39 with no elevator. How far do you want to climb?" I said, "How about the second floor. I don't really want to climb up three floors." So he comes back out with the key and instructions to drive around back to park. Suddenly, we find ourselves eye-level with the second floor—no climbing at all! I said, "Why are these rooms $6 less? There is no climbing involved!" Had we known, we would have taken a third-floor room and climbed the flight of stairs that we originally envisioned. But at this point, it would take too much time to redo and I'm afraid of what their crazy answer might have been! People are really nutty!

Week 42 | Tennessee, Missouri, and Iowa

Half a day of travel brought us to Nashville, Music City USA. On our way there, we realized—by looking in our AAA guidebook—that the Grand Ole Opry only plays on Friday and Saturday nights. This being Saturday, we decided that would be our first stop. I called ahead to make sure tickets were available, and we headed for Opryland. Our tickets are for the late show at 9:30, so we had time to get settled and have dinner.

We had no preconceived notions about what the Opry was going to be like. It is a large venue with church-type pews for seats. Tonight it was quite full on the main floor, which created a good audience, probably 800 people. The Opry is actually the live performance of their long-running radio show of 75-plus years. People are wandering all over the large stage. Performers are coming and going and watching from the wings, friends and family are watching from seating on the stage, and the "host" is standing at a podium reading commercials that are projected on large screens around the theater. It was quite a scene, very different from most concerts.

In the course of two and a half hours, over twenty-five different acts performed, so they were changing instruments, performers, and backup bands every five to seven minutes! But it all happened without a hitch. It was interesting that the Opry provided certain common elements to every act—all the audio/amplification equipment, a large drum set, four backup singers, and probably more that we couldn't see. That is what allowed the groups to move in and out quickly. At each change, a bevy of techies descended on the stage to help each group get unconnected and the new group get connected, adjust microphone heights and locations and amp settings, etc. It was kind of controlled chaos!

One more "must-see" stop before heading out of town—the Ryman Theatre, where the Grand Ole Opry played for thirty-seven years. Originally built as a church (thus the pews carried over into the new venue), it has been restored to its original majesty. It now houses many traveling acts, theater productions, and yes, the Grand Ole Opry returns there for a couple of months each year. It is right in the heart of the convention area and has a special place in the hearts of Nashville residents and Grand Ole Opry stars.

Off to a totally different kind of adventure. That's what makes this trip so fun. We never get bored of one type of sightseeing. It is always something different. We are now headed for Mammoth Cave National Park. Not Phil's favorite thing, but he agreed to a two-hour historic tour tomorrow morning.

The day dawned rainy and cool—perfect weather to head into a cave.

The Ryman Theatre is the ideal place for these budding country singers to find a back-up band.

This one was dry, no stalactites or stalagmites. This cave was formed by water and is the largest known. Over 350 miles of cave have been discovered so far. (The park ranger's favorite stupid question: "How many miles of the cave are undiscovered?") The water has hollowed out huge tubes in the limestone underground—ranger's second-favorite stupid question: "Is all the cave underground?"—and made some truly beautiful formations. A "capstone" of shale covers the entire area and keeps most water from seeping into the cave, although several active rivers still are in the deepest areas of the cave.

Once we got settled in St. Louis, we headed for their light rail and off to town. We explored the historic area called Lacleide's Landing, mostly restaurants and nightclubs. Decided we would come back this evening for dinner. We walked on down to the Arch, 630 feet tall and the same width from one base leg to the other. There was a wonderful Westward Expansion museum inside the visitor center. It tells the story from the Louisiana Purchase to the Lewis and Clark Expedition and a bit about the California Gold Rush. Good exhibits, and it puts things in a timeline perspective.

Of course, we had to take the tram up to the top of the Arch. Quite a view from up there, but I thought the tram was even more interesting. How to you devise an "elevator" to go up the inside of that curved space? It was an engineering dilemma. They came up with something like a Disneyland ride that lifts and then moves inward, lifts and moves in, and so on. You sit in cramped little cars, five people to a car—it's a good thing it only takes a few minutes each way. It's a bit claustrophobic.

We had to choose between Ulysses S. Grant and Daniel Boone. Of course, we choose Daniel Boone! We are off to find his last home. Most of his life was spent in Kentucky, but his last years were in Missouri. It was a real trek to find this place. I was sure we would be the only ones there! But actually quite a few people had ventured forth. An interesting diversion, and we learned a lot about his life.

Off to the scenic road, the Great River Road, up the Mississippi to Hannibal, Missouri, the home of Mark Twain. But this early in the season, they close everything at 4 p.m., and we didn't make it until 4:30. We looked around, but there wasn't really much to see without getting the full tour. We actually had a hard time finding the place, as there were absolutely no signs directing you. And they pride themselves on this being their big attraction and claim to fame—couldn't believe we finally had to stop and ask. This is not a large town, so that really amazed us. We decided not to stay over and see it tomorrow but pushed on toward St. Joseph's, the home of the Pony Express.

A quick night in the middle of nowhere and we were on the road again for what turned out to be our longest driving day of the trip. We had planned to go to Omaha and then into Sioux City the next day to rendezvous with our friends from Brookings, South Dakota. We got to Omaha mid-afternoon, and since we will come back this way, we decided to push on for Sioux City, especially since the temperature was hovering near freezing and we could get snow flurries! Who knows what the morning will bring.

We have wanted to know the weight of the RWH for the entire trip. The Pleasure-Way handbook says we weigh about 8,500 pounds, but it is unclear as to whether that includes gas, water, people, possessions, etc. So when we saw the highway sign saying "Trucks over 6,000 pounds must exit" at the truck stop, we thought, good, now we'll know. The inspector waved us on, but we stopped and I went back and asked him if he could weigh us, as they weren't busy. He said sure. Now we know that we weigh 8,120 pounds with about a quarter tank of gas and a half tank of water. Apparently, any weigh station will weigh you on request.

Phil-osophies

This morning, as is my normal ritual, I went down to get the proverbial continental breakfast at the motel and my morning newspaper. I came back to the room just cracking up. "Look at the date on this paper." (I've learned to always check.) "It says Tuesday, March 20, but today is Saturday, March 24!" Carol, thinking I was losing it, says, "Why did you buy this?" That's the laugh. The news is current—sports headlines that happened yesterday. They just didn't change the banner—for several days now! Welcome to our heartland!

Right now we are wishing that we hadn't sent our heavy winter clothes home with the Mardi Gras stuff. It is sunny and beautiful—until you step outside! Fortunately, we still have some sweatshirts, jeans, boots, and windbreakers!

Speaking of clothes, we are really sick of our meager wardrobe! We may burn everything when we return home! I have four pairs of pants—black cotton, black wool, cords, and jeans. That's it for over two hundred days so far! Oh, I forgot, I do have a few pairs of shorts for those sunny days! Two long-sleeved shirts, one turtleneck, two sleeveless tops (one bought along the way), and three or four golf shirts make up my inventory! Phil's is similarly skimpy, but our storage is so limited, this is what has to be.

Our friends arrived right on schedule bearing a "book" made by her first graders who are using our website as part of their education this year. There was a picture on the front and letters from each of them about what they have liked most and thanking us for teaching them. The whole thing is precious and will be one of our favorite mementos from this trip.

Week 43 | Zooming through the heartland

Sioux City was really cold, around 12 degrees last night. When we started down the road in the RWH, we kept hearing this thumping sound. We finally realized it was our fresh-water tank with a chunk of ice in it! It had actually frozen last night! Hope it doesn't break a hole in the tank with its banging around in there!

We did a drive-by on Omaha. It is still quite cold, and we didn't see anything to inspire us to get out of the van! A cute historic district, but other than that, a medium-sized city in the middle of the prairie, and we decided to head on down the road. Headed for Abilene, Kansas, the home of Dwight D. Eisenhower.

We sure would like to see some leaves on the trees. We haven't seen leaves since last October or November, except for palm trees in Florida. The landscape is so barren without leaves on the trees. There are hardly any evergreen trees in this part of the country, so it makes it very bleak. It really is making me homesick for spring. So many of you have mentioned the flowers, trees budding out, and the beautiful sunny weather we've had back in Oregon.

Sing along now: "Abilene, Abilene, prettiest little town that I've ever seen"—remember that one? It is a pretty little town at the end of the Chisholm Trail where the Texans brought their cattle to the railroad for several years until the railroad was connected farther south, and that ended Abilene's tenure as a bawdy cow town! Agriculture took over and has been their economic base ever since. But of course, their real claim to fame is "Ike."

We knew Tulsa was probably a stretch for tonight from Kansas City, since I got my hair cut and we didn't get on the road as early as we expected. We made it to the border and a little town called Coffeyville, Kansas. We found out the next day that their claim to fame was the demise of the Dalton Gang at the hand of locals when they tried to rob a bank! They have preserved the bank building, the jail, and the alley where they had the getaway horses!

Off to experience Route 66 on our way to Oklahoma City. This is supposed to be one of the best-preserved parts of the route. There was quite a bit of old 1960s kitsch left, but surrounded by lots of 1990s schlock! It was more difficult to find the old among the new.

We are both really tired. We feel like we have been continually on the go this month. I just looked it up on the itinerary, and we have been in eleven different states this month, and we've been in and out of several of them—Missouri, Tennessee, and Mississippi—more than one time! We need a rest!

Today was quite a day. We expected to be able to cover the four things we wanted to see in Oklahoma City in one day, but the Oklahoma City National Memorial was so compelling that we spent most of the day there. They have done a fabulous job of telling the story. The outdoor memorial is stirring with the 168 empty chairs lined up in nine rows, representing the nine stories of the building and the probable location of the victims, along with the survival tree, an elm that was within 250 feet of the blast which was felt thirty to fifty miles away but that survived the bomb and fires. A beautiful pool of water fills the area that was once the street running in front of the Alfred J. Murrah Center. Granite saved from the building outlines the former structure, and the survivors' names are emblazoned on a wall that endured the blast. People still come to leave memorials on a portion of the fence that has been preserved.

But that was nothing compared to the memorial museum that has been carefully built with input from families, survivors, rescue workers, and ordinary citizens. It is done in a dramatic timeline starting with "any other day" that shows the ordinary nature of this momentous day. It then takes you through sitting in a water-board meeting as the blast occurs, the pandemonium and confusion that ensued, and then the rescue days and all the aftermath up to building this museum. It was heartbreaking, sobering, and encouraging. The way everyone pulled together in this city was incredible. The man who gave the boots off his feet to a fireman who needed them, the schoolchildren who gave 168 pennies in classes all over the country to eventually raise $450,000 toward the museum, to the outpourings of emotion written on buildings and attached to the fences. The exhibit ended with a beautiful fountain with children singing, "Let their be peace on earth, and let it begin with me." An incredible experience. An absolute must-see for every American. Nothing could be horrible enough for Timothy McVeigh to endure. His execution next month in Indiana is nowhere near a fitting punishment for the havoc he created upon this city. After seeing this exhibit, all American citizens will be committed to peace and the end of terrorism.

Chapter

Spring Has Sprung

Week 44 | Oklahoma and Texas

What a crummy way to start our week. Phil realized yesterday while we were in OKC (that's how they abbreviate Oklahoma City here—everybody does it!) that he left his wedding ring in the shower. He had a barbecue sandwich for lunch the day before and some of the sticky sauce was still under his ring, so he took it off in the shower. He never takes that ring off! When I got in, I saw something golden on the shampoo bottle, but thought it was foil or something on it. Without glasses on, I didn't think anything of it—he never takes his ring off!

When we returned, it was gone. Our hearts both sunk. We called the front desk and told them. They called the head housekeeper. She would talk to the person cleaning our room in the morning. Of course, the housekeeper denied even seeing the ring. The general manager at the motel suggested we file a police report, which we did, but I'm afraid it is gone. The manager didn't even express an "I'm sorry." She was very defensive. The lady at the police department says they will notify the pawnshops. It may show up there, and she says they have a really good relationship with all the shops in town. It will be easy to spot due to the inscription and date on the inside. She says it will probably get traded for drugs or cash but will most likely turn up in a pawnshop. She also says, "Gee, we haven't had a complaint from up there for a while." Makes me wonder what goes on there.

Let's see, we've had a traffic accident, a medical emergency, and now a theft. What else is left?

Having done everything we could, we headed for the National Cowboy Museum and Hall of Fame, another terrific attraction. OKC should be very proud of their facilities for visitors. This place is first-class and covers everything about the West. Cowboys, Indians, rodeos, weapons, living on the trail, Frederick Remingtons, Charles Russells, Western wear (old and new), a Western town, and just about anything else you can think of that is Western.

We are on our third audio book. This one is *Into Thin Air*—a fascinating recount of an assault on Mount Everest that goes bad. The miles just fly by. Before we knew it today we were in Dallas. We almost wanted to keep going just so we could keep listening!

Dallas is a happening place, the eighth-largest city in the country and relatively easy to get around in. We stayed one night in the "burbs" just to avoid rush-hour traffic and gather ourselves for what we wanted to do. The next morning we headed for downtown to a Hampton Inn right in the heart of everything for less than $100 a night—a real find in a big city like this! It is also right on their light-rail line and next to the West End and all the JFK attractions.

We enjoyed the cloudy but warm, breezy, and humid day exploring the West End Marketplace area, the Dealy Plaza area where Kennedy was shot, the sixth-floor museum where Lee Harvey Oswald fired the shots, the grassy knoll, and the Kennedy Memorial. It was quite eerie to see the place; it is still essentially just like it was that day in 1963. We continued on to the Book Depository building to see all the information about everything related to the tragedy. What struck us as odd—as it did the other people at the museum—is why Oswald waited to shoot until Kennedy was in that location. Oswald had a much better opportunity (straight-on shot) before the motorcade turned the corner onto Elm Street. It was almost like he waited until the last possible second before he was out of range. Why?

After a day walking around town, we were pooped and still had more sight-seeing to do the next day. We went over to the convention center, as we wanted to see the park around it. There is a really wonderful sculpture of a cattle drive down a hill, several cowboys and lots of cattle, all life-size. It is very well done. We went to see the Dallas City Hall, which was designed by a famous architect, I. M. Pei. It is a triangle sitting on its edge—kind of.

Austin is our next stop. It's frequently rated as one of the top ten cities in the country, and we were interested to see what this was all about. The Texas Hill Country. Finally trees with leaves, and lots of them. Austin is a very pretty town—lots of parks; a nice, alive downtown; and suburbs that are growing too fast. Everyone we talked to agreed this is a wonderful place to live. The weather was uncharacteristically windy, hot, and humid, but you could feel the energy and pride in their city.

Our last stop was the Lady Bird Johnson Wildflower Garden. Enjoyed talking to yet another former Oregonian in the gift shop. We seem to find someone every few days who has connections to Oregon.

We have discovered that something went wrong with our last roll of film. Upon development, we find that we've lost all our pictures in Nebraska, Kansas, and Oklahoma. Phil lost his stadium pictures and several other things. Fortunately, we have digital pictures of many of the attractions. I had a photo-repair shop look at the camera, and it seems to be working perfectly. Neither of us can explain why the film quit winding yet kept acting like it was winding. It must have been something in the way I attached it to the spool.

Today we took more back roads to a small German town called Fredericksburg via Luckenbach, of Willie Nelson fame. What a trip back in time that was! Not really a town at all, but a wide spot on a side road that is totally funky, a real Willie kind of place. You can just imagine the craziness that goes

Phil sizes up the roots of "Willie and Waylon" where "everybody's somebody in Luckenbach" (Texas).

on in their largest of five buildings, the dance hall. A small store, an outhouse building, a house, and another unidentified building make up the rest of "town" nestled under a canopy of comforting oak trees where "everybody's somebody in Luckenbach." A visit by a bevy of Harley riders while we were there added to the ambiance.

When we arrived in Fredericksburg, we discovered that most of our motel was filled with more middle-aged Harley riders!

Not like the Harley groups of yore. They are quiet, well-behaved, and busy keeping those bikes shiny clean. Some even brought their bikes to town in trailers pulled by Volvos and BMWs! Since Phil has a cold and is not feeling very well, we enjoyed a leisurely afternoon just poking around the town and watching the Masters on TV in the evening.

Phil-osophies

First, Florida is not, I repeat, not part of the South. It is a place and culture all of its own! Having now passed through the "Real South," I can look back and see that the South is a very special place with a rich history and culture not seen in any other part of our country. The people have a way about them that is more genuine, less protective of self. They are more willing to laugh both at themselves and situations, but they are also more sure of their opinions and experiences. There is almost a melodramatic or flamboyant air about their delivery, but in a positive way. Yet there is a softness and acceptance that isn't seen in other places. The pretensions of the North and West seem absent from their way. I enjoyed the South and its people greatly.

As we headed out of town, bound for Fort Stockton on our way to Big Bend National Park, the scenery began to change. First the lovely trees started shrinking in size into stocky, bushy formations. The bluebonnets were still stumbling along the roadways, hanging over the rocks, and mixing with other spring wildflowers to make a variegated carpet as we drove along. Somewhere west of Sonora, even the bushy trees left us, replaced by classic desert plants. Yuccas, heavy with their white jutting blooms, cactus of various types, and pinions that made a contorted image along the road. The bluebonnets were gone, but fields of brilliant yellow replaced them, as did occasional outcroppings of other lovely wildflowers, unidentifiable as we zoomed along.

With traffic as sparse as the landscape, we were in Fort Stockton, 260 miles later, in no time. Yesterday had brought them a terrible windstorm, even closing parts of the highway at times, and the thick dust from that storm still clung to the air, blocking all views of the mountains in the distance. Another week behind us.

Week 45 | Texas and New Mexico

Palm Sunday in Fort Stockton, Texas, a godforsaken place, remembered only by the massive amount of truckers stopping for refreshment, fuel, or sleep right across from our motel. But in spite of its desolate location, we are taking an extra pause here because it is the first really nice weather we have seen since Florida—sunny, a little breeze, and about 85 to 90 degrees today. The deserted pool is calling our names and the sunshine is just too inviting. We also want to watch the final round of the Masters this afternoon during what would normally be our drive time. Big Bend will have to wait until tomorrow.

Contemplating what to do with an entire unscheduled day was too much for us. We decided we had to accomplish something! One look at the Rolling White House and we knew what we needed to do. Its last bath, other than rain, was in Columbus, Ohio, in September! Her new color is a dim gray. The local self-service car wash was brimming with customers, lined up waiting to place their quarters in the soap-and-water machine. I'm sure the awful dust storm yesterday has something to do with it, and the fact it is a glorious Sunday. Five dollars worth of quarters later, we got at least the first layer of grime off. What an improvement!

Big Bend National Park gets only a few thousand visitors a year, low for a national park. It is *way* off the beaten path—only the determined visit here. But what a treat for those who make their way here, and an even bigger treat for those who make their home in this area. You have to be a pioneer, as nothing in this area is easy, but the people are wonderful. The scenery that they enjoy every day is beyond breathtaking, but making even a meager living here is difficult. Those of us who are "trespassers" on this beauty are the lucky ones.

We have arrived during the most beautiful part of the year. There are three distinct areas here: the mountains, the desert, and the river—the infamous Rio Grande. We knew we wanted to experience one of the canyons on the river and enjoy the best display of desert flowers in years. They were spectacular!

A stop at the visitor center yielded the information that the campgrounds and lodge were full—spring break for some schools. I had scoped out this resort at Lajitas, even more off the beaten path, but they have a golf course! So off we went. Now, this place is a trip. It was about 99 degrees at five o'clock in the afternoon and seventeen miles from even the most minimal idea of civilization, but we were here. The golf course was closed due to remodeling, the pool was freezing cold, but the rooms were reasonable ($58). We checked in and made plans for the river trip tomorrow. "Big Bend Adventures—Feel the Magic!" There would be no rafting, as the river is too low, but a canoe trip, called the boomerang, is possible. The chipper twenty-year-old explained, "Three hours upstream with not much current—you can do it! Then some hiking in the canyon and a nice drift back down." OK, we'll bite.

We are apprehensive. Our last encounter with boats that we personally managed was not a happy experience. The guide cheerfully reminded us that canoes are also called "divorce boats." That's reassuring. Phil decided that the solution was to let me pilot the boat in the rear, and he will take orders—he knows what a control freak I am about things like making it safely down rivers! Instructions: paddle on the side opposite the direction you want to go. The pilot can control direction by dragging the oar on the side you want to turn towards, and—this is the best part—the rower in front takes direction on which side to row from the pilot!

We're in the water and paddling upstream. Stay out of the current and follow the guide. Some places are too low even for canoes. Now paddling like crazy—did I mention upstream?—and additionally, we have to drag the canoes across sandbars and gravel bars! Thankfully, it was a cloudy day, as opposed to yesterday of hot, high temps. The scenery is spectacular! Canyon walls 1,500 feet above us and totally silent here. Beautiful.

Not only is the Rio Grande low, but they warn, don't swim in it. We were the only canoe of five that didn't overturn at some point during the day! I attribute it to my skillful maneuvering and fear of my camera meeting the Rio Grande up close and personal! One could not drown in this river—it's not swift and not deep! The real "aha" of how bad the river is was the guides' insistence of using a waterless hand cleaner before we could eat lunch! This was not recommended, it was mandatory. A little scary!

The lunch stop was a welcome site. A green site with Mexico on one side, 1,500 feet up, and the park 1,500 feet up on the other. After eating, a hike up to a fern grotto was planned. Phil and I only went part way as old age, out of shape, and a bad case of "the tireds" had set in. We had to save our meager strength for the return trip and its portages ahead of us.

On the return, we not only had the river current to help but also a nice wind blowing down the canyon speeding us along. Amazing how much more quickly we got back to the put-in location. Even the portages were easier downstream! We even learned how to navigate mild rapids, and we executed them without tipping or slamming into other boats. Poor Phil—near the end and with our strength totally sapped, an even older couple in our group got into trouble and was stuck crosswise between two rocks. We were behind them and needed to go through the same channel that was blocked. Phil got out of our canoe and helped free them, complete with them *in* the canoe! He said later that he's not sure how he got the energy! Except we knew our exit from the river lay ahead of getting them going again!

We fell into bed very early after a nice long shower to remove the Rio Grande from our bodies! It was a beautiful trip and a wonderful remembrance of this park, but oh the aching bodies! A raging dust storm had greeted us upon our return from the canyon. We thought it might blow our casita off the foundation, and the poor RWH, what would become of it? We drove the few blocks to dinner instead of walking, as the visibility was only a few yards and the dust was horrific, stinging the body and getting in our hair, clothes, etc.

As we were leaving the park, there was something in the road. *Thunk, thunk.* "Phil, you just ran over a huge snake!" This guy was stretched out across the entire lane, at least eight feet long! It was red and pink and probably six to eight inches in diameter. We stopped as we were exiting the park and asked what it was. The ranger said there are lots of them here. It is a Coach Whip. While not poisonous, it was quite spectacular and big!

We've been out of cell-phone range for two days now, and there are no phones in our rooms! They are wonderful new little cottages with a fireplace, Jacuzzi tub (for those still-aching muscles), a sitting area with bay window, and a nice lawn to sit out on. But no phones and no e-mail now for four days. We are starting to go a little buggy.

We got into Carlsbad in time to still see the caves today, thanks to the change to Mountain Time—only one time zone from home! As Phil says, "This is the Disneyland of caves!" The largest by far, and all types of formations—huge rooms of beautiful forms. We just gawked at everything, and the walking was very easy. Phil didn't have to duck down once! It took a couple of hours and was a little over a mile stroll.

We could have camped tonight, but we really needed to get e-mail and wanted to see *Survivor*, so we checked into a motel, once more. *Can you believe it?*—this motel's phone system is so cheesy that we can't even get online! Even with all my special "motel" gadgetry, we couldn't get a connection. We both groan. I want to update the website, get e-mail, and do a few other Web chores, but again, not tonight. I even went to the office to see about their fax line. Even that goes through the same funky system!

OK, I'm chilled out over last night. We decided not to go to Tucson this weekend and headed for one of our favorite cities instead, Santa Fe. From Carlsbad, it is a good four-and-a-half- to five-hour drive through absolutely nowhere! Oh, I take that back. Roswell is part way up the road—you know, UFOs and the like. We decided that this is not really our "cup of tea," and we made a beeline for Santa Fe.

We are getting really road-weary, so we decided that maybe a few days break was what we needed. We made a great deal on a hotel right downtown at the Inn of the Governors. It has a fireplace, balcony, great Santa Fe–style furnishings, hand-decorated lamps, neat tin accessories, hangers that you can take off the rod, a secluded walled-in lovely pool—and it's in the heart of everything. We have been here before, so some of the immediate tourist things have already been done. It is a great small town with so much to see. The Santa Fe walking tour is not to be missed. It was fun to just re-walk some of the things we had learned earlier.

There is definitely something to be said for staying in the heart of a city. We have noticed it several times along our way. You seem to have a closer connection with what is going on than when you stay out in the suburbs. It is just a different "touch point." Even though the rooms cost more, you save money on driving, parking, and general frustration, and usually you can walk everywhere, especially in Santa Fe.

We have lined out our Easter weekend here. Attend church Sunday in the old cathedral, St. Francis of Assisi, have brunch in the hotel, and golf mid-afternoon. Today, Saturday, we will explore some of the galleries, sit by the pool, go to the Georgia O'Keeffe Museum, have a massage, and find a low-key local restaurant for dinner. Sound perfect?

I think maybe my favorite thing this weekend was Easter Sunday morning. It dawned sunny and crisp. We got our showers and headed out across the square and the narrow little streets, already filled with people of every description. Many of them were, like us, following the sounds of the church bells reverberating through the town to the very old Catholic church, just a couple blocks off the square and quite beautiful inside. We arrived right at the stroke of 10 a.m. and found ourselves, along with another hundred or so worshippers, standing in every available nook and cranny listening to the age-old story told in this ancient city, where so many cultures come together in life and in spirit. This will be etched in our minds.

Week 46 | Arizona

The sixteen miles across gravel roads dissuaded us from the Chaco National Historic Park—maybe sometime in a rental car!—and we headed for the western border and the town of Gallup, another "get your kicks on Route 66" place. It is one of the best-preserved areas of the route, with many old signs, hotels, and other memorabilia still intact in a beautiful surrounding of red hills and mesas.

We had planned to camp, but the campgrounds were pretty dismal, and the call of an historic old hotel named the El Rancho, from the early Route 66 days, intrigued us. One of our favorite guidebooks, *Road Trip USA*, called it "lovingly restored." It had been a real hot spot for Hollywood stars in town for the many Western movies shot here during the '40s and '50s. Each room is named after a star that stayed here. We're in the Alan Ladd room, and wonderful Southwestern art adorns the walls of the generous rooms.

After enjoying some of the old-time sights around town, we headed for a national monument that spans five different periods of Indian history, dating back to 2500 B.C. The Canyon de Chelley (pronounced *shay*) is filled with fairly well preserved artifacts from the Anasazi, Hopi, and Navajo occupations of the canyon. Even though this is a part of the National Park system, the Navajos still own property and occupy farms in the canyon. We drove one of the rim drives and hiked down into the canyon—it's not the going down, it's the coming back up, six hundred vertical feet in a half mile of switchbacks! The next day we took a jeep tour into the canyon, right through the river, along the sandbars, and right up next to these wonderful petroglyphs, pictographs, and ruins of their homes and other buildings.

We needed gas coming out of the remote town of Chinle, but the price was $1.64 a gallon. We decided we could get to the interstate and hopefully better prices. The freeway brought $1.74! Phil dug his heels in and said, "We're not paying it! We still have almost a quarter tank. Let's keep going." A few miles later, we had to turn off to the Petrified Forest National Park. We had decided to just get a little bit of gas, if the price is still so high. One gas station at the exit, and it is within the National Park complex—looks bad. Lo and behold they are having a "Route 66 rollback sale" in honor of the 75th anniversary of the highway! $1.39! We scored big-time on this tank! We get the biggest amusement out of the smallest things. We need to get off the road!

We can tell we are getting closer to home—more license plates are from Oregon and Washington. Today on the jeep tour with nine other couples, two of the nine are from Oregon—nice people who have second homes in the Tucson area and are still wintering down here. Oh, while we were at the $1.39 gas station, a couple from Coos Bay was asking about our vehicle. They may be interested in buying it from us, so we were sure to get their name and phone number!

The Petrified Forest National Park was a nice half-day type of park. The sad thing about this park is that it is disappearing into people's pockets at the rate of one ton a month! Even though there are stiff fines, signs everywhere, and park rangers pleading, the loss continues. A couple of years ago, the rangers placed some invisibly marked rocks near an accessible path, and within one week 20 percent of them were gone! Amazing. You look at pictures of how it used to be and how it is today, and it is really sad. And you can buy rocks outside the park that have been harvested legally in other areas, but still the loss continues. What is wrong with people!

Another unexpected situation has sprung on us. My mom has been diagnosed with breast cancer at age 81. She is going in for a double mastectomy after several weeks of debating the options available to her. We will be going home for about ten days to get her through that and get additional care arranged. We will fly home from Phoenix on April 28 and continue our trip May 10. We are running a couple of weeks ahead of schedule, so we should still be home by our anticipated mid-June time frame. It would be better if we could stay home, but we are determined to finish what we have started, and Mom is very supportive of us doing that. So, we will have a short interruption to the Great American Adventure, but things do happen over which we have no control. We can only control our response to the situation and make the prudent arrangements.

We didn't make it all the way to Tucson, Arizona, stopping short in a tiny town called Florence. AAA lists only two motels, and for the first time, we could find no others. The first one looked a little scary, so we went in search of the other one quite a ways out of town, but what a find! The Rancho Sonora Inn has six B&B style rooms, all named, around a lovely courtyard with lots of trees, a fountain, and cactus gardens. Breakfast, of course, is available on the patio, and soft music discreetly enhances the background. A lovely pool and spa a few steps away and a steak house just down the highway where we had the best steak of the trip for about $10 or $12, a filet mignon! We could easily have stayed here longer. You just never know what waits around the next corner.

Evening found us a lovely campground on the way back to Tucson, complete with lake, clubhouse, pool and spa, and nice grounds. Our first camping since Florida! It was really nice to cook again and just putter around in the van.

Week 47 | Arizona

We had heard about this great campground near Saguaro National Park, so we set out to find Gilbert Ray. It was truly another find, private sites set right in the desert landscape with the Tucson Mountains as a backdrop. With the cactus all in bloom and the saguaros standing guard, it was one of the best places we've stayed. We didn't discover until the morning that there were no showers, but we survived with a sponge bath! Electric only, so we had to use our onboard fresh water—fortunately we had some!

A nice drive through Saguaro National Park and all the sentinels standing guard over the desert, and we were off to find downtown Tucson and the University of Arizona for Phil and his picture-taking of stadiums. I had spotted an inexpensive yet interesting motel in the AAA book. Score! For $44 we are ensconced in the Ghost Ranch Lodge on the Miracle Mile. It has beautiful grounds, a great pool area, nice rooms, a laundry for Phil, and a nice restaurant and bar. After a couple of camping nights, we were ready, so we spent the remainder of the day around the pool just enjoying this beautiful place.

Even though we have really enjoyed our time in Tucson, Phoenix is calling us. We need to get ready to head for home for ten days and figure out what we're going to do with the van. We are going to take some time to just regroup, pack, run a couple of errands, see a couple of things—Karsten Golf and Taliesin West are on the agenda—and be ready to head out on Saturday morning. Talk to you when we get back.

Weeks 48 and 49 | Home again

Another whirlwind trip home, but with a more solemn purpose than the holidays. Mom came through her double mastectomy like a trooper. Surgery on Tuesday, home on Thursday, out for a walk the same day, showering and moving around remarkably well. Her spirits were buoyed, as were the family's. I was even able to get away to attend a friend's wedding shower on Saturday and host a small dinner party on Sunday night.

Most days were taken up with running errands, helping Mom around the house, and getting her ready to be self-sufficient again, with a little help during the day. Then, unexpectedly, on Monday morning a raging red rash developed on one side, but we were due to the doctor that afternoon. The doctor was a bit alarmed at how quickly it came on. He gave her a big shot and started antibiotics immediately. The next day was no better, and on Wednesday, with us back on our way to Phoenix, Mom lands back in the hospital with a roaring infection. We couldn't have left, except daughter Andrea was on her way down from Seattle for her turn with Grandma. Little did we know she would be tending to her in the hospital. By Thursday, her fever had broken and the doctor says she was much better.

Meanwhile, we arrive in Phoenix to 106-degree temperatures. We planned to stay and golf, but Phil was too hot and just wanted to get on the road again, so we headed for the hills, literally.

By late afternoon we arrived in Prescott (*press-kit*), Arizona, at 5,600 feet, much cooler and very pleasant. We looked at a development here as a potential winter getaway but found it is too cold in the winter here for our liking, even though they boast over 350 days of sunshine a year! They have

What Phil won't do to amuse the grandchildren on the website! Yes, he's actually in all four states at the same time!

twenty inches of snow in the winter with an average high of 55. That just doesn't do it for us—scratch another location off our list!

Flagstaff, Arizona, is another stop on Route 66 that still has many of its attractions in operation. We found a room at the Monte Vista Hotel in historic old Flagstaff. They have taken a lot of pride in preserving this piece of Americana, in a town that values its roots on Route 66. The old train station is still there, only a couple of blocks from the hotel, and the trains still come through regularly. In fact, I think every train in the United States came through the night we were there! Between the trains and the reveling North Arizona State grads who enjoyed their graduation that night, we were a little short on sleep! But it was still fun, probably more so because of the graduation and all the excitement in town. We sat on the balcony of the Wetherill Hotel and watched the sun go down and the kids enjoying their big evening.

In Cortez, Colorado, we enjoyed a pleasant evening in a campground with a million-dollar view of the mesas and the southern end of the Rocky Mountains. Big clouds rolled all around us and you could see rain and thundershowers in the mountains, but we got to be just spectators to a dramatic sky.

Mesa Verde hides its face behind a highway of hairpin turns and switchbacks up and down the mesas, but what a special treat when you get there. The Cliff Palace, the largest ruin of its type in the country, the Spruce Tree House, and other well-preserved ruins peek out all over this World Heritage site. We spent most of the day crawling up and down ladders and stairs as we took advantage of this one-of-a-kind location. The end of the day took us back through these winding roads and on to Durango, Colorado, where we nestled in for what was left of our Mother's Day.

We made a call to Mom to make sure the kids had gotten her out of the house and out for a nice Mother's Day dinner. She seemed pretty perky, but tired after her first outing in over two weeks. She seemed to enjoy visiting with them, but she was ready to hit the sack. We're just glad she is home and doing better.

Week 50 | Colorado

Our plan is to be home by mid-June, and to do that we need to get a move on! We also are planning to meet some of the grandchildren at Disneyland toward the end of the month. All of this means we have to choose *carefully* where we spend our time—a new experience for us.

Today we drove one of our longest days—315 miles from Durango to Colorado Springs, over beautiful mountain passes and through "valleys" at 7,000-plus feet. We stopped at a rest stop for lunch at 9,000 feet with a waterfall tumbling down from a thousand feet higher yet. Awesome!

Before retiring for the evening in Manitou Springs, we made arrangements to take the cog railroad to the top of Pike's Peak the next morning. Even though it was showering and not looking too promising, the motel owner assured us, "This is Colorado; tomorrow will be great." And she was right. The morning dawned beautiful, so our layers were reduced to a fleece over our golf shirts. 14,130 feet is *high*! We weren't cold with the snow all around us, but we could hardly breathe! The view from Pike's Peak is incredible—mountains, lakes, cities, and views into neighboring states. Just don't move too fast or you will be panting—a very weird experience.

Phil-osophies

I had spied a volleyball exhibition to be held at the U.S. Olympic Training Center. After trying to find it in this large complex, we found it was actually in downtown Colorado Springs—so off we went. We missed the team workout, but we enjoyed watching the players working with kids and teenagers to promote the sport of volleyball. Even ran into a guy from my volleyball days at the club.

We decided to end our day at the Garden of the Gods. In the middle of this granite mountain range, you have a whole valley of red-rock formations. This park is fabulous, and you can tell that the locals also enjoy it. We were there late in the afternoon after an 80-plus-degree day, and the rock climbers were out in force, clambering up many of the faces rising from the valley floor. Moms walking their babies, joggers, bicyclists, hikers, and horseback riders filled the park with late-day enjoyment. It was an invigorating way to end a glorious day.

Today we are off for Denver to see a few sights there, as Phil has never been there. I've been there so many times I could throw up! After a quick look at downtown and the state capitol, we were off for Boulder in rush-hour traffic. Fortunately we weren't in any hurry. Today has been rainy all day, so this made the traffic even worse, and more importantly, we couldn't see the mountains! Again, the desk clerk at the motel assured us that tomorrow could bring a 90-degree day. We'll see.

Well, it is a lot like Oregon. The day dawned sunny and bright with most of the mountains in view. We headed for the University of Colorado to see the campus and the stadium. This would be a great place to go to school. The campus is lovely and the town small and intimate, perfect for a campus town. Boulder Creek meanders through it all. After wandering around the campus, we headed for the historic area. As one local said, "What is historic about it? They have torn everything down and rebuilt it!"

We have had another camera catastrophe and needed to find a real camera shop. When I was rewinding the 35mm, the film went "snap." I knew it had broken, so we found a shop with a darkroom where they could remove it safely from the camera. This roll will get developed when we get home, as it will take special handling. But hopefully the pictures will be OK.

With over half the day gone, we are off to Rocky Mountain National Park. Estes Park is a darling little town. Checked out the Stanley Hotel and realized we had been there before, when we went to Fort Collins, back when we were dating. Wasn't that at least a hundred years ago? Rain has been threatening all day, but there were so many great RV parks here. However, we don't like rain camping, so we ducked into one of the many cabin motels in the area. Don't even think of staying in some chain location here—the cabins are so cute and there are lots of them. We found the Big Thompson Timberlane Lodge and thoroughly enjoyed the cabin and their lovely grounds.

It was pretty funny, as we headed down the driveway to cross the river, I yelled at Phil —something I rarely do—"*Stop!*" The bridge ahead of us with the raging water below did not look RV-friendly, and sure enough there is a small sign with a weight limit of 7,000 pounds. Phil sprinted across the bridge to the office and found that there is a back entrance for behemoths like us. Both they and we were grateful that we didn't attempt the crossing. Lovely grassy grounds, a pool, a play area for kids, BBQs and picnic tables, and several inviting hot tubs made this a perfect place to stay.

Saturday morning was partly sunny and partly cloudy, but we were on a mission to enjoy the park. The road through the park isn't open yet, due to snow, but we went as far as we could and then also took in the area around Bear Lake. Even this very traveled trail had snow on the north side. It was a nice hike around the lake, and we enjoyed our lunch while we were there.

Today we are off for Grand Junction or Montrose to see the newest national park, the Black Canyon of the Gunnison. The drive from Vail to Grand Junction is without a doubt the most spectacular interstate drive we have had. You go through Glenwood Canyon and through many wonderful little towns, all along the Colorado River. In many places the freeway is actually a long bridge clinging tenuously to the mountainside. In a couple of places the traffic going the other way was actually under us, the canyon was so narrow. Besides the beauty, we noticed that there is a bike/walking/ skating path the full length of this incredible route.

Week 51 | Utah

The afternoon took us out of Colorado and into southern Utah. What a change of scenery in a short period of time! We stopped at the Utah visitor center to try to get a handle on the route for all these parks in Utah. They actually call it the Grand Circle and have a well-laid-out path to follow, no matter where you enter the circle. Some of the roads look a little scary, but it appears that this is the only way to really see everything. So we're off.

Our first stop in the late afternoon is Arches National Park. They say go early in the morning or late in the afternoon for the best photography and views. The sky is clear blue and the scenery out of another world. The red rock against the azure blue sky can barely be captured in pictures. And talk about personalities—some of the tall "figures" have faces and expressions that you can easily see! It was quite shocking!

Today is my birthday. Mom checked in early, feeling bad that she couldn't even send me a card! Tonight I got an e-card and e-gift-certificate from the grandchildren—what a difference a generation or two makes! Now I have to figure out how to access it and use it! We were out of cell range most of the day in Canyonlands Park and missed several calls from friends with good wishes. It helped make the day more special out here in the middle of nowhere. Tonight we are in Blanding, Utah, a dry town! We couldn't even toast my birthday, except in our room!

Canyonlands was a fun way to spend my birthday. We hiked and photographed more of this crazy country. We went into the Needles area, one of three separate locations within a giant park. It almost becomes overwhelming after a while when one thing is more spectacular than the last. Your eyes almost go numb!

We spent all day on a scenic byway, only 190 miles, but it takes us all day. A stop at Natural Bridges and Capitol Reef to see the wonders of both of these locations. We are in and out of the red rocks, with fabulous white rock faces leaping out of the river floor. There are roads that thread their way through canyons with creeks and rivers, long plateaus with small green shrubs as far as the eye can see, and formations that reminded us of all kinds of statues and strange things to see.

This is the kind of scenery that cameras can't really capture. Your eyes see the panorama, but the lens can't take that all in, so all a photographer can do is try to focus on a representative sample of the terrain, but that seems so inadequate and flat on the lens. You have to see it for yourself—that is the only way to truly "see" it, and you have to get out of your car to see at least some of the backcountry. Today we took a short hike with a 200-foot drop/rise and a two-mile hike through a wash in a canyon. Totally different experiences, but both gave us a better appreciation of the areas.

It suddenly dawned on us that this weekend is Memorial Day. It is easy to lose track of time! And we realized that we are in one of the most popular locations in the country. We had to sit down and plan, oh horrors! We made reservations for Friday through Monday at appropriate locations. Then we'll be on a beeline for Southern California to see the grandbabies. We feel like we are under a lot of stress! We actually have to *be* somewhere on a certain date!

What will happen when we get home? We are so used to our own schedule, I can't imagine having *obligations* again! I told Phil today, "We have got to get a calendar. People are already working on filling our days!" We're starting to get worried about the "reentry" to normal society!

At what point can the eyes and senses not take anymore? This country is so eye-popping at every turn. Hour after hour, you see one setting after another that changes from reds to greens to whites to combinations; from plateaus to deep valleys to rolling slicks to peaceful valleys. Today we ventured down what has been called one of the most scenic highways in America, Highway 12 from Torrey, Utah, to Bryce National Park. It is only a little over a hundred miles, but it took us at least three hours of time. Up and down we went, twisting turns, vistas that force a stop, and then—the Hogsback. It is a strip about a half mile long at 15 mph, across a narrow two-lane road with minimal shoulders and no guardrail where you see into the depths below on *both* sides about 1,000 feet lower than you are as you creep across this unbelievable ridge. The original road through this area around Boulder, Utah, was hand-built by the CCC (Civilian Conservation Corps, part of Roosevelt's "New Deal"), every shovel-full built by hand, creeping up and down canyon walls. It is the last place in the United States where the mail was delivered by mule. It is part of Escalante Grand Staircase National Monument. You are too awed to be scared.

We pulled off the road for lunch at the Kiva Koffeehouse with a view that wouldn't quit. It was built in the mid-1990s by an artist fulfilling his dream. His family is now completing his vision. The food was fresh and homemade and the feeling intimate. The materials for the structure came mostly from the surrounding land and looked like an Indian kiva. We had a delightful conversation with a couple about our age from San Francisco, another possibility of interest for the van. They "toured" the rig and really thought it was perfect! They have traveled extensively in both the United States and the rest of the world. A very interesting life they have had, and now in retirement it sounds like "no-holds-barred" traveling for them!

We have been over a mile high for two-plus weeks and still can't breathe comfortably! It's just a matter of how uncomfortable we are. We are doing well up to about 8,000 feet now; another few weeks and maybe we'll be like the locals! All of these parks are just begging you to hike.

A few hours drive and we arrive at the North Rim of the Grand Canyon. We had reserved a cabin for the night at the Grand Canyon Lodge. What a wonderful choice! A historic lodge built right on the rim, I don't know how they built it this way, but the building is literally the edge of the canyon. Two big terraces with old rocking chairs beckon you to stop and just enjoy the vista. This is Friday night of the busy Memorial Day weekend, and the two hundred lodge cabins are full, but the place is still not overrun with people. It is just pleasant to wander around, take a hike, look through the gift shop, meander through the cabins, or go take a nap!

Bright Angel Point—visible from the South Rim—was recommended for sunset, so off we went, camera in hand. It is truly not to be forgotten. The canyon was in constant transformation as the sun changed the shadows throughout the rock. I'm so glad I sucked it up and went out onto this point with the canyon falling all around me.

Little did we know what was ahead of us. Nothing I had read had prepared us for the east entrance to Zion National Park—the most-visited of the parks in the Grand Circle. Whereas at Bryce and Canyonlands, you look down into the valley, at Zion you are in the valley looking up. But first you have to get from the 6,000-foot elevation outside the park to the 3,700-foot floor in the park. Are you getting the picture? The Zion–Crescent Junction highway at the park entrance is considered one of the great engineering marvels of the 1920s. Two tunnels (now one-way traffic at a time only), one over a mile long, guard the valley. Strenuous height, weight, and length restrictions keep much of the traffic out completely, and anything much bigger than we are requires

an "escort" through the tunnel at $10 a pop and a wait in a long line the day we were there! Once you get past the tunnel, you switchback down the side of the mountain at 15 to 25 mph, white-knuckle all the way. But the scenery—we pulled over at several turnouts just to look—was beyond description. Walls going straight up into the blue sky a thousand feet above and a riverbed with lush vegetation lining the small valley floor. Rocks of red next to ones almost white or stained nearly black from minerals. Just too amazing for words—and this wasn't even the "scenic drive" part of the park!

Can you believe this scenery? Zion is just one of many eye-popping national parks in southern Utah.

It almost made us forget we didn't have a place to stay tonight since we had cancelled our reservations because we weren't ending up where we thought we would. We did drive straight through the park on into Springdale, Utah, and stopped at the first RV/motel we saw. Thankfully, they found room for us and we were set! A warm night in the campground caused us to be up early and off to see Zion. This park allows only their own buses into the canyon—a very good idea after looking at the number of cars and the narrow road. It actually works very well. Buses run each direction about every five to six minutes and stop at all the places to see. Plus the drivers are a wealth of information about the park and are very accommodating. We hiked on three different trails, had lunch, took pictures, and just generally enjoyed this most magnificent of parks. Even with all the Memorial Day madness, it was still an enjoyable day.

Week 52 | California

We are looking forward to today's adventure. We are off to Death Valley and the famed Furnace Creek Inn, definitely in the off-season right now! Hope we don't melt before we arrive!

We had about a half tank of gas but decided to fill up before leaving St. George. We had found $1.48 and weren't sure what would lay ahead down the road. Some California tourists at Zion had told us the prices in California were awful. They had seen $1.56 and thought it was a great bargain, so we thought $1.48 looked pretty good.

It is a really hot trip to Death Valley—only 109 degrees here today! The RWH was working its heart out trying to keep us moving, keep the engine cool, and keep us cool. Poor thing, it was a champ, though.

Leaving St. George you go through the Virgin River Gorge, another really pretty interstate drive. It is actually in Arizona. You travel about thirty miles before entering Nevada.

We explored the park on the way in and stopped at the visitor center with the most enthusiastic park ranger we have encountered to date. He loves his job and really enjoys sharing Death Valley with visitors. We had passed the

Furnace Creek Inn on the way into the valley and were anxious to see this bit of green in a sea of brown.

What an oasis in the desert! A neat Spanish-mission-style lodge with wonderful rooms with stone patios looking over the green oasis with running water and ponds. You *almost* forgot how hot it was. The pool is filled with ideal 85-degree water directly from the springs, crystal-clear and no need to treat it after it travels through natural volcanic filtration. A beautiful sight overlooking the Death Valley salt flats and mountains beyond. I loved this place and could have stayed here much longer. Dinner in the dining room was fabulous. I don't know how they do it out here two hours from anywhere! It was definitely a four-star experience.

Gas in the park was $2.45, so we decided to try to get to a town, of which there were very few for hundreds of miles. We are headed for Joshua Tree National Park, almost three hundred miles away, but we have the "inside scoop" on the best route from our friendly ranger. Not sure what today will bring, but it can't be worse than the gas price in the park!

By the time we reached Shoshone, the first town outside the park, we had to have gas—$2.35! So we got just $10 worth, hoping for better prices down the road. Another 100 miles and we came to Baker—home of the world's largest thermometer, registering 104 today—and gas for $1.99. Never did we think we would view that price as good! We bought $20 worth at this juncture and hoped for still better prices further down the road.

Poor Joshua Tree National Park got kind of a "drive-by shooting." We spent only about an hour driving through the most scenic portion of the high plateau where the Joshua trees are. We justified it by saying that when we get our house down here, we can come back anytime, and it was getting late. We were bound for Palm Springs with no gas and no place to stay!

The smog being blown into the valley from LA was unbelievable! A thick brown/white haze hung in the valley, partially obscuring the beautiful mountains. I've never seen it that bad. Oh well, we can deal with the gas tomorrow—let's find a place to stay. I had scoped out some of the older, historic motels in downtown Palm Springs. We had never stayed in "the Springs" before, so we thought that would be fun. We landed at the Estrella Inn with its three pools, two spas, tile-roofed casitas, and whitewashed hotel rooms set against the mountain backdrop. All nestled around manicured grounds in a quiet area one block off Palm Canyon Drive, so we could walk to everything. A real find at a great price this time of year.

It's predicted for 110 degrees today, and Phil wants to play golf! I told him, "Knock yourself out and have a great time; I'm heading for the pool!" And I was in bad need of a pedicure, so I found a place to get that done, and a haircut, also badly needed! We made a trek down to El Paseo to my favorite swimsuit shop. It had been three years since my last purchase, also at this same place! I found two new numbers that will get me through a few more summers!

We had an interesting conversation with a couple visiting from Switzerland. It was fun discussing everything from Clinton, Bush, technology, pensions, Social Security, the economy, the environment, and AAA and AARP. They have been asked everywhere if they "have AAA or AARP" and had no idea what these even were! A fun afternoon soaking in the pool and talking. Their English was impeccable. Their first language was German, but you'd never know it!

After a week of 100-plus temperatures, we were saddened to get into the smog-filled valley and temperatures in the low 70s with no sunshine. Give us the clear days and the 100-degree temps! We had dinner with the kids and plotted our strategy for Disneyland tomorrow. The new Downtown Disney outside the park is really nice—good restaurants, fun shops, entertainment, etc. The kids were enthralled by the Rain Forest Restaurant.

Tomorrow starts our second year on the road! Hard to imagine!

Week 53 | California

What is it about Disneyland that makes everyone feel like a kid? Is it the upbeat, happy music? The Disney characters? The wonder of little smiles on the grandchildren's faces? The perfectly maintained, hassle-free grounds? The fairy-tale rides? I think it may be all of those things. No matter how many times you've been there, there is always something more to see, another laugh to be enjoyed, and more pictures to be taken. The scared/excited squeals of

"Honey, I shrunk the audience" were outdone only by the broad smiles from atop the rocket ships, yelling down at Mom and Dad to look, while Grandma and Grandpa took them to outer space!

Another short drive up the coast and we were preparing for our assault on the Channel Islands, one of the most difficult national parks to see. We will be on an all-day adventure tomorrow with a bunch of schoolkids to see Santa Cruz Island, one of the five islands in the park.

What a perfect day! We arrived at the boat with our water, food, sunscreen, and jacket ready for a fun day. The weather was beautiful, a nice tropical breeze, sun in and out of the clouds keeping the temperature just right, deep-blue waters that are so clear and vistas from the bluffs that make you know you are in very special place. Indian artifacts are still being found all around the islands, and the geology is interesting.

The boat ride was half the fun. We saw a pod of six beluga whales, a big school of dolphins who played all around the boat for about five minutes, sea lions, and all kinds of birds. The whales were a big thrill, as they are not often seen in this area. They were quite close to the boat a couple of different times. The adults were more thrilled with them than the kids! I guess nature just can't compete with Disneyland and video games!

We wanted to see the mission at San Luis Obispo, so we made a beeline up the road to see that. It dates back to 1792 and is the fifth in the chain of twenty-one missions throughout California. It is now right downtown and still much like it would have been in the 1800s. The museum has many of the original pieces of the original mission, and downtown San Luis Obispo has lots of charm. They have done a nice job with the shops and with the creek that runs through the town.

Today we have a long trek to Kings Canyon and Sequoia National Parks, so we left our cozy room on the beach before they kicked us out. Somehow our guidebooks didn't mention that the road going in the southern entrance was another one of "those" roads. It is called the Generals Highway after Lee and Grant, and I think it was forged when they were still alive! No vehicles over twenty-two feet are allowed, and most switchbacks are the 10 mph variety, for seventeen very *l-o-n-g* miles! We climbed from about 1,000 feet to over 6,000 feet, but the views were spectacular and the sequoias awesome. Just to stand near the largest living thing on this planet—the Sherman tree—has its own sense of reverence at 107 feet around the base and an estimated 2,300 to 2,700 years old. A thirteen-story building would come to only the first of its huge eight-foot-diameter limbs. You can't get a sense of it without being there.

Fortunately the road improved after the Sherman Tree. We drove on to Grant Grove Village, the location of the original part of the park. Here we made a strategic mistake. They wanted $130 to stay at the lodge—contrary to what the book says—and the guy was a jerk to boot. So, we said to ourselves, every national park has lodging just outside the park, and this one had lots of places coming in the south entrance. So, we thought, we'll just grab something and continue into Kings Canyon tomorrow. Well, an hour and a half later we were in Fresno, still with no place to stay. Now we have to drive all the way back in tomorrow! It was one of the worst misjudgments we've made on the whole trip!

We thought seriously of not going back, but we're glad we did. It was over 100 degrees in Fresno and yet only in the 80s in the park. We saw more sequoias today and drove part way down the King's Canyon Gorge before we had to turn back to get to my friend's house by 5 p.m. King's Canyon is the deepest gorge in the United States. How did I always think it was the Grand Canyon? We had a really nice day just exploring the park.

What a time we always have with friends. Once again, you would think we see each other all the time. We are able to just get right back into our lives and cry and laugh about what has happened and where we are in our lives. We yakked and yakked, then went for dinner and a movie, and then more yakking. First with the guys, and then we sent them to bed and kept going a while longer.

We knew when we left Fresno that we were within sniffing distance of home. We pushed on for Red Bluff, the entrance area to our final park, Lassen. We can't believe two things—that we have been out for over a year and that we will really be home this next week. We talked and cried over all we've seen and all we've learned. We know we have some wild days ahead of us as we try to reorient ourselves to "normal" life, but we are looking forward to that and to working on the book about everything we've done.

Week 54 | Home again

An early start out of Red Bluff and off to the last of our forty-three national parks. Not many people can say they have seen all forty-three of our parks in the forty-eight contiguous states. The only parks we are missing now are American Samoa and the seven parks in Alaska. We have previously seen both of the Hawaiian parks and the one on St. John in the Virgin Islands. Plus we have seen over forty of the more than three hundred monuments, seashores, historical parks, etc.

The Rolling White House just chugged right over those passes like it too was anxious to get home. Little does it know that we are going to sell it!

Our last night was a remembrance of our first night. Exactly one year and one week—June 3, 2000, and June 10, 2001—and we were back in the campground we site started out in! It was just the same. We toasted, reminisced, and began to look forward to what would come next in our lives.

Splish, splosh, splish, splosh. The rhythm of the windshield wipers welcomed us back to our home state and the final leg of the trip. Was it raining because it is Oregon?—or perhaps because it is so sad that the Great American Adventure is, indeed, coming to an end.

The adventure of a lifetime comes to an end—the last night the same as the first at RiverPark RV Resort, Grants Pass, Oregon.

Epilogue

The most commonly asked question we hear now is, "In hindsight, would you do it again?" The answer: "Absolutely."

Every minute of the planning and all the anxious moments, calamities, loneliness, homesickness, and road-weary days of the trip are but a footnote to the knowledge, personal closeness, and fabulous memories that we carry with us every day of our lives.

Not a day goes by that we don't pick up the newspaper or watch television and see someplace featured that we have visited. When you have personal knowledge of a place, then everything that happens there becomes more interesting, thus furthering your understanding of the world we live in.

Although we were already a close couple before we left, we learned so much more about each other as a result of the trip. When you have only each other to depend on day after day, you learn new information about the other person and how he or she handles situations under circumstances both funny and dire. There is no one else to lean on or to interfere; it is truly just the two of you. When you return from the trip, these new skills and understandings will spill over into your normal daily routine, creating a "new" couple from the one that started the trip.

We both feel that we are so much more well-rounded as a result of our adventure. We approach everything with more confidence in our abilities and with a more spirited sense of adventure. We can conquer anything!

If your life up until now has created little chance for you to travel, a trip of this type will take on special significance. Until you actually venture forth from your safe and comfortable environment, you just can't imagine all the things you have missed.

Phil says he felt like a kid in a candy store—so much to choose from, and all of it good!

Our educational background has been broadened immeasurably. We both grew up on the West Coast, and our knowledge of history was strong on cowboys and Indians but weak on the Revolution, the Civil War, and other historic events. Visiting all the places we did throughout the East Coast made everything so much more meaningful to us.

Even with everything that we saw and experienced, there is so much more that we could have seen. We could go a whole additional year and never visit places where we have already been. You just can't imagine the breadth and depth of the culture, history, natural beauty, and people in this country. Whatever your particular interests, there is so much to experience.

After taking a trip like this, you will never again be at a loss for something to talk about. All you have to do is mention that you took off and traveled for a year, and you can fascinate people for hours—well, at least for more than a few minutes, depending on the setting.

So, would we do it again? You bet! We will never have another experience in our lifetimes as awesome and memorable as *our* road trip dream.

About the Authors

Phil and Carol White are experts on the topic of yearlong travel. They have lived and experienced every word of *Live Your Road Trip Dream*.

The Whites are recently retired from the everyday work world and have begun travel writing as their new vocation. This trip was a year in the talking, learning, researching, and planning stages and another year in the execution of the actual adventure.

During Phil's twenty-six-year career, he was the small-business owner of a retail men's clothing store, and he has extensive sales and marketing experience from that endeavor as well as a comprehensive understanding of what it takes to run a successful business. His skills in listening to people and engaging them in informative conversation were invaluable on the trip.

Carol comes from the other end of the sales and marketing spectrum, having retired from the corporate giant Lucent Technologies in 1999. Her thirty-five years in the telecommunications and computing fields with Lucent and AT&T have garnered her a wealth of experience.

Both Phil and Carol are graduates of Portland State University in Oregon. Phil has a broad-based degree in general studies, and Carol graduated magna cum laude with a double major in business administration/marketing and psychology.

When they are not traveling, Phil and Carol live in Wilsonville, Oregon, where they enjoy golf, community activities, and most of all, their eight grandchildren.

Appendix

Master Budget Worksheet
An MS-Excel template is on our website at www.roadtripdream.com.

Sources of income for your trip

Item	Computation	$ per month	Annual
Rental of house	Monthly income	$_____	$_____
Proceeds from sale of home	Net amount to spend divided by months on trip	$_____	$_____
Rental from other properties	Monthly income	$_____	$_____
Proceeds from sale of cars or other assets	Net amount to spend divided by months on trip	$_____	$_____
Social Security	Amount of monthly check from Uncle Sam	$_____	$_____
Pension	Amount of monthly check from former employer	$_____	$_____
Trust fund	Amount of monthly check from Daddy—or whomever!	$_____	$_____
Gifts	Amount of gifts from friends divided by months on trip	$_____	$_____
Investment income (IRAs, annuities, etc.)	Monthly income	$_____	$_____
Sabbatical income	Monthly income from current employer—good job!	$_____	$_____
Income from your business while traveling	Monthly income or estimated income	$_____	$_____
Credit cards and other lines of credit	Estimated monthly usage to be paid after trip is complete	$_____	$_____
Savings or withdrawals from investments	Estimated amount needed monthly	$_____	$_____
Total income for your trip		$_____	$_____

(Continued on next page)

Master Budget Worksheet (*continued*)

Expenses while on the road

Item	Computation	$ per month	Annual
Gasoline	Miles driven per month, divided by mpg times the cost per gallon	$_____	$_____
Motel lodging	Average cost per night times days per month	$_____	$_____
RV lodging	Average cost per night times days per month	$_____	$_____
Food—restaurant and groceries	Average cost per day per person, times 30.5 days, times number of travelers	$_____	$_____
Attractions and entertainment	Estimated average cost per day times 30.5 days	$_____	$_____
Dry cleaning, laundry, personal	Estimated cost per month	$_____	$_____
Cards, postage, gifts sent home	Estimated cost per month	$_____	$_____
Souvenirs and photo developing	Estimated cost per month	$_____	$_____
Clothing	Estimated cost per month	$_____	$_____
Cell phone, long distance, Internet access	Estimated monthly billings	$_____	$_____
Travel vehicle payment	Cost of monthly payment	$_____	$_____
Vehicle maintenance, repairs, insurance	Estimated monthly costs	$_____	$_____
Additional transportation en route (buses, tolls, etc.)	Estimated monthly costs	$_____	$_____
Miscellaneous (newspapers, treats, etc.)	Estimated monthly costs	$_____	$_____
Deduct for trip home— if planning one	Deduct items not incurred while home	– $(_____)	$(_____)
Total expenses on the road		$_____	$_____

Master Budget Worksheet

Expenses while preparing to go

Item	Computation	Cost
Equipping vehicle to go	Initial cost for supplies and equipment	$_____
Purchase of electronics (cameras, GPS, etc.)	Initial cost	$_____
Marketing home for sale or lease	Estimated cost	$_____
Advertising cars for sale	Estimated cost	$_____
Clothing	Estimated cost	$_____
Other	Estimated cost	$_____
Total preparation expenses		$_____

Expenses at home while on the road

Item	Computation	$ per month	Annual
Property management of rental properties	Cost to property management firm or friend	$_____	$_____
House repairs of properties	Estimated cost per rental property—including your home	$_____	$_____
Mortgages (or any ongoing rental costs)	If you included total rent (not net of mortgages) in revenues, include mortgage cost here	$_____	$_____
Second mortgages	Cost of any second mortgages	$_____	$_____
Homeowner's fees	Monthly cost, if applicable	$_____	$_____
Property taxes	If not in monthly payment	$_____	$_____
Homeowner's insurance	If not in monthly payment	$_____	$_____
Utilities that you are continuing to pay	If leaving home empty or paying for renters	$_____	$_____
Yard work, pest control, housekeeper or other work to keep property safe and kept up	If leaving home empty or paying for renters	$_____	$_____
Security service	Monthly cost, if applicable	$_____	$_____
Travel club membership	Annual fee	$_____	$_____
Club memberships (athletic, country club, etc.)	Any ongoing expenses	$_____	$_____
Consumer loans	Payments you are currently making that will continue	$_____	$_____
Insurance (health, life, etc.)	Monthly cost, if applicable	$_____	$_____
Care for others while you are gone	Monthly cost, if applicable	$_____	$_____
Total expenses at home while gone		$_____	$_____

(Continued on next page)

Master Budget Worksheet (*continued*)

Expenses for trip home during year

Item	Computation	Annual
Airfare or transportation cost	Estimated cost	$_____
Hotels and lodging	If applicable	$_____
Parking for travel vehicle (distant end)	If applicable	$_____
Rental car or local transportation	If applicable	$_____
Meals and groceries	Estimated cost	$_____
Holiday gifts, decorations, etc.	Estimated cost	$_____
Miscellaneous (personal services, doctor appointments, etc.)	Estimated cost	$_____

Total expenses for trip home $_____

Putting it all together

Total sources of money   Annual

Total sources of money $_____ *

Total expenses on the road	$_____
Total preparation expenses	$_____
Total expenses at home while gone	$_____
Total expenses for trip home	$_____

Total expenses of trip $_____ *

These two numbers should be close to the same.

Sample "To Do" List for Trip

This timeline assumes an early June departure.

December

Stop renewing magazine subscriptions

Take house pictures for website

January

Work on house website; get pictures scanned and ready to go

Get list together for advertising the house

Go to AAA and get them started on "trip tik" research

February

Send flyer to colleges and corporations about the house for lease

Get bank signature cards to Andrea and Amy

Start cupboard cleaning

March

Check on insuring the van and check on AAA motorhome coverage

Place an ad for the house in the club magazine

Continue cupboard cleaning

Follow-up with corporations, leasing agents, and colleges—send invitations to open house

Get taxes done

Build trip website (contract out?)

April

Second round of advertising for house, if needed

Open house for high-potential firms—corporations, leasing agents, local realtors, colleges

Purchase van

Expand house list to include other avenues—newspaper, magazines, etc.—if needed

Get financial affairs in order

Get Volvo 850 ready to sell and advertise it

Finish cupboard cleaning

(Continued on next page)

Sample "To Do" List for Trip (continued)

May

Cancel all standing orders for products, including vitamins

Get Volvo 740 ready to sell and place ad

Change athletic club to non-resident; change locker to Christopher

Send letter to renters; change address for rent money

Change cell plan to full U.S. coverage and add voice mail

Have furnace serviced

Get windows washed and carpet cleaned (near end of month)

Start packing

Get reciprocal club lists and cards of introduction

Figure out voting and mail-forwarding issues

Apply for direct-billed phone card—or get prepaid phone card, whichever is better

Take trial-run trip

Give rental and bill stuff to Andrea (passwords and safe-deposit box key)

Give Tom's information to Amy

Finish packing and take storage items to Andrea's house

Pack "Christmas box"—things we may want to take back on the road with us

Change all utilities to renter

Get title from safe-deposit box

June

Forward mail to Andrea

Get traveler's checks ($500)

Make list of all Internet-access numbers

Finalize all packing in RV

Home at Christmas

File tax extensions on all accounts—personal taxes, corporation taxes, Tom's trust, family trust—and pay any estimated taxes on each account

Doctor and dentist visits

Haircut

Sample Itinerary

State	Month	High / Low / Rain	City
Leave Oregon	**June**		
South Coast highway and Oregon Caves—monument			
Medford—Donna (phone number)			
Salmon Run golf course			
Northern California	**June**	93 / 60 / 1	**Fresno**
Lassen Volcanic National Park (NP)			
Redwood NP			
San Francisco—visit Wendy (phone number)			
June 12–18, U.S. Open—Pebble Beach—condo in Carmel			
Steve and Joyce—Fresno (phone number)			
Sequoia and Kings Canyon NP			
Yosemite			
Dick and Lori—Clio (phone number)			
Nevada	**June / July**	83 / 47 / 3	**Reno**
Great Basin NP			
South Idaho	**July**	90 / 58 / 2	**Boise**
Sun Valley			
Craters of the Moon—monument			
Wyoming	**July**	88 / 54 / 8	**Casper**
Yellowstone NP			
Grand Teton NP			
River rafting trip?			
Jackson Hole			
Sheridan—Dick's mom (phone number)			
Montana	**July**	85 / 57 / 6	**Billings**
Central/Eastern Montana			
Fairmont Hot Springs			
Beartooth scenic highway (Marianne told us)			
Little Big Horn—monument			
North Dakota	**July**	84 / 56 / 9	**Bismark**
Theodore Roosevelt NP			
Lewis and Clark stuff?			
South Dakota	**August**	84 / 57 / 2	**Rapid City**
Badlands NP			
Black Hills—Mount Rushmore—monument			
Wind Cave NP			

(Continued on next page)

Sample Itinerary (*continued*)

State	Month	High / Low / Rain	City
Minnesota Voyageurs NP Isle Royale NP Mall of America Minneapolis/St. Paul	**August**	**81 / 53 / 11**	**Minneapolis**
Wisconsin Green Bay Packers, pre-season game—Green Bay? Door County	**August**	**80 / 57 / 9**	**Madison**
Michigan Monica and Leon—Traverse City (phone number) University of Michigan—Ann Arbor	**August**	**81 / 58 / 9**	**Grand Rapids**
Indiana Speedway—Indianapolis Abraham Lincoln sites	**September**	**78 / 56 / 8**	**Indianapolis**
Ohio Ohio State football game—Columbus Akron (Cuyahoga Falls) Cincinnati Pro Football Hall of Fame—Canton Rock and Roll Hall of Fame—Cleveland	**September**	**74 / 54 / 10**	**Akron**
Upstate New York Lake Placid Fall colors Niagara Falls Adirondacks—Sagamore Lodge (news article) Baseball Hall of Fame—Cooperstown	**September**	**73 / 49 / 10**	**Albany**
Vermont Fall colors	**September**	**69 / 49 / 12**	**Burlington**
New Hampshire Fall colors	**September/October**	**72 / 46 / 9**	**Concord**
Maine Acadia NP Maine coast—lighthouses? Portland	**October**	**59 / 38 / 9**	**Portland**

Sample Itinerary

State	Month	High / Low / Rain	City
Massachusetts	**October**	63 / 47 / 9	**Boston**
Red Sox baseball game—Fenway Park—Boston			
Freedom Trail—Boston			
Kennedy Library			
Cape Cod, Martha's Vineyard, Nantucket			
Harvard, MIT—Cambridge			
Rhode Island	**October**	64 / 43 / 9	**Providence**
Mansions			
Newport			
Connecticut	**October**	64 / 41 / 9	**Hartford**
Karly and Jerry—Westport (phone number)			
Mystic			
New York City area	**October**	65 / 40 / 11	
Theater			
Central Park			
NASDAQ Tours—Times Square			
New Jersey	**November**	55 / 39 / 10	**Newart**
Boardwalk—Atlantic City			
Pennsylvania	**November**	55 / 38 / 9	**Philadelphia**
Penn State football game—State College			
Historic sites—Philadelphia			
Amish country			
Gettysburg			
Valley Forge			
Delaware	**November**	56 / 37 / 9	**Wilmington**
No specific plan			
Maryland	**November**	57 / 37 / 9	**Baltimore**
Star Spangled Banner Flag house—Baltimore			
Annapolis			
Washington D.C.	**November**	58 / 41 / 9	
Redskins football game			
Smithsonian and the usual sights			
Vietnam Memorial			
Ford's Theater			

(Continued on next page)

Sample Itinerary *(continued)*

State	Month	High / Low / Rain	City
Virginia	**December**	**50 / 30 / 9**	**Richmond**
Shenandoah NP			
Mount Vernon			
Monticello			
Civil War			
Williamsburg			
West Virginia	**December**	**46 / 28 / 14**	**Charleston**
The Greenbrier, White Sulphur Springs			
North Carolina	**December**	**53 / 32 / 9**	**Raleigh**
U of North Carolina or Duke—basketball—Raleigh			
Blue Ridge and Great Smoky Mountains			
Biltmore Estate—Asheville			
Cape Hatteras			
Home for Christmas (from Raleigh, N.C.?)			
About December 20 to January 5?			
South Carolina	**January**	**55 / 32 / 10**	**Columbia**
Hilton Head			
Grand Strand			
Historic Charleston			
Georgia	**January**	**50 / 32 / 11**	**Atlanta**
Savannah			
Stone Mountain			
M. L. King National Historic Site			
Florida	**January/February**	**73 / 50 / 7**	**Orlando**
Everglades NP			
Dry Tortugas NP			
Biscayne NP			
LeAnne and Joaquin—Miami Lakes			
Kennedy Space Center			
Key West			
Golf Hall of Fame—St. Augustine			
TPC at Sawgrass—Jacksonville			
Alabama	**February**	**69 / 46 / 10**	**Birmingham**
U of Alabama—Tuskaloosa			
Civil-rights exhibits—Birmingham? Selma?			
Robert Trent Jones Golf Trail			

Sample Itinerary

State	Month	High / Low / Rain	City
Mississippi Mansions Natchez Trace	**February**	60 / 36 / 9	**Jackson**
Louisiana John and Nerissa—Monroe (phone number) New Orleans—Mardi Gras Mansions	**February**	64 / 43 / 9	**Baton Rouge**
Arkansas Hot Springs NP	**February**	54 / 33 / 9	**Little Rock**
Tennessee Great Smoky Mountains Grand Ole Opry	**February/March**	61 / 39 / 12	**Nashville**
Kentucky Mammoth Cave NP Horse racing—Churchill Downs Abraham Lincoln birthplace	**March**	55 / 35 / 13	**Lexington**
Illinois Oak Park—Frank Lloyd Wright Lincoln tomb—Springfield	**March**	46 / 29 / 13	**Chicago**
Iowa No specific plan	**March**	47 / 28 / 10	**Des Moines**
Nebraska No specific plan	**March/April**	63 / 34 / 8	**North Platte**
Missouri Branson St. Louis	**April**	67 / 44 / 11	**St. Louis**
Kansas Eisenhower Center—Abilene	**April**	68 / 45 / 8	**Wichita**
Oklahoma Oklahoma City Memorial Tulsa	**April**	72 / 49 / 8	**Oklahoma City**

(Continued on next page)

Sample Itinerary *(continued)*

State	Month	High / Low / Rain	City
Texas	April	76 / 55 / 8	**Dallas**

Big Bend NP
Guadaloupe Mountains NP (*see also* Carlsbad, N.M.)
San Antonio—been there, go again?
Space Center—Houston

New Mexico	May	80 / 49 / 5	**Albuquerque**

Carlsbad Caverns NP
Albuquerque/Santa Fe/Taos
Bandelier—monument
Aztec ruins

Colorado	May	71 / 44 / 11	**Denver**

Rocky Mountain NP
Mesa Verde NP
Debbie—Vail (phone number)
Leadville—(mining town/Mocks told us)
Pikes Peak

Utah	May	67 / 33 / 5	**Flagstaff, AZ**

Arches NP
Canyonlands NP
Bryce Canyon NP
Zion NP
Capitol Reef NP
Salt Lake City—Mormon Temple

Arizona	May	94 / 64 / 1	**Phoenix**

Grand Canyon NP—maybe north rim; been to south rim
Petrified Forest NP
Saguaro NP
Sedona
Tombstone
Tucson

Southern California	May	85 / 57 / 2	**Bakersfield**

Channel Islands NP
Death Valley NP
Joshua Tree NP
Getty Center—Los Angeles
Paul and Tara (phone number)

Sample Motorhome Checklist

Make a list similar to this one from your owner's guide.

Prior to leaving on a trip

- Start refrigerator 24 hours before leaving
- Chassis fluids are at proper levels
- Batteries are charged and water is at proper level
- Detectors are working properly—smoke, fire, LP, carbon monoxide, GFI
- Tire pressure is at recommended levels—55# front, 70# back
- Air shocks are at recommended levels—50-55#
- All exterior lighting is functional
- Review "Breaking camp" items

While in motion

- Propane is off to all appliances and at central valve
- Refrigerator is on 12V
- OK to use generator—but verify that you have at least a quarter tank of gas
- Switch refrigerator to propane if leaving coach for sightseeing, etc., for more than a couple of hours

Upon arrival at site

- ***Ensure that headlight switch is turned all the way to the right and off so your battery won't drain!***
- Level the motorhome
- Ensure that all exterior vents are clear from obstructions
- If connecting to sewer, make sure black and grey water tank valves are *closed*
- Hook 110V power to site receptacle, check voltage on meter by stove, and use circuit analyzer to check polarity
- Check to make sure that water-pump switch is off and all faucets are closed before connecting water
- Hook up fresh-water line to *city fill*, if available, check pressure with water-pressure gauge (no more than 20-30 PSI), and place purifier filter inline—or fill *fresh-water tank*, if water not at site, drop chemicals in, and start pressure pump
- Turn LP gas on at valve
- Turn on generator, if using—make sure that you have at least a quarter tank of gas
- Turn refrigerator to 110V power (or LP, if no 110V available)

(Continued on next page)

Sample Motorhome Checklist *(continued)*

Upon arrival at site *(continued)*

- Turn water heater on—make sure there is water in the tank (pump switch is on or city water is hooked up)
- Switch TV to 110V power, if not dry camping; otherwise leave on 12V

Breaking camp

- Turn off LP gas at main valve
- Wait until at least half full to dump—black water first, then grey—and then flush lines with water from inside, replace chemicals, and run in a little water
- Turn water-heater switch off
- Turn city water off, release pressure at sinks, disconnect hose; turn water pump on if needing fresh-water tank en route
- Turn off 110V appliances (including air conditioner) before disconnecting 110V power
- Store electrical cords and exterior hoses in compartments
- Secure and close all exterior and interior components (roof fan?)
- Make sure that furnace-control switch under thermostat is off
- Make sure that TV 12V switch is in off position
- Change refrigerator to 12V from LP or 110V
- Remove leveling devices from wheels and store them

A Primer to RV Systems

Just like your "land" home, your traveling home has all the systems you need to make your life comfortable. (Some of these will vary from one unit to another.)

System	Home	RV	
		Hookup	Onboard
Electrical	110V (circuit breakers)	110V–30/50-amp circuit (can step down to 15-amp connection)	Generator (converts to 110V) and a separate 12V battery system (fuses)
Heat/air conditioning	Furnace/air conditioning	When connected, you can use an electric space heater*; for air you have a separate air conditioner on roof	Propane furnace (with thermostat); separate air conditioner on roof (110V)
Fresh water	City water or well	City water hookup	Pressurized tank
Hot water (sinks and shower)	Hot-water tank	Propane hot-water tank	Propane hot-water tank
Sewer (toilet)	City sewer system or septic tank	Connect to sewer at site or use dump station as needed	Tank—dump when over half full (black water)
Drains (sinks and shower)	City sewer system or septic tank	Dump station or empty at site (after you empty sewer)	Tank—dump when over half full (grey water)

Not part of built-in systems—but when hooked up, why not use the site's electricity!

(Continued on next page)

A Primer to RV Systems (*continued*)

In many ways, your RV is more flexible and provides more options than your home systems.

Appliance	110V (plug-in or generator)	12V	Propane
Microwave	•		
Refrigerator	•	•	•
Stove			•
Hot water			•
TV/VCR	•	•	
Outlets	•		
Lights	•	•	
Overhead fan	•	•	
Air conditioner	•		
Furnace			•

Remember, when running the generator, you need to have at least a quarter tank of gas, and you can't run all the appliances and outlets simultaneously on the generator!

Supplies for a One-Year Trip

This is what we took—or ended up with along the way. Obviously your list will vary depending on your habits, interests, and lifestyle. Use this only as a memory jogger and adapt it to fit your trip.

Kitchen

- Dishes, silverware, cups, glasses (4)
- Pots and pans (2 saucepans, 2 skillets, 1 large pot, griddle)
- Large mixing bowl (doubles as ice bucket, salad bowl, etc.)
- Spatula, big spoon, tongs, strainer, corkscrew, bottle opener, can opener
- Measuring cups (4-cup liquid and dry set), measuring spoons
- Large and small sharp knives
- Trivet, hot pads, cutting board
- Toaster
- Coffee pot and filters
- Folding dish drainer, soap, scrubber, sponge
- Paper plates, napkins, rattan plate holders
- Foldable BBQ grill and self-lighting briquettes
- Windproof candle
- Insulated pop-can holders
- Spices, condiments, salt and pepper

- Basic canned goods (soups, tuna, syrup, etc.)
- Oils and vinegar
- Dry mixes for sauces, dips, salad dressings, etc.
- Zip-lock bags with flour, sugar, oatmeal, rice, noodles, breakfast cereal, pancake mix, etc.
- Extra zip-lock bags (in several sizes)—we used them for everything!
- Assorted plastic containers (for mixing and storage)
- Aluminum foil, plastic wrap
- Extra paper bags
- Paper towels
- Picnic-table cover and clamps
- Flower vase—one of our luxuries!
- Blue ice
- A few clothespins (for hanging up clothes or reminders)
- Fly swatter

Cleaning supplies

- Sponges, rags, etc.
- All-purpose cleaner
- Bathroom cleaner
- Glass cleaner
- Handiwipes—a must!
- Rechargeable hand vacuum
- Bug spray

- Whisk broom and dustpan
- Paper towels
- Dish soap
- Laundry soap
- Swiffers
- Fabreeze

(Continued on next page)

Supplies for a One-Year Trip *(continued)*

Linens

- One set of towels per person
- Swim towels (can double in a pinch if the regular towels are in the wash)
- Sheets, pillows, pillowcases, comforter
- Kitchen towels
- Tension rod to hang wet towels, swimsuits, etc., in bathroom

Personal

- Extra glasses—a must!—and your prescription
- Sunglasses and straps to hold them on
- Heating pad
- Sunscreen
- Moisturizing lotion
- Makeup bag and perfume
- Bactine or other antiseptic, sunburn remedy
- Prescriptions and over-the-counter meds
- "Shower caddy" containing
  Toothbrush and toothpaste
  Soap in a container
  Shampoo and conditioner
  Brush
  Deodorant
  Shaving cream and razor
  Lotion

Electronics

- Cell phone
- Laptop PC, printer, paper, extra ink cartridge
- Boom box
- Digital camera
- Surge protector
- GPS (optional)
- Two-way radios
- Two-prong adapter
- Analog/digital converter for motel phone systems
- Extension cord
- Altimeter and compass
- Owner's manuals for all products

Recreation

- Golf clubs, shoes, bags
- Board games
- Cards
- Yoga mats and tapes
- Audio books
- Novels and magazines—trade along the way!
- CDs, tapes, favorite videos
- Backpack (small), water bottles
- Cooler (small)
- Cameras, tripod, lots of film
- Folding chairs and folding table
- Blanket for picnics, concerts, etc.
- Binoculars

Supplies for a One-Year Trip

Navigation

- AAA maps, campground guides, and tour guides (or equivalent)
- *Road Trip USA*
- RV campground guide (CD-ROM) from Trailer Life
- Camping-club guides
- KOA guide
- *National Geographic's Guide to the National Parks of the United States*
- *National Geographic Guide to Small Town Escapes*

Tools and van supplies

- Owner's manuals for all systems and products
- Extra set of all keys
- Exterior hide-a-key in a non-locked compartment
- Book on van maintenance and repair—even if you don't do it, it helps to understand what the problem may be
- Flashlight
- Kneeling pad—we called it the "prayer rug"; you pray everything comes out OK!
- Toolbox with hammer, screwdrivers, pliers, special square screwdriver that all RVs use, etc.
- Jack and spare tire—make sure you know how it works! (If spare is exterior-mount, get a heavy-duty lock for it!)
- Leather gloves
- Bungie cords (various lengths)
- Extra sewer hose (for when you have to go a ways to the outlet)
- Disposable rubber gloves—a whole box—makes sewer duty easy!
- Water hose (at least one), filter, pressure valve
- Cable for TV
- Chemicals for tanks (gray, black, fresh)
- Toilet paper for RVs
- Battery-operated drill, bits, screwdriver, extra battery and charger
- Wheel levelers
- Polarity checker
- 110V gauge
- Bubble levels
- Heavy-duty (exterior) extension cord
- Duct tape
- Sun screen for windshield
- RV wash equipment (brush, soap, etc.)
- Extra bulbs for interior lights
- Flashlight
- Wastebasket and liners
- Exterior doormat—saves lots of vacuuming!

(Continued on next page)

Supplies for a One-Year Trip *(continued)*

"The Organizer"

- Envelopes (long and regular)
- A few big manila envelopes (folded)
- Stamps (first-class and postcard)
- Paper clips and clamps (various sizes)
- Stapler and staples
- Scotch tape
- Extra velcro strips
- Double-sided sticky pads
- Small sewing kit
- Small first-aid kit
- Band-Aids
- Nail polish and remover pads
- Rubber bands
- Wire ties (for plastic bags—many uses)
- Floss and picks—got to keep those teeth healthy!
- Calculator
- Marking pens

- Batteries (all sizes—and don't forget the camera batteries)
- Extra pens and pencils
- Scissors
- Post-It notes
- Nail files
- Antacids
- Single dose of occasional-use drugs
- Aspirin, first-aid cream, and other over-the-counter drugs
- Copies of prescriptions
- Extra set of credit cards
- A few nails and other fasteners
- Measuring tape
- Extra washers, etc.
- Glasses repair kit
- Anything small you may need!

Clothes—Phil

Shorts (4)

Jeans (2)

Cotton khakis

Cords

Wool dress slacks

Microfiber slacks (golf or dress)

Various belts

Sweater vest

Sweatshirt

Light jacket

Heavy jacket

Fleece

Long-sleeved knit shirts (2)

Turtlenecks (2)

Golf shirts (4)

T-shirts (4)

Underwear (10 days)

Various socks

Swim trunks

Sports jacket, dress shirt, tie, belt

Tennis shoes (2)

Tevas

Hiking boots

Dress shoes

Hats, gloves

Duffel bag—for taking into hotels or on the train, airplane, etc.

Zippered suit cover

Supplies for a One-Year Trip

Clothes—Carol

Shorts (2)—black, khaki

Gym shorts—black

Workout tights—black (wear underneath when cold!)

Wool pants—black

Cotton pants—black

Jeans

Various belts

Cords—khaki

Cotton sweater—black

Light jacket—black

Sweatshirt—color

Fleece—color

Rain jacket—color

Long-sleeved shirts (2)—color

Turtlenecks (2)—black and color

Golf shirts (3)—color

T-shirts (2)—color

Underwear (10 days)

Light robe

Sweats outfit—color

Swimsuit

Cotton casual long sundresses (2)

Dress—black (dress it up or down)

Scarves (2)—(for warmth or dress)

Long skirt—black

Dressy sweater—gold

Costume jewelry (don't bring expensive things)

Tennis shoes

Hiking boots

Aqua sox (or Tevas—for rivers)

Sandals (2)—black, white

Loafer—black

Dress shoes—black

Various socks, one pair nylons

Everyday purse and evening bag

Warm hat and gloves

Duffel bag—for taking into hotels or on the train, airplane, etc.

Ideas for a Flyer to Lease Your Home

Decide who your audience is and develop the flyer with them in mind!

Use bold colors and some appropriate graphics (many computer programs have templates for flyers).

Include a few pictures and mention that additional pictures are available via e-mail or on your website.

Be sure to include all the pertinent contact information—everything you have!: e-mail addresses, regular mail address, cell phones, home phone, fax, pagers, etc.

Use short, bulleted, descriptive statements:
- Fabulous executive home in desirable neighborhood
- Great golf-course location
- Restful master suite
- Quiet neighborhood pool

Mention the most desirable features:
- 1,800 sq. ft., one level, two bedrooms and den, two baths
- Cozy fireplace
- Includes weekly housekeeper
- Sunny skylights
- Spacious double garage
- Vaulted ceilings

Tell when it is available (from when to when) and state the price.

Don't make it too cluttered. Make it easy to read, and let the pictures tell the story with a little text.

Six to eight well-written bulleted points should be plenty—one line each!

Have additional information ready to discuss when someone calls to inquire:
- How much are the utilities?
- Is there bus service close-by?
- Do you allow pets?
- How much are the deposits?
- Are you flexible on your dates? On the price?
- Can you fax me the floor plan?
- Prepare for the many other questions you might be asked.

Follow-up Letter to Leasing Agent

(date)

(name)
(address)
(city, state, zip)

Dear _____:

Thanks for talking with me today regarding our property for lease. Enclosed please find the specifications on our home.

This house would be ideal for a visiting or relocating executive or other professional. We will be traveling for a year, and we would like to have a responsible couple or small family enjoy our fully furnished home for that year. We are advertising it for occupancy from (date) to (date), but we are willing to consider some deviation from those dates.

If you have a candidate for this home or have questions, please feel free to call us at any time to discuss it.

Sincerely,

Phil and Carol White
(telephone number)
enclosures

Renter's Move-out Reminder List

(date)

Dear _____:

Thanks for being such good tenants. We really appreciate you caring for our home during our absence.

We just want to review the items that we expect from our tenants, in order to avoid any confusion in receiving the deposits back. Your pet deposit will be fully refundable, as long as no damage is found, and $_____ of the cleaning/repair deposit is refundable, provided the house is returned in good order and no damage is found when we check you out. The key deposit of $_____ will be returned in full. We are expecting to receive two house keys, two mailbox keys, and two garage-door openers.

Since we have found over the years that our expectations do not always match those of the tenants, we have prepared a list of items you will want to review prior to moving out to avoid any confusion on deposit refunds.

- ☐ All appliances cleaned and in good repair
- ☐ Kitchen, laundry, and bathroom cabinets wiped out thoroughly, and outsides wiped down, as needed
- ☐ Both bathrooms cleaned thoroughly
- ☐ Carpets vacuumed and cleaned
- ☐ Vinyl floors mopped
- ☐ Windows washed inside and out
- ☐ Window coverings cleaned as needed (dusted or wiped down)
- ☐ Walls, closets, ceilings, light fixtures, window frames, etc., free of cobwebs, as well as around entry doors on the outside, please
- ☐ Countertops, door and window frames, ledges, shelving, etc., dusted
- ☐ Garage and workshop completely cleaned out and swept, and work surfaces wiped down

Renter's Move-out Reminder List

☐ Yard mowed and weeded, and any annuals, vegetables, etc., removed

☐ Walkways swept

☐ Fireplace cleaned out

☐ All debris and moving "throwaways" removed from premises—any normal garbage-pickup materials OK

We will fumigate for any possible fleas, spiders, etc., after you leave.

Thanks again for renting from us, and please let us know if you have any questions about the move-out procedure.

Sincerely,

Phil and Carol White

(telephone number)

Index